METROPOLITAN AREA SCHOOLS

Resistance to

District Reorganization

BASIL G. ZIMMER
Brown University

and

AMOS H. HAWLEY
University of North Carolina

SAGE PUBLICATIONS, INC. / BEVERLY HILLS, CALIFORNIA

THE RESEARCH REPORTED HEREIN WAS SUPPORTED BY THE
COOPERATIVE RESEARCH PROGRAM OF THE OFFICE OF
EDUCATION, U. S. DEPARTMENT OF HEALTH, EDUCATION
AND WELFARE UNDER COOPERATIVE RESEARCH PROJECT
No. 1044.

For information address:
SAGE PUBLICATIONS, INC.
275 SOUTH BEVERLY DRIVE
BEVERLY HILLS, CALIFORNIA 90212

Standard Book Number: 8039–1005–3

Library of Congress Catalog Card Number: 68–57144

FIRST PRINTING

Acknowledgments

IN A STUDY OF this type, many persons contribute in a variety of ways to its outcome. As much as we would like to, it is clearly impossible to name everyone; however, we do wish to single out a few for special recognition. First of all, we are deeply indebted to the United States Office of Education, Department of Health, Education and Welfare, for financial support of the study, and to Professor Peter Rossi, Mr. Galen Gockel, and Mr. William Simon of the National Opinion Research Center, University of Chicago, for their contribution in the selection of the sample, the collection of the data, and the coding and preparation of the data for analysis. A special debt is owed the 110 interviewers in the various metropolitan areas who actually talked to the respondents in the field and carefully recorded their responses, and to the hundreds of residents and public officials who were kind and generous enough to take the time to respond to a rather lengthy interview.

We are indebted to the Department of Sociology Computer Laboratory, Brown University, for the use of their tabulation equipment. We also wish to thank Mr. Thomas McGlew, a graduate student research assistant, who was responsible for most of the tabulations, and Mrs. Norma MacDonald and Miss Jane Wilkenson, departmental secretaries, for their help in typing the early drafts of some of the tables. Special thanks are extended to Janet M. Zimmer, who helped with the calculations and typed earlier drafts, as well as the final copy of the report.

B.G.Z.
A.H.H.

Table of Contents

List of Tables

METROPOLITAN AREA SCHOOLS

Resistance to
District Reorganization

1

Introduction

THERE IS A MARKED tendency, in any society, for established behavioral patterns as well as organizational structures to persist in their present form long after social and economic conditions have reached the point where change is necessary for the system to function effectively. In a sense, the present administrative structure of education and government in metropolitan areas in the United States typifies this situation. This is the type of problem that sets the stage for the present study, which is an attempt to identify the factors that account for resistance to reorganization of school districts in metropolitan areas.[1]

There are few problems in American society more crucial and of more immediate concern than those related to the present administrative structure of education at the elementary and secondary levels, particularly in the rapidly growing metropolitan areas. A great deal of research attention has been focused on the consequences of segmentation of school districts and local governments within metropolitan centers. Invariably such studies conclude that there is a need for "reorganization." School and municipal problems have reached acute form in many metropolitan areas throughout the country. And it is in these areas that the nation's population is becoming increasingly concentrated. The consensus among qualified observers is that many of the difficulties confronting public education in metropolitan areas are traceable to the multiplicity of small-scale governments in suburbia. Yet efforts to effect change

[1] This is part of a larger study concerned with local government in metropolitan areas, which will be reported separately.

to a more efficient and equitable administrative arrangement have met with uniform failure. Local residents resist reorganization even when by all objective standards it would be to their own self-interest to accept such a proposal.

Even though the need for reorganization is usually well documented, proposals for change fail due to lack of support not only from the residents of suburban areas, but also from the officials of their governmental units. In fact, it seems fair to say that failure rests not so much on apathy as on strong opposition to reorganization proposals. On the other hand, central city officials and residents tend to support such programs. Although there is a great deal of supposition, there is little dependable knowledge about what lies at the roots of the opposition to administrative change.[2] This study will attempt to uncover some of the factors which account for the failure of such proposals to get the necessary popular support, and will also probe the nature of resistance found among school and municipal officials.[3]

Clearly one of the major trends of the present century has been the rise and development of the metropolitan community. This new population aggregation has been so thoroughly documented that it needs no further elaboration.[4] Moreover, within the metropolitan community in recent years there has been a marked and consistent trend in the redistribution of population. Suburban areas have been growing at a much more rapid rate than central cities.[5]

[2] B. G. Zimmer and A. H. Hawley, "Approaches to the Solution of Fringe Problems: Preferences of Residents in the Flint Metropolitan Area," reprinted from *Public Administration Review*, XVI (Fall, 1956), pp. 258–268, in George A. Theodorson (ed.), *Studies in Human Ecology* (Evanston, Ill.: Row Peterson, 1961), pp. 595–606. See also Hawley and Zimmer, "Resistance to Unification in a Metropolitan Community," in Morris Janowitz (ed.), *Community Political Systems* (N. Y.: Free Press, 1961), pp. 146–184.

[3] "In most states the procedures for reorganization of school districts have been cumbersome and difficult to set in motion. With few exceptions a favorable majority vote has been required in each of the districts in the proposed new district —that provision alone has always been sufficient to restrain reorganization progress to a snail's pace." C. O. Fitzwater, *School District Reorganization: Policies and Procedures*, Office of Education, U. S. Department of Health, Education and Welfare (Washington: U. S. Government Printing Office, 1957), p. 7.

[4] R. D. McKenzie, *The Metropolitan Community* (N. Y.: McGraw-Hill, 1933); Donald J. Bogue, *The Structure of the Metropolitan Community: A Study of Dominance and Subdominance* (Ann Arbor: University of Michigan, 1947); Amos H. Hawley, *The Changing Shape of Metropolitan America* (Glencoe, Ill.: Free Press, 1955).

[5] Philip M. Hauser, *Population Perspectives* (New Brunswick, N. J.: Rutgers University Press, 1960).

According to the 1960 Census, nearly 85 percent of the total growth in the nation's population during the previous decade occurred in metropolitan areas. This is a continuation of a trend that has characterized the present century. Suburbia has been absorbing increasingly larger proportions of total metropolitan growth. The growth rate for the territory in metropolitan areas lying outside of central cities was 48.5 percent during the 1950–1960 decade, as compared with only a 10.7 percent increase in the central cities. Thus, during this period, the outlying population increased nearly five times as rapidly as the central city populations.

As the population in suburban areas continues to grow at increasingly rapid rates, and as young families with children become more and more concentrated in suburbs of metropolitan areas, there is an expanding need for school facilities and programs. But the needs cannot be met in many school districts because of the lack of an adequate tax base, while in other, adjacent, districts the resources for school financing may be abundant—a circumstance preserved by the obsolete and inefficient type of school organization found in most areas.[6] In suburban areas throughout the country, demands for school facilities to keep pace with population growth have raised local taxes for school purposes to burdensome levels, especially where the district contains no industrial or commercial property. Only in rare instances is it possible to support an adequate school system through local resources where the tax base is limited to residential property.[7]

Despite the limitations of financial support at the local level, most, if not all, districts attempt to provide full kindergarten through the twelfth grade programs. The problem is most acute at the high school level, for there the burden on fiscal resources is heaviest. Thus James B. Conant argues, in his report on *The American High School Today,* that "in many states the number one

[6] In St. Louis County, for example, "one school district has an assessed valuation (the basis for all property taxes) which is twenty-eight times the tax base per capita of another. The first suburb pays one of the lowest tax rates in the area, the second one of the highest. But the school systems are far apart in quality. The first is a superior school system, the second is struggling to maintain its accreditation." Scott Greer, *Governing the Metropolis* (N. Y.: John Wiley, 1962), p. 116.

[7] This is the type of problem one observer referred to as the "segregation of resources from needs." Robert Wood (with the assistance of Vladimir V. Almendinger), *1400 Governments, the Political Economy of the New York Metropolitan Region* (Cambridge: Harvard University Press, 1961).

problem is the elimination of the small high school by district re-organization." [8]

The importance and significance of this situation can be illustrated by the consequences of segmentation of school districts in a single metropolitan area. In our earlier studies in the Flint metropolitan area, in the late 1950's, we found that the suburban districts combined contained only 25 percent of the taxable wealth in the urbanized area, but 34 percent of the children in school. And, more importantly, there were great differences among school districts in the suburban area; one district contained 36 percent of the taxable wealth in the suburbs, but only 10 percent of the children in school. The range in per capita taxable wealth was from $42,379 to only $4,408, nearly a tenfold difference. The one suburban district assessed only 8.35 mills and realized more than $350 for each child in school, whereas a neighboring district assessed 18.35 mills and obtained only $81.[9] Although the state's contribution decreased the differential between the districts, the gap remained large nonetheless. In the one district the total per capita expenditures for school operations came to $475, but only $258 in the other district.[10] Such differences were reflected in the quality of program offered. The need for reorganization of school districts in that area was apparent. Yet efforts to accomplish this met with uniform failure. This is the type of problem that led us to the present study.

In a democratic society, when change can come about only through popular support and is urgently needed, as it is in the administrative structure of our metropolitan areas, the factors involved in resistance become of paramount importance.[11] Thus the present study attempts to determine the amount of resistance to change, and why residents and officials are opposed to joining an integrated

[8] James B. Conant, *The American High School Today* (N. Y.: McGraw-Hill, 1959).

[9] B. G. Zimmer, "A Report on Education in the Flint Metropolitan Area," *Flint Area Study* (mimeographed report, 1957), chap. 9.

[10] In a more recent study in St. Louis County, it was reported that "one school district spends $308 per pupil in average daily attendance, others attend school in a district where the comparable expenditure is $337, and still others go to school in a district that spends $615 per pupil." John C. Bollens (ed.), *Exploring the Metropolitan Community* (Berkeley: University of California Press, 1961), p. 44. See also Roscoe C. Martin, *Government and the Suburban School* (Syracuse, N. Y.: Syracuse University Press, 1962).

[11] For a discussion of the general problems of school district reorganization, see Fitzwater, *op. cit.* note 3.

unit so as to be able to more effectively and efficiently provide the education function. Knowledge of the factors related to resistance will not only contribute to our understanding of social change as such, but will also permit the concentration of future efforts toward improvement where they are likely to be effective. The basic question is: "What are the roots of the resistance to the establishment of a single administrative unit for the larger area?" When this question is answered, effective solutions will be less difficult. Present attempts at reorganization are limited, since no systematic data are available on the resistances that must be overcome before change will be accepted.

Theoretically, the unification of administrative units would be the last stage in the natural development of metropolitan areas.[12] However, even though in all other stages of development many metropolitan centers in the United States have attained maturity, this last stage is yet to develop either in respect to the educational or municipal functions.[13] Thus, in a very real sense, both theoretically and practically, there is a need to know what factors impede the development of the final stage that would integrate the larger functional community into a single governmental and educational unit. The present study will focus only on the organization of school districts, which is a crucial dimension of the overall problem.[14]

Segmentation of Administrative Units

The segmentation of local government in metropolitan areas in the United States is extensive. According to the last Census of Governments report, there were more than 19,000 local units of

[12] See Hawley and Zimmer, op. cit. note 2; Henry S. Shryock, Jr., "The History of Metropolitan Areas," American Journal of Sociology, XLIII (1957), pp. 163–170.

[13] In Amos H. Hawley, Human Ecology: A Theory of Community Structure (N. Y.: Ronald Press, 1950), the problem of metropolitanization was stated thusly: "An expanding organization engulfs and spreads over many political subdivisions, such as smaller cities, villages, townships and school districts and parts of states. But there is no redistribution and reorganization of administrative or governmental functions comparable to that we observed in connection with manufacturing and service functions. Each political entity tends to persist as a semi-autonomous unit, retaining the powers granted in its charter or constitution. . . . The net result is a confusion of jurisdictional boundaries, of unequal governmental powers, and of conflicting administrative policies in what in other respects is a functionally integrated unit" (pp. 425–426).

[14] The local government problem will be presented in a separate study.

government in the 212 Standard Metropolitan Statistical Areas in 1962.[15] This figure includes some 6,600 separate school systems. Among the latter there were slightly more than 6,000 independent school districts and another 600 dependent school systems.[16] That there is a disproportionately large number of school districts in metropolitan areas is evident when we note that the number of school systems outnumber the separate municipalities by more than 50 percent. There are two and one-half times as many school systems as townships, and more than twenty times as many school systems as counties, in the 212 metropolitan areas.

While the nation's metropolitan areas, on the average, have some 31 school districts apiece, they nonetheless contain a disproportionate number of the larger systems. Metropolitan areas contain three-fifths of the population, but they have less than 20 percent of the total number of school systems in the nation. Yet these areas account for more than two-fifths of the systems enrolling 1,200 or more pupils. And while the larger districts account for most of the public school enrollment in metropolitan areas, we nonetheless find a slightly larger number of small school systems in such areas enrolling fewer than 300 pupils each. Such systems account for 40 percent of the districts in metropolitan areas. Perhaps the most significant point here is that approximately one system out of six in metropolitan areas enrolls less than 15 pupils each or is a non-operating district—that is, it does not have any schools of its own.[17]

For the most part, size of school system varies directly by size of metropolitan area. That is evident from the data presented in Table 1-1. In the largest metropolitan areas, nearly half of the

[15] U. S. Bureau of the Census, Census of Governments, *Local Government in Metropolitan Areas* (Washington: U. S. Department of Commerce, 1962).

[16] A dependent school system is one that is under the direct financial control of another unit of government. They operate as adjuncts of other governments. For example, in both Buffalo and Rochester the school systems are dependent on the city.

[17] Non-operating districts have developed historically when very small districts with inadequate facilities closed their one-room schools and transported their pupils to an adjacent district, paying tuition to cover the cost of their education. The district remains, however, legally independent, and continues to have its own school board. There were 912 such districts in metropolitan areas at the time of the 1962 Census of Governments. Another 127 districts continued to operate their own schools, even though less than 15 pupils were enrolled. Not only have these districts remained independent legal entities, but they have resisted even a functional relationship with other districts.

TABLE 1-1

PERCENT DISTRIBUTION OF SCHOOL DISTRICTS BY NUMBER OF PUPILS
ENROLLED BY SIZE OF STANDARD METROPOLITAN STATISTICAL AREA*

By Size of Enrollment	Total	1,000,000 or more	500,000 to 999,999	300,000 to 499,999	200,000 to 299,999	100,000 to 199,999	50,000 to 99,999
Total	6604	2591	892	812	1096	914	299
	%	%	%	%	%	%	%
1200 plus	38.7	49.2	48.4	32.8	25.7	28.7	13.0
300–1199	21.4	21.2	27.2	24.4	18.2	24.8	13.0
50–299	16.2	12.1	16.1	18.4	17.5	22.2	21.4
1–49	10.0	4.4	6.3	9.5	17.6	15.7	25.4
0	13.8	13.1	7.0	14.9	21.0	8.6	27.1
Total	100.0	100.0	100.0	100.0	100.0	100.0	100.0

* SOURCE: U. S. Bureau of the Census, Census of Governments, *Local Governments in Metropolitan Areas* (Washington: U. S. Department of Commerce, 1962), Table B, p. 5.

systems have an enrollment of 1,200 or more, but that declines by size and reaches a low of only 13 percent in the small metropolitan areas. At the other extreme, while 10 percent of the total operating systems in metropolitan areas enroll fewer than 50 pupils, this ranges from less than 5 percent in the largest to some 25 percent in the smallest metropolitan areas. Thus as the size of metropolitan area declines, there is a sharp increase in the number of small school systems. It is noteworthy, however, that there is not a corresponding increase in the proportion of pupils enrolled in the smaller districts. For when we look at total enrollment, we find that in each metropolitan area size class more than 90 percent of the pupils are enrolled in districts with 1,200 or more pupils. Stated in somewhat different terms, this means that in the largest metropolitan areas, half of the systems account for 96 percent of the enrollment; and in the smallest metropolitan areas, 13 percent of the districts contain more than 90 percent of the pupils enrolled in public schools in those areas. Perhaps the significance of the multiplicity of school districts in metropolitan areas is best indicated by the converse—that is, in the smallest metropolitan areas, 87 percent of the districts enroll less than 10 percent of the pupils attending public schools. And even in the largest metropolitan areas, half of the school systems combined enroll less than 4 percent of the pupils in the public schools in these areas.[18]

For the most part, school district organization is largely independent of the boundary lines of other levels of government. Of the 6,604 school systems in metropolitan areas, the boundaries of only 1,854 (28 percent) were coterminal with some other local government areas, whereas the remaining 4,750 (72 percent) were not coterminal.[19] In other words, there are nearly 5,000 school systems in the 212 metropolitan areas which in one way or another overlap the jurisdictional boundaries of other local governments. And since these districts are independent units of government with taxing powers, this condition can only further com-

[18] For a discussion of the relative costs of education by size of enrollment, see Washington State Planning Council, *A Study of the Common School System of Washington* (Olympia, 1938); Iowa State Department of Public Instruction, *A Report to the People of Iowa on the Present Problems and Future Goals of Reorganization in Your School District* (Des Moines, 1952).

[19] U. S. Bureau of the Census, Census of Governments, *op. cit.* note 15, Table 2, p. 24.

plicate the problems resulting from governmental segmentation.

While the population in the United States is increasingly becoming concentrated in the highly urbanized metropolitan centers, this new population aggregate has been largely superimposed on a structure of school districts created for an earlier time when the conditions of life were much different. We have already noted that more than 15 percent of the districts in these metropolitan clusters are non-operating systems. That is, there are more than 900 school districts which do not provide schools for the pupils living within the district and must arrange to have the education of their children provided for in some other area. Another 10 percent of the districts enroll fewer than 50 children. Clearly these are the types of systems that once served sparsely settled agricultural areas. And yet we find that they continue to persist in our metropolitan areas in the late twentieth century. We find further that some 40 percent of the operating districts in metropolitan areas have only a single school, and another nearly equal proportion operate between two and nine schools each. Only a small proportion of the school systems in metropolitan areas are sufficient in size to operate ten or more schools within their system.

It is noteworthy that more progress has been made in reference to school district reorganization than in respect to the reorganization of local governments in metropolitan areas. For example, during the five-year period 1957–1962, the number of independent school districts in the 212 metropolitan areas declined from 7,486 to 6,004. By way of comparison, the number of municipalities in these same areas increased from 3,844 to 4,144, and special districts jumped from 3,736 to 5,411.[20] Thus, while the number of independent school districts declined by 20 percent, municipalities increased by 8 percent and special districts by 45 percent. These data suggest that the school problem has shown at least some improvement in the direction of reducing the number of independent districts, while the problems of local government are becoming increasingly segmented in metropolitan areas.

It seems ironic, at least to some, that in a society where an increasing proportion of the children continue their education into the college level, many school systems continue to function when

[20] *Ibid.*, unnumbered table, p. 2.

they do not provide any training beyond the elementary level. Yet in the 212 metropolitan areas we find that, in 1962, there were more than 2,500 independent school systems, 45 percent of all operating districts, providing the elementary grades only.[21] The residents of these areas have maintained local control over education, but only at the elementary levels. For the crucial college preparatory training, they must depend on secondary schools outside of their own districts. In perpetuating the "status quo," they have forfeited control over the education of their children in the secondary grades. This curious anomaly exists in almost half of the school districts in metropolitan areas.

Of all of the functions of government in metropolitan areas, education is clearly the major activity. From the point of view of number of people employed by local governments, we find that the education function accounts for nearly half the total. For example, in the Census of Governments report for 1962, it was reported that 48.2 percent of all full-time equivalent government employees were engaged in education.[22] And when we look at the general expenditures of local government, education accounts for 42 percent of the total.[23] However, education expenditures as a percent of the total tends to decrease as size of metropolitan area increases. While education accounts for half (49.6 percent) of the direct general expenditures in the metropolitan areas below 100,-000 population, the proportion declines to less than two-fifths (38.7 percent) in the metropolitan areas in the one million and over class. Government costs are generally higher in the larger metropolitan areas because services are more extensive. Although education accounts for a lower proportion of the total, it is noteworthy that the per capita expenditures for government tend to increase in the larger areas.[24] Thus on any dimension, it is clearly evident that the school problem in metropolitan areas is a highly

[21] *Ibid.*, Table 1, p. 21.

[22] This figure does not include the more than 200,000 members of local school boards. The economic magnitude of public education is fully discussed in Charles S. Benson, *The Economics of Public Education* (Boston: Houghton Mifflin, 1961), Appendix A.

[23] The general expenditures for education in all metropolitan areas exceeded the amount for all of the following functions combined: highways, public welfare, sanitation, health and hospitals, police and fire protection, housing and urban renewal, and parks and recreation. See U. S. Bureau of the Census, Census of Governments, *op. cit.* note 15, Table D, p. 10.

[24] *Ibid.*, "Graphic Summary," M/13, p. 19.

significant one. It is a function that places a heavy economic burden on the residents of the area. Yet it tends to be organized on a basis which is inconsistent with the pattern of settlement in metropolitan areas. And we find that little effective progress has been made toward the establishment of a more efficient type of system.[25] Small districts persist. The multiplicity of separate districts continues.

We are concerned first with how views regarding reorganization vary by place of residence within the metropolitan community, and secondly with how these vary by size of metropolitan area. A classification by type and size of place of residence is carried throughout the following analysis. Within the context of the different community settings, we are also concerned with how views regarding reorganization vary among different population subgroups and how these views vary by different life patterns within the community. Still another aspect of this study pertains to how local public officials view reorganization of school districts in metropolitan areas. Here, too, there is a particular concern with the reaction of officials in different parts of the metropolitan area. Consequently, in selecting a sample of officials, care was given to having each segment of the community represented by sufficient numbers so as to be able to examine differences by size and type of area. The selection of the sample as discussed below was designed to meet these needs.

Areas Selected for Study

In selecting the areas to be included in the study, several broad and general criteria were set forth. Of prime importance was that the areas should have comparable forms of local government and that state legislation should be similar in respect to school district and governmental organization. Since we were concerned with views on the reorganization of school districts and local government, we wanted metropolitan areas where a popular vote was usually needed in order to bring about change. We wanted areas which included a multiplicity of independent governmental units, including unincorporated townships as well as school districts.[26]

[25] Fitzwater, op. cit. note 3.
[26] This limited the study to the North Central and Middle Atlantic states.

We also wanted metropolitan areas that varied substantially in degree of complexity, regarding both local governments and the number of school systems. For example, the small metropolitan areas should represent the simplest form of governmental organization—that is, the area contiguous to the city should be largely unincorporated, but there should be multiple school districts. In the larger areas, an attempt was made to select metropolitan areas that were similar in the number of incorporated and unincorporated units of government in the urbanized areas contiguous to the city. In this way the level of complexity of reorganization would be approximately similar in each of the metropolitan areas in each size class, but would differ among size groups. Yet we did not want the areas to be so large and complex that the size of the problem would become unmanageable. Thus the largest metropolitan areas such as New York, Chicago, and Detroit were excluded from the study, on the assumption that the resolution of local government problems in such areas was of a dimension so complex in scope, and limited to only a few areas, that it would be more beneficial to concentrate our attention on the smaller, more representative metropolitan areas. On the basis of an educated judgment, we decided that we would work with metropolitan areas in three different population size classes where the population of the urbanized areas ranged in size from approximately 150,000 to around 800,000. This range would permit a test of the significance of size of area in resistance to change.

In the selection of the specific metropolitan areas to be included in each size class, a number of further requirements were established. In each size class, the two metropolitan areas included should be approximately matched for size of urbanized population and the proportion of the population that lived in the central city.[27] Within each size class, the central cities should differ in rates of population growth and the ratio of satellite to central city growth. In each area an attempt was made to include one city that was gaining population and one that was either declining in size or increasing at a much lower rate.[28] In addition to this, we also

---

[27] In addition, the two cities selected in each size class were similar in the percentage of white collar workers, economic base, employment-residence ratio, and proportion employed in manufacturing.

[28] In both the large and medium-sized metropolitan areas included in the study, one city in each actually lost population during the last decade, but in the small metropolitan areas the cities differ only in rate of growth.

wanted suburban areas in each size class that differed substantially in their rates of growth. Accordingly, data were compiled for all of the metropolitan areas, based on the 1960 Census, for the regions having comparable local governments in metropolitan areas. In each size class we selected the two metropolitan areas which seemed to best approximate the general criteria that we had set up. The cities selected were: Buffalo and Milwaukee, Dayton and Rochester, and Rockford and Saginaw.[29] The metropolitan area populations for these areas range from 1,300,000 to slightly less than 200,000.

Selection of Sample

The study is based on a random sample of nearly 3,000 residents and a sample of 630 public officials in central city and suburban areas in the six different metropolitan areas in the three different population size classes. So as to be able to maximize the possibilities of analysis and to be able to do the same depth of analysis for each area, different sampling rates were used in each size class and in various segments of the metropolitan areas. The sample was designed so as to have an approximately equal number of respondents in each city and suburban area, regardless of the size of the population. In each of the six metropolitan areas, the original design for the random sample called for about 500 interviews equally divided between the central city and the suburban areas.

City directories constituted the basic sampling frames in all of the central cities and in a number of the minor civil divisions in the suburban areas. In portions of the latter areas not covered by up-to-date city directories, conventional areal probability sampling procedures were employed.[30]

The boundary of the study in each metropolitan area was larger in scope than the urbanized area but less inclusive than the entire metropolitan area. The survey population was defined as the central city and all minor civil divisions contiguous to it. Included as contiguous were all incorporated areas completely surrounded by

[29] The number of incorporated cities and unincorporated townships in each of the areas are: Buffalo 7–5, Milwaukee 8–5, Dayton 3–6, Rochester 2–8, Rockford 1–5, and Saginaw 0–7.
[30] For a detailed description of the sample, see Appendix A.

an unincorporated minor civil division contiguous to the central city.[31]

The sample of public officials was also designed so as to have approximately the same number of interviews in each of the cities and a slightly larger number in each of the suburban areas. The latter were to be equally divided between school and municipal officials. Since the number of officials is rather limited in the cities, an attempt was made to draw a matched sample for each of the cities in the study. Consequently, the minimum number of officials of a given type in any of the city areas placed the upper limit on the number of officials of that type who could be included in the sample of officials in any of the other cities. Officials were equally divided between elected and appointed positions. The reason for employing this method in selecting the officials to be studied is that we were primarily interested in how the responses of officials would differ by size of city. Thus an attempt was made to hold the composition of officials constant in all of the areas. Similarly matched samples of officials were also selected in each of the suburban areas. In the latter areas, officials were equally divided between school and municipal officials. Lists of all officials, municipal and school, were compiled for each of the city and suburban areas from which matched samples of the officials to be interviewed were then selected. Here, too, samples of the same size were selected from each of the areas, even though there were differences in the total number of officials. In the city areas, the research design called for approximately 90 elected and appointed officials in each size class. In the suburbs the sample was limited to approximately 125, and these were equally divided between school and municipal officials in each size group. In all, 630 public officials were interviewed.

Since this study is concerned with how people in the different parts of the metropolitan area would respond to a proposal for change in terms of their knowledge, their attitudes, and their level of involvement in the community, it is important that we first note some of the salient characteristics of the population. We would expect behavior, as well as responses, to be largely in-

---

[31] While this particular areal delineation is not congruent with any established statistical unit, it was deemed optimal for the present study, owing to its relevance to the problems of metropolitan integration.

TABLE 1-2

SELECTED CHARACTERISTICS OF SAMPLE POPULATION
BY PLACE OF RESIDENCE AND SIZE OF METROPOLITAN AREA

Selected Characteristics	Large		Medium		Small	
	City	Suburb	City	Suburb	City	Suburb
	%	%	%	%	%	%
Residential Experience						
Lived in opposite area	18.5	67.9	24.7	64.6	26.3	73.4
Never lived in opposite area	80.9	31.5	73.7	24.5	72.6	26.2
Tenure						
Home owners	45.9	73.1	55.8	84.6	66.2	84.1
*Education**						
Grade school level	33.4	20.6	32.0	15.2	28.9	30.0
College or more	15.5	26.3	18.1	31.1	13.5	15.9
Occupation						
White collar workers	30.9	52.0	34.6	53.1	34.6	34.9
Professional-managerial	17.4	34.6	19.7	39.5	19.2	21.3
Age						
Household heads 65 years and over	17.4	12.5	19.7	9.1	18.6	10.8
Income						
Median income	$4,728	$5,778	$4,906	$5,792	$4,513	$5,612

* Refers to education of respondent. Throughout the study, with the exception of occupation and income, personal characteristics are those of the respondent. Occupational status and income are based on the head of household.

fluenced by the set of characteristics borne by the population in the different residential categories. Accordingly, attention is focused on the distribution of selected characteristics of the sample populations in the central city and suburban areas in each metropolitan size class. These data are shown in Table 1-2.

Population Characteristics

It is readily evident that the historical boundary line between city and suburbs effectively segregates populations which differ consistently and markedly in many characteristics. First of all, the previous residential experience of the population indicates that a very large proportion of the residents in the suburbs have previously lived in the city, while only a small minority of the city residents have ever lived in the surrounding suburban areas. From two-thirds to nearly three-fourths of the suburban residents have lived in the city, whereas one-fourth or less of the city residents have ever lived in the suburban areas. This movement pattern characterizes each metropolitan area, but movement across the city-suburban border in both directions occurs most frequently in the small metropolitan areas. At any rate, residential experience of the suburban residents has been such that a substantial majority are familiar with city living. However, from the point of view of metropolitan reform, which would consolidate the suburbs with the city, this movement history may prove to be one of the obstacles to change.[32]

To the extent that home ownership is any measure of the ties people have with the local community, it is clear that suburban residents would exceed those living in the city. At any rate, suburban residents are much more likely to own their homes. However, the city-suburban difference declines substantially by size of metropolitan area. Home ownership increases in both city and suburban areas as the size of the metropolitan area declines, though the proportionate increase is much larger in the cities than in the suburbs. While only 46 percent of the households in the large cities own their home, this increases to two-thirds in the small cities. In the suburbs, where the frequency of home ownership is much higher, the variation is only from 73 percent to 84 percent. In this respect city and suburban populations again differ substantially. But the populations also differ in respect to a number of socioeconomic characteristics.

Except in the small metropolitan areas, the sample populations typify the usual city-suburban differences. The city populations tend to be made up disproportionately of persons in the lower

[32] In an earlier study concerned with local government in a single metropolitan area, the authors found that "those who have never lived in the alternate place are considerably more in favor of a solution involving some sort of joint action by central city and fringe than are those who have lived in both places. And, conversely, residents who have lived in both places are more strongly inclined toward solutions through local action independently of the central city." Zimmer and Hawley, op. cit. note 2, p. 598.

socioeconomic groups, while suburban residents tend to be those who are at the upper levels. When we look at the proportion who have only a grade school education in both large and medium-sized areas, the proportion in the cities exceeds the suburbs by two-thirds or more; no differences, however, are found in the small metropolitan areas. Similarly, in respect to the proportion who have at least some college training, no differences are found between city and suburbs in the small metropolitan areas, but sizable differences in favor of the suburbs are found in the other metropolitan areas. The same pattern is also observed in respect to the proportion in white collar occupations, as well as in the proportion in the higher white collar groups, that is, the professional and managerial workers. In both the large and medium-sized areas, the proportion in the suburbs exceeds those in the city by more than 100 percent, but this difference disappears in the small metropolitan areas.

It is only in the small metropolitan areas that the typical "class" differences between city and suburbs are not found. For the most part, the city and suburban populations in the small areas tend to be very similar, at least in terms of educational and occupational composition. And to the extent that these variables help to account for resistance to change, we would expect least city-suburban difference in the small metropolitan areas. But the issue is not quite that straightforward or clear, for when we focus on age composition and income, the usual city-suburban differences are found even in the small areas. Without exception, cities in each size class have a disproportionately large number of household heads who are sixty-five years of age or over. On the other hand, median income is consistently higher in the suburban areas. The city-suburban gap fluctuates around $1,000 in all areas in favor of the suburban residents. These income differences we would expect because of differences in occupational structure, but even in a more detailed analysis, where occupation was employed as a control, the suburban areas consistently showed higher incomes within each occupational category. Apparently suburban areas tend to select out the upper income levels within each occupational category.

That the movement out from the city disproportionately attracts the new generation of households is evident when we look at the family life cycle stages of the suburban population as compared with the cities in each metropolitan area size class. The young childless couples are found twice as frequently in the cities as in the suburbs. Apparently in the early formation of the family there is a tendency to settle first in the city. No doubt this is largely due to the greater availability of small rental units. However, with the arrival of children people seek out a home on the periphery of the built-up areas, where less expensive and newer housing is available. They become home owners. Consequently the suburban areas are made up primarily of couples with young children. Our sample data show that couples with young pre-school-age children and couples with children of school age—that is, between six and seventeen years of age—predominate in the suburbs. The proportion of such households increases as size of metropolitan area declines. Families at these stages of the life cycle account for less than one-half of the households in the city, but they make up from 53 percent to 67 percent of the household units in the suburban areas. On the other hand, the cities, regardless of size, contain a disproportionate number of the couples with no children or with all children over seventeen years of age. Also incomplete family units are much more concentrated in the cities than in the suburban areas.[33]

The data for the present sample indicate that the centrifugal movement of population within metropolitan areas results in the effective sorting of populations between city and suburban areas so as to lead to marked differences in population composition. Not only are the families in the early stages of the family life cycle moving away from the city, but there is also a substantial withdrawal of the upper occupational, educational, and income levels. This pattern of movement has produced a governmental segregation by social class.[34] Similarly, city and suburban school districts are also likely to reflect social class differences. And while the larger community is closely integrated in the daily economic and social

[33] Here, too, the greater availability of rental units in the city likely accounts for much of this. However, another factor is that when family units are broken by the death of one of the partners, there is a tendency for the survivor to continue to live in the original home. Since such persons tend to be old, these homes would have been established during a much earlier period and would be concentrated in the cities.

[34] Scott Greer, *op. cit.* note 6, p. 109.

activities of life, it is segmented into parts for both the governmental and educational function. And as pointed out earlier, integration at the administrative level continues to lag behind the growth and development of the metropolitan community in all other respects. This final stage in the progressive and logical development of the metropolitan community meets with strong and persistent opposition. Although it is a stage felt to be necessary by many, it has failed to develop.[35]

The present structure of the suburb in relationship to the city in metropolitan areas has been appraised by one observer thusly: "There is no economic reason for its existence and there is no technological basis for its support. There is only the stubborn conviction of the majority of suburbanites that it ought to exist, even though it plays havoc with both the life and government of our urban age." [36] And since the reorganization of school districts is a crucial dimension in the more general problem, this provides sufficient justification for focusing on the factors that account for resistance to change.

Focus of Study

The primary purpose of this study is to investigate the factors accounting for resistance to change in the organization of school districts. Before addressing ourselves to this question, we shall focus our discussion on the level of involvement, the views shared, and the amount of knowledge the metropolitan population has concerning their schools. The major emphasis will be on city-suburban and size of metropolitan area differences. The first several chapters will report on the use of the schools, the level of knowl-

[35] It is of interest to note that much more progress has been made in adjusting school district organization to the depopulation of rural areas than to the new pattern of settlement in metropolitan areas. For example, the total number of school districts in the United States declined from 52,913 in 1957 to 37,019 in 1962. Thus during the five-year period the number of districts declined by nearly 16,000, which is a 30 percent decrease. However, during the same period the number of school districts in the 212 metropolitan areas declined only 20 percent. Consequently, while the metropolitan areas accounted for only 14 percent of the total districts in 1957, this had increased to 18 percent by 1962. Data taken from Census of Governments reports in 1957 and 1962.
[36] Robert C. Wood, *Suburbia: Its People and Their Politics* (Boston: Houghton Mifflin, 1958), p. 19.

edge and participation in schools and school-related activities, the views residents have regarding school taxes and the level of government that should support schools, and how residents compare their schools with those in the opposite parts of the metropolitan community. Since these are all important aspects of the school problem in metropolitan areas, they have descriptive merit, but in addition we will attempt to determine how variations in each of these respects among the residents account for resistance to change. The second part of the discussion will be concerned with the views that residents in different parts of the metropolitan area have regarding district reorganization. And lastly, attention will be focused on how public officials compare with the general population in respect to school issues and the question of reorganization.

2

Use of the Schools

BY VIRTUE OF THE manner in which public schools are financed, they are or should be a concern of every taxpayer, whether his tax payments are made directly or through the intermediary of a landlord. But an additional element of vested interest attaches to those taxpayers who are the immediate beneficiaries of school services, those who have children in school. No great exercise of the imagination is required to anticipate that the two sectors of the population, the direct and the indirect beneficiaries of school services, are not only variously composed but also differentially distributed over metropolitan areas. Nevertheless, we need to know what these differences are, for we assume that they underlie the collective attitude toward the administrative organization of schools. In this and the following two chapters we shall examine the structure of the population in which school issues are debated and resolved.

First of all, it is evident from our data that a very large proportion of the household units in all residential sub-areas do not have children in school at the present time. This factor must be taken into account when attempting to seek community support of school-related issues. Of course these data do not mean that all such households have not had any previous contact with the schools or will not have children in school in the future. On the contrary, those in the older ages may have had children in school in the district at some earlier period, and the younger couples likely have or will have children who will enter schools at a later date. Consequently, the latter in particular would be concerned about the future of the schools in their area. Also, many of those living in the areas may have attended schools in the district in earlier years. At any rate, at the present time a substantial proportion of the population have no formal contacts with the schools in their area.

However, marked differences are found in use of the schools by both place of residence and size of metropolitan area. For example, the proportion of households in the central city with no children in school exceeds the proportion in the suburbs by more than one-fifth in each size class. In the large metropolitan areas, where the central city-suburban difference is least, we find that nearly two-thirds (63.9 percent) of the households in the city have no children in school, as compared with slightly more than half (52.9 percent) of the suburban households. Thus the city exceeds the suburban proportion by more than 20 percent. The proportion of households with no children in school ranges from a low of 43 percent in the small suburbs to a high of 64 percent in the large cities. Thus the latter area exceeds the former by nearly 50 percent.

Not only are the suburban area households more likely to have children in school than central city residents, but they are also more likely in each size class to have several children in school at the same time. Considering all grade levels, the proportion with two or more children in school ranges from a low of 22 percent of the city households in the large metropolitan areas to a high of 39 percent of those living in the suburbs of the small metropolitan areas. The latter area exceeds the former by some 80 percent. While the differences between central city and suburbs tends to be similar in each size class, the proportion with two or more children in school tends to increase in both residential areas as the size of the metropolitan community decreases. In the city, the proportion increases from 22 percent in the large areas to 29 percent in the small areas. Among suburban households, the proportion for the respective areas increases from 29 percent to 39 percent.

Differences by place of residence are much more marked at the elementary than at the high school level. At both school levels in each population size group, we find a larger proportion of households with children in school, and with two or more children in school, among suburban than central city households. Whereas only slightly more than half of the suburban households in the small metropolitan areas have no children in elementary school, this proportion increases to nearly three-fourths of the households in the large cities. At the high school level, the range for the same areas is only from 82 percent to 85 percent. Thus, at the elementary school level, the proportion with no children in school in the large cities exceeds the proportion in the small suburbs by 45 percent, but the difference at the high school level is only about 3 percent.

It is of particular interest to note that more than eight households out of ten in all residential areas do not have any children in high school. This makes it readily apparent that the proponents of any proposal regarding the high schools in the area that needs the support of the whole community, could effectively reach only a small minority directly through the high schools themselves. Thus at any given point in time, only a small segment of the population makes use of the high schools in the district, whereas a much larger proportion, but still not a majority of the households, have children in the elementary schools.

Type of School Children Attend

Another dimension to be considered in describing the use of schools in metropolitan areas is the type of school attended. Whether residents use the public or non-public schools is likely to be a significant factor in their willingness to support the local school system; and more particularly, in terms of the focus of this study, type of school attended may be an important factor in how the residents would react to any proposal to reorganize the school districts within the metropolitan area. Although we have already observed that suburban households are more likely to have children in school than city households, particularly at the elementary level, the differences in use of the public schools is even more marked. For total households, the proportion with children in public schools tends to increase as the size of the metropolitan area decreases. The same pattern is observed in both residential areas. Among central city residents, the proportion of total households with children attending a public elementary school ranges from a low of 14 percent in the large areas to a high of 26 percent in the small areas. Medium-sized areas fall midway along this range. Small cities exceed the large cities by approximately 85 percent. Among suburban areas, households with children in public schools range from 24 percent in the large areas to a high of 42 percent in the small metropolitan areas. Here, too, the medium-sized areas fall approximately midway between the extremes. A very similar pattern by place of residence is found at the high school level also, but the size of the differences is much less marked.

These differences are due to a combination of at least three factors. One, of course, is the greater use of schools among suburban residents, which is a function of the composition of the population; and secondly, suburban residents, when they do have children in school, are more likely than city residents to use public than non-public schools. Thirdly, the religious composition of the population varies markedly by size of metropolitan area. We also find small differences between central city and suburban residents in religious affiliation. In short, the large metropolitan areas have a much larger proportion of Catholics than is found in either of the other two size classes. The smallest proportion of Catholics is found in the small metropolitan areas, particularly in the suburbs. The proportion of households that are Catholic ranges from only 23 percent in the small suburbs to 51 percent in the large cities.

Not only are suburban households more likely to have children in school, but the proportion in public school as opposed to non-public is also substantially higher than is found among central city residents. The same pattern of difference is found within each population size group. For example, only slightly more than half of the children in school in the large cities attend public school, as compared with more than two-thirds of the children in the suburbs of the same areas. In the small metropolitan areas, 72 percent of the families in the city have their children in public schools but the proportion increases to 86 percent among the suburban families. In neither of the above instances is there a substantial difference in the proportion of Catholics living in the suburbs as compared with the city.

Even at the high school level, the tendency is for the suburban families with children in high school to use the public schools more so than central city families. However, it is noted that in all residential zones families are more likely to send their children to public high schools than to public elementary schools. The difference is substantial except in the small suburbs where children are least likely to attend a non-public school at any grade level. In the latter areas, more than 85 percent of the families with children in school have their children in public schools. The greater use of the public schools at the high school level in most residential areas is likely a function of both the large proportion of Protestants in these areas as well as the unavailability of non-public facilities at these grade levels, particularly in the suburban areas. It would seem quite obvious that the reaction to school issues would vary considerably among these areas as a result of differences in the use of public schools.

It is to be expected that use of the schools would vary markedly by age of the respondent, in that only certain age groups are likely to have children of school age. This is clearly shown by the data presented in Table 2-1. For the respondents under 25 years of age only a very small percentage have any children in school, and almost without exception when they do have children in school they are in the public schools. These doubtlessly are kindergarten children for which only public facilities are generally available. The peak use of the schools occurs in households where the respondent is in the middle age category, that is, those between 35 and 44 years of age. But even in this category suburban residents are more likely to have children in school than central city residents.

The proportion of households with children in school shows the same pattern of variation by age in all residential zones. With only one exception in each age group we find that more than 90 percent of the households under 25 years and over 55 years do not have any children in school. Neither place of residence nor size of population appears to have any significant affect on this proportion. Within each age group, suburban areas in each size class tend to have not only a larger proportion of families with children in school, but also a larger proportion with children in public schools. Focusing on the age group most likely to have children in school, that is, those 35 to 44 years of age, we find that 44 percent of the households in the large metropolitan areas have children in public schools as compared with 56 percent of the suburban households. Families with children in non-public schools in the

TABLE 2-1

USE OF SCHOOLS BY TYPE OF SCHOOL CHILDREN ATTEND BY AGE OF RESPONDENT
BY PLACE OF RESIDENCE AND SIZE OF METROPOLITAN AREA

Age and Size of Metropolitan Area	Central City					Suburban Area				
	Number	Public	Public	None	Per-cent*	Number	Public	Public	None	Per-cent*
		%	%	%	%		%	%	%	%
Large										
Under 25 years	45	6.7	2.2	91.1	100.0	25	—	—	100.0	100.0
25–34	83	26.5	8.4	65.1	100.0	126	38.1	11.1	50.8	100.0
35–44	104	44.2	32.7	21.2	100.0	117	56.4	27.4	16.2	100.0
45–54	72	19.4	23.6	55.6	100.0	93	30.1	18.3	61.3	100.0
55 years plus	169	4.7	2.4	92.9	100.0	118	3.4	3.4	93.2	100.0
Medium										
Under 25 years	28	7.1	—	92.9	100.0	26	7.7	—	92.3	100.0
25–34	78	30.8	11.5	57.7	100.0	136	46.3	9.6	41.9	100.0
35–44	108	53.7	15.7	29.6	100.0	142	62.0	17.6	20.4	100.0
45–54	97	30.9	9.3	58.8	100.0	91	42.9	8.8	48.4	100.0
55 years plus	144	4.2	2.1	93.7	100.0	100	5.0	1.0	94.0	100.0
Small										
Under 25 years	34	11.8	—	88.2	100.0	37	8.1	—	91.9	100.0
25–34	101	50.5	14.9	34.7	100.0	133	63.2	8.3	28.6	100.0
35–44	112	58.9	20.5	19.6	100.0	133	72.9	11.3	15.8	100.0
45–54	94	36.2	12.8	51.0	100.0	88	43.2	12.5	44.3	100.0
55 years plus	144	3.5	1.4	95.1	100.0	99	10.1	—	89.9	100.0

* May not add to 100 percent because the "no answer" category is not shown but it was included in the calculations.

same areas ranges from a high of 33 percent in the city to 27 percent in the suburbs. In the medium-sized areas we find that 62 percent of the suburban households in this age group have children in public school as compared with 54 percent of the central city households. And in the small metropolitan areas the proportion with children in public schools ranges from 59 percent in the city to 73 percent in the suburbs. At no other age level or in any sub-area does the use of the school equal this latter proportion.

Accessibility to School

Although suburban residents are more likely to have children in school than are central city residents, they are less accessible to the schools their children attend. These data are shown in Table 2-2. Within each size class, central city households with children

TABLE 2-2

DISTANCE TO ELEMENTARY SCHOOL CHILDREN ATTEND BY
PLACE OF RESIDENCE AND SIZE OF METROPOLITAN AREA

Distance	Large		Medium		Small	
	City	Suburb	City	Suburb	City	Suburb
Total number	125	173	130	214	180	241
	%	%	%	%	%	%
Within ¼ mile	72.8	45.1	53.1	38.8	57.2	28.2
¼ to ½ mile	12.0	18.5	18.5	19.2	22.8	15.4
½ to 1 mile	9.6	13.3	16.2	18.2	11.7	17.0
More than 1 mile	1.6	22.5	9.2	22.9	7.8	37.8
No answer	4.0	0.6	3.1	0.9	0.6	1.7
Total	100.0	100.0	100.0	100.0	100.0	100.0

in school live much closer to the elementary school attended than do suburban households. The differences by place of residence are striking. In the large metropolitan areas, nearly three-fourths of the city households with children in school live within one-quarter mile of the elementary school, whereas less than half of the suburban households do so. This is a difference of more than 60 percent in favor of the city. At the other extreme, less than 2 percent of the city households live more than one mile from the elementary school, but nearly one-fourth of the suburban households are found in this distance category. In this distance category, the suburban area households exceed the cities by 130 percent.

A similar but even more marked pattern of difference is found in the small metropolitan areas. In the first distance zone we find nearly three-fifths of the city households, but only slightly more than one-fourth of the suburban households. While only 8 percent of the city households are in the more distant zone, we find nearly five times that proportion among suburban residents. It is readily apparent from these data that suburban residents are much less accessible to schools than are central city residents.[1] We also find that accessibility varies directly by size of area. This is observed in both segments of the metropolitan community. Viewing only the large and small metropolitan areas, we find that while 73 percent of the residents of the large central city live within one-fourth mile of their school, this declines to only 57 percent in the small cities. In the suburbs, the proportion in this distance zone declines by size from 45 to 28 percent. These differences are largely the result of variations in density of settlement by size of metropolitan area and as between central cities and suburbs. Proximity to school also varies by type of school attended, but that is of less importance than place of residence. Regardless of the type of school attended, distance to school tends to decrease as the size of the community increases, and within each size class suburban residents must travel a greater distance to school than central city residents.

Method of Transportation to School

Since distance to school varies by place of residence, it is to be expected that method of transportation would also vary. In examining our data, marked differences are observed in how the children get to school. In the cities nearly all of the children walk to elementary school. It is only in the small metropolitan areas that a substantial number use some other method of transportation. Here

[1] These observations are consistent with earlier findings based on a single metropolitan area, reported by the authors in "Suburbanization and Some of its Consequences," *Land Economics*, XXXVII, No. 1 (Feb., 1961), pp. 588–593, where it was noted that "suburban residents sacrifice the accessibility and convenience of city living. They must travel greater distances in the journey to work, to church, to shopping areas, to elementary schools, and to friends."

more than 8 percent are taken to school by car, as compared with 5 percent in medium central cities and 3 percent in the large cities. Only a very small proportion of the children in any area use public transportation at the elementary school level. The most frequent use occurs in the small cities, but even here it is used by less than 3 percent of the families with children in school.

Similarly, school buses are rarely used by elementary school children in the city, but this is the method of transportation used by one-third or more of the elementary school children in each of the suburban areas. In the small suburbs this is the most frequently used method of transportation. Nearly half of the suburban families report this as the method used by their children in getting to school. In the cities, school buses are used rarely. This difference is, of course, partly a function of distance to school, but it is also due to the availability of such facilities in the suburbs. In the cities, school districts do not provide such facilities, since there is less need for school buses and the policy regarding the provision of transportation is different.

At any rate, the proportion of elementary children that walk to school in the suburbs tends to decrease directly as the size of the metropolitan area decreases. The proportion ranges from a high of 60 percent in the large suburbs to a low of 45 percent in the small suburbs, while the proportion using the school bus increases from 33 percent to 45 percent in the same areas. In both instances, the proportion in the medium-sized area suburbs is approximately midway between the large and small areas.

In all areas, children are much less likely to walk to high school than to elementary school because of the greater distances involved. But here, too, the proportions are higher in the cities than in the suburban areas. While the same pattern is found in all size classes, the proportion varies by size of metropolitan area. For example, in the large suburbs about one-third of the high school students walk, but this declines to only one-fifth in the small suburbs. On the other hand, the proportion riding the school bus increases from 43 percent to 52 percent. And while the proportion using public transportation decreases with size of area, the proportion that travel to school by car varies from 12 percent in the large suburbs to nearly 20 percent in the small suburbs. In the cities, the difference by size is even more marked. Use of the car increases inversely by size of area, ranging from 16 to 30 percent. The most frequent use of the car occurs in the small cities and, to a lesser extent, in the small suburbs.

Public transportation is much more likely to be used by central city than by suburban high school students. Whereas elementary school children rarely use public transportation, this is the method reported by one-fourth or more of the city households with children in high school. The most frequent use of public transportation is found in the large cities, where approximately one-third of the households report this as the method used by their children to get to high school.

One of the major differences observed between central cities and the suburbs is that high school students in the city tend disproportionately to use public transportation, whereas comparable suburban students are much more likely to ride school buses. Thus, in the large metropolitan areas, one-third of the city students use public transportation, while less than 3 percent use school buses. In the suburbs, school buses are used by more than two-fifths of the students, whereas public transportation is used by only slightly more than one-tenth. Differences are even more marked in both the medium and small suburbs. In the latter areas, while less than 3 percent of the city students use school buses, this is the method of transportation reported by more than half of the suburban households with children attending high school. And while public transportation is reported by one-fourth of the city families, it is reported by only 5 percent of the households in medium-sized suburbs and by 8 percent of those in the small suburbs. Thus public transportation is rarely used by high school students in the suburbs. In these areas, school buses tend to be the most frequent method of transportation used. However, the latter are rarely used in the city.

Similarly, at the elementary school level, school buses are frequently used in the suburbs but rarely, if ever, used in the city. Although we do not have any data on this, it is quite likely that the school buses reported by city residents mean something quite different from school buses reported by suburban residents. In the latter these are probably buses provided by the school district without charge to the students, while in the city this reference may be to buses that carry only school children but do so on a fee basis. This distinction is important, because it may be that part of the reason suburban residents resist change in organization is that this may result in the loss of "free" school bus transportation, since it is largely the non-city school districts that provide such facilities. Transportation is an important issue in the suburbs, since the schools are much less accessible and beyond walking distance. Consequently, some form of transportation is needed. And the regular public transportation generally available to city residents may be lacking in the suburbs, and even if available in these areas it would tend to be quite inaccessible for use by school children because of the more widespread settlement pattern in the suburbs. To join with the city may mean the end to school buses. Accordingly, residents may resist change and prefer the existing system.

Summary

In this chapter we have attempted to describe the extent to which the population is currently using the schools in the community at both the elementary and secondary levels. We have found that only a small proportion of the households have children in school, particularly at the high school level. Also, even among the segment of the population with children in school, a substantial proportion are not using public facilities but have elected rather to send their children to non-public schools. This is most likely to occur at the elementary school level. Use of non-public facilities varies by size of community, but the differences are largely due to variations in the proportion of the population that is Catholic in the different-sized metropolitan areas. But even apart from religious composition of the areas, suburban residents are more likely than city residents to use public rather than non-public facilities. Suburban households are not only more likely to have children in school than are city households, but they are also more likely to have children in the public schools. Use of the school increases as size of the community decreases. This pattern persists even when we control for differences in the composition of the population in the residential zones. The implications of the findings regarding use of the schools are many, but the one of importance here pertains to the question of how lack of immediate contact with the schools will influence the position people will take concerning school issues. Since reorganization of school districts generally requires the support of the population of the communities or districts involved, we are interested in how concern over this issue varies by the amount of use people make of the schools. One such issue concerns the extent to which resistance to change is due to ignorance resulting from lack of familiarity with school problems, since residents do not have any direct contact with the schools.

We have also found that schools tend to be much less accessible to suburban residents, as compared with those living in the city. Also, accessibility tends to decrease with size of community. Consequently, the method of transportation used also varies by size of community, and large differences are found between central cities and the suburbs. Of particular significance is the more widespread use of school buses in the suburbs. Since these facilities tend to be provided in the suburbs without cost to the residents using the buses and are not provided in the city, this could well be one of the factors accounting for resistance to change, since this service would likely be discontinued if the suburbs joined with the central city into a single district. Yet some form of transport is needed, since schools tend to be beyond walking distance—as is evident from the much lower proportion of children who walk to school in the suburbs.

In the foregoing discussion we have noted several differentia which would seem to bear on interest in school organization. First, very substantial proportions of the households, ranging upwards from two-fifths of the totals, have no children in schools, though they contribute in one way or another to the costs of schools. Conceivably the adults in these households might be more amenable to proposals directed at achieving improved efficiency and lowered costs of school operation. Yet the lowest proportions of households without children in school are found in suburbs, which is where the problems of school financing and administration are most severely felt. Second, over one-fifth of all households send their children to non-public schools. They, in other words, pay two school bills. The majority of that group, however, do have to turn to the public schools when their children reach high school age. Third, suburban residents are inconvenienced by relatively greater distances to schools.

3

Knowledge of and Participation in School-Related Activities

ULTIMATELY, ANY BASIC CHANGES in the organization of school districts in metropolitan areas, under existing legislation, can come about only when the change has the support of the population in all segments of the community. There are, of course, a multitude of dimensions to the factors that may influence the decisions of the residents of the area when faced with a proposal for change. Certainly, important dimensions in the response of residents to any school issue would be their level of knowledge concerning the schools and the extent of their involvement in school-related functions. In the analyses to follow, particular attention will continue to be directed to central city-suburban differences as well as to differences by size of metropolitan area. The indices used to measure both knowledge of schools and participation in school-related activities are admittedly crude, but they will provide at least a rough measure for comparative purposes.

Only households that have children in school at either the elementary or high school level were asked if they knew the name of the principal of the school their child attended. The responses, which represent one dimension of knowledge of the schools, are shown in Table 3-1. It should be emphasized that these findings apply to only a segment of the population. It is quite certain that the proportion not knowing the name of the principal would have been much larger had the responses been obtained from all house-

TABLE 3-1

KNOWLEDGE OF THE PRINCIPAL BY SCHOOL LEVEL CHILDREN ATTEND
BY PLACE OF RESIDENCE AND SIZE OF METROPOLITAN AREA*

Know Name of Principal and School Level	Large		Medium		Small	
	City	Suburb	City	Suburb	City	Suburb
Elementary School						
Total Number	125	173	130	214	180	242
	%	%	%	%	%	%
Know	73.6	82.1	77.7	79.9	78.3	76.9
Not know	23.2	17.9	20.0	20.1	21.7	20.2
No answer	3.2	—	2.3	—	—	2.9
Total	100.0	100.0	100.0	100.0	100.0	100.0
High School						
Total Number	70	89	69	84	79	87
	%	%	%	%	%	%
Know	67.2	80.9	69.6	75.0	74.7	55.2
Not know	31.4	19.1	29.0	25.0	24.1	39.1
No answer	1.4	—	1.4	—	1.2	5.7
Total	100.0	100.0	100.0	100.0	100.0	100.0

* These data refer only to those households that have children in school at each grade level.

holders in the sample.[1] With very little variation either by place of residence or size of community, we note that approximately one-fifth of the households with children in elementary school report that they do not know the name of the principal of the elementary school attended by their children. There is, however, a slight tendency for the proportion knowing the name of the elementary school principal to be higher in the suburbs than in the city. The only exception occurs in the small metropolitan areas.

At the high school level, the pattern of difference is similar but the size of the difference is more marked, particularly in the large metropolitan areas. Again, with the exception of the small metropolitan areas, suburban residents are more likely to know the principal of the high school than are central city residents. While in the

[1] For example, the 74 percent who know the name of the elementary school principal in the large cities make up only 19 percent of the total households, and the 67 percent who know the high school principal includes less than 10 percent of the households. Similar ratios obtain in all of the other areas.

cities the proportion not knowing the name of the high school principal increases directly by size of area, the opposite pattern is found among suburban residents. However, it is noted that a distinct majority in all areas knows the name of the principal at both school levels. But residents are more likely to know the elementary than the high school principal. Of particular significance is the disproportionately large number in the small suburbs who do not know the name of the high school principal. The reasons for this are not readily clear, but one possible explanation is that in such areas students may have to go outside of their own district to attend high school, whereas in the larger suburbs residents have their own high school. At any rate, on this dimension of knowledge of schools the small suburbs rank lowest, while the large suburbs rank highest.

Quite the opposite is found regarding level of knowledge by place of residence and size of metropolitan area, when the total population is considered and the question pertains to the superintendent of the local school district. Admittedly this position is much further removed from the population, particularly among those with children in school, than the position of school principal, yet in view of the importance of the position it would seem reasonable to expect that residents would know the name of the superintendent and how he obtains his position. At any rate, we have assumed that variations in such knowledge represent differences in awareness of school issues.

Whereas suburban residents were more likely to know the school principal, they seem to have less knowledge than city residents concerning the superintendent. In each size class, the proportion not knowing the name of the superintendent of schools is higher in the suburbs than in the cities. The most marked differences are found in the large metropolitan areas, where 56 percent of the city residents report that they "do not know," as compared with 69 percent of the suburban residents. The latter were also more likely to report the wrong name. That is, they thought they knew the superintendent but did not give the correct name when asked to do so.

Viewed differently, nearly two-fifths of the large city residents reported the correct name of the superintendent, while only slightly more than one-fifth of the suburban residents did so. In the medium-sized metropolitan areas, little difference is found between central city and suburban residents, but in the small metropolitan areas city residents again exceed the proportion of correct responses in the suburbs. The point to be emphasized here is that a majority of the population in each area do not know the name of the superintendent of schools in their districts. The proportion is highest in the large suburbs and tends to decline with size, but the range is only from 75 percent to 65 percent. No such clear pattern of difference by size is found in the cities. However, the proportion "not knowing" is lowest (49 percent) in the small cities. It is in the small cities that the largest proportion gives the correct name of the superintendent of schools, but even here the proportion is less than two-fifths.

The level of knowledge is even more limited when we view the proportion of residents who know how the superintendent of schools obtains his position. Although the level of knowledge is substantially lower, we find that suburban people have more knowledge of this than do city residents. The pattern of difference is the same in each size class but the size of the difference is most marked in the large metropolitan areas, where only 11 percent of the city residents give the correct answer, as compared with 19 percent among suburban residents. The higher proportion of correct responses in the suburbs may be due in part to the larger proportion of households with children in school than is found in the city. While the residents in the large metropolitan area cities and suburbs have the lowest proportion of correct responses, the highest proportions are found in the medium-sized areas. But as important as this position is to a school district, since it is the superintendent who provides the leadership for developing the school program, it is somewhat surprising that in none of the areas do we find that even one-third of the households know how the position is filled.

A further examination of the data reveals an interesting cleavage in the possession of knowledge. While the proportions of suburban residents who know how the superintendent is selected are larger than the corresponding proportions in central cities, suburbs also include larger proportions who confess that they are ignorant in that respect. This latter may be a consequence of shorter durations of residence. Yet larger proportions of central city residents have incorrect knowledge of how school superintendents obtain their positions. At this juncture we can only guess that such knowledge may be affected by direct involvement in school activities. This, of course, could not account for the greater readiness to give an incor-

rect answer rather than to admit ignorance. Perhaps the most significant finding here is not so much the variations in knowledge by
place of residence or size of metropolitan area, but rather the substantial proportion of households in all areas that are lacking in
knowledge concerning this important official position.

Continuing the same type of inquiry, similar questions were asked
concerning the school board, or board of education, as it is frequently called. The first question asked for the name of the chairman
of the board and the second question was concerned with how he
obtained his position. The responses to these questions are shown
in Table 3-2. The most striking observation here is the almost complete lack of knowledge as far as that position is concerned. The
proportion of people able to give the correct name of the chairman
of the board of education is higher in the cities than in the suburbs
in both small and medium-sized metropolitan areas. But the highest
proportion, found in the small cities, is only 14 percent. At least in
the cities, there is a steady increase in the proportion who know the
name of the chairman as size decreases. The range is from a low of
only 2 percent in the large cities to a high of 14 percent in the small
cities. Approximately one in twenty gave the wrong name, and
three-fourths of the residents reported that they did not know who
was chairman. In the small suburbs, only 5 percent gave the correct
name, while 8 percent gave the wrong name and 86 percent are in
the "don't know" category. The proportion in the latter category
tends to increase slightly with size, reaching the highest proportion
in the large suburbs. The same pattern by size is found for the city
residents. Among the latter, the range is from 76 percent in the
small cities to 84 percent in the large cities. The proportion reporting the wrong name in the suburbs varies inversely with size. It may
be that the turnover in chairman is more frequent in the smaller
areas and the residents are reporting a recent incumbent of the
position without knowing that the position has passed on to another
member of the board.

More residents know how the chairman obtains his position than
who currently occupies the position. But again we find that only a
small proportion answered the question correctly. In no area does
the proportion reach 20 percent. Except for differences in the large
metropolitan areas, where suburban residents exceed the central
city in the proportion knowing how the chairman is selected, there

TABLE 3-2

KNOWLEDGE OF SCHOOL BOARD BY PLACE OF RESIDENCE
AND SIZE OF METROPOLITAN AREA

Knowledge of School Board	Large		Medium		Small	
	City	Suburb	City	Suburb	City	Suburb
Total Number	477	495	457	493	488	492
	%	%	%	%	%	%
Who is Chairman of the Board?						
Total	100.0	100.0	100.0	100.0	100.0	100.0
Gives correct name	2.3	4.4	11.8	7.5	13.9	5.1
Gives wrong name	11.7	3.4	4.2	5.3	5.3	7.9
Don't know	83.6	89.7	77.9	86.2	76.4	85.6
No answer	2.3	2.4	6.1	1.0	4.3	1.4
How is Chairman of Board Selected?						
Total	100.0	100.0	100.0	100.0	100.0	100.0
Selected or Appointed:						
by Board	9.9	16.2	19.0	19.1	17.8	15.4
Non-specified	27.0	13.5	14.7	7.9	19.5	8.3
Elected	8.6	14.1	11.2	12.2	6.4	13.4
Don't know	51.4	52.9	48.4	58.2	51.8	60.2
No answer	3.1	3.2	6.8	2.6	4.5	2.6
Know Any Member of the Board?						
Total	100.0	100.0	100.0	100.0	100.0	100.0
Yes	11.5	19.4	14.9	24.7	19.5	28.9
No	85.7	77.8	78.6	73.6	76.2	68.7
No answer	2.7	2.8	6.6	1.6	4.3	2.4

seems to be little or no difference by place of residence. In each size group, city residents are more likely to give an incorrect response, whereas suburban residents tend to be concentrated disproportionately in the "don't know" category. Thus, again we find that city residents are more likely to have faulty information whereas suburban respondents are likely to realize that they do not have the knowledge at hand.

As measured by knowing the names of persons who occupy rather key positions in the local school system, the level of knowledge in all metropolitan areas is very limited. To the extent that differences are found, knowledge tends to be somewhat more frequent among suburban households than among those living in the city. There is also a tendency for knowledge to increase with decrease in community size, but the size of the differences and the pattern of differences are neither consistent nor striking.

The questions to this point have been administrative in character. The lowest panel of Table 3-2 reports data of a more personal kind. Individuals may be acquainted with school board members without knowing their specific responsibilities as members of boards. The proportion of residents who know members of the local board of education follows a distinct pattern both by place of residence and size of metropolitan area. Suburban households are more likely to know a member of the school board than are city households. The pattern of difference as well as the size of the differences between cities and suburbs tends to be approximately the same in each size class. In both segments of the metropolitan community, the proportion reporting that they know a board member increases as the size of the community decreases. Of all the subgroups included, the level of acquaintance is highest in the suburbs of small areas and lowest in the central cities of large areas. The range is from a high of 29 percent to a low of only 12 percent.

But again the striking observation is the large proportion of households that do not know a member of the school board. Even in the suburbs of small areas, where one would expect informality and neighborliness to prevail, particularly in reference to the local school districts, we find that more than two-thirds of the residents do not know a member of the school board. In the large cities, the proportion increases to 86 percent. This means that in the large cities only slightly more than one household out of ten, as compared with one in three in the small suburbs, knows at least one of the current members of the board of education. This would seem to support the stereotype that an advantage of small districts is that it functions closer to the people. At least in the smaller districts more of the residents feel that they know some of the people holding important offices, whereas in the city, contacts as well as acquaintances are more limited. This might well be one of the factors involved in resistance to change, since suburban residents may feel that in the larger district they would lose the closeness of association they now have with school leaders. If so, it bears upon a small minority of residents.

Knowledge of Course Offerings

Still another measure of knowledge of schools is found in the responses to a series of questions asking whether or not specific types of courses were offered at the high school level in their district. To answer such questions correctly demands a rather thorough familiarity with the programs provided in the high school. There is uncertainty, however, in such questions, for the respondent may give either a "yes" or "no" answer based on incomplete or even faulty knowledge. Nonetheless, the "don't know" responses at least represent householders who do not know and report that they do not know whether a specific course, program, or facility is provided by the local high school. It is to be noted, however, that the question as asked fails to distinguish those who give an incorrect answer. For this reason we report only the frequencies of "don't know" answers in Table 3-3.

TABLE 3-3

PERCENTAGE OF RESPONDENTS REPORTING "DON'T KNOW" IF COURSE
IS OFFERED IN HIGH SCHOOL BY PLACE OF RESIDENCE
AND SIZE OF METROPOLITAN AREA

Course Offerings	Large		Medium		Small	
	City	Suburb	City	Suburb	City	Suburb
	%	%	%	%	%	%
Latin	32.2	26.3	28.9	35.5	21.3	35.6
Foreign language	27.2	18.1	24.7	30.6	20.0	32.5
Trigonometry	40.7	25.1	36.3	37.5	31.3	38.8
Geometry	28.7	15.1	24.7	28.8	19.1	29.5
Calculus	59.1	50.2	58.2	62.5	55.4	58.8
Physics laboratory	36.6	22.2	27.8	35.1	24.4	31.9
Chemistry	31.4	18.5	23.4	29.6	18.2	28.3
Advanced placement	53.0	51.5	57.1	59.6	56.2	60.3
Gymnasium	21.8	11.3	15.5	20.9	9.9	19.3
Swimming pool	29.5	13.9	23.9	28.7	11.7	23.9
Shop work	28.2	19.9	21.1	30.7	13.3	25.8
Average	35.3	24.7	31.1	36.3	25.5	35.0

There is a marked tendency for the proportion of "don't know" responses to be highest in respect to the more specialized and less obvious subjects or programs. Thus in all areas, the proportion is highest regarding calculus and advanced placement courses. And for these two offerings there is a slight tendency in both cities and suburbs for the proportion of "don't knows" to increase as the size of the community decreases. But there is no consistent pattern of difference by place of residence. It is only among these offerings that a majority of the households report that they "don't know" if these are provided in their high school. The proportion of "don't know" responses is substantially lower for the other offerings, but in most instances the proportions are quite high. It is interesting to note that in respect to the three course offerings in mathematics covered in the interview, the lowest proportion of "don't knows" is reported for geometry, while trigonometry falls in between this and calculus. The same pattern is found in each area and in each size class. But again, we do not find any consistent pattern of difference in the "don't know" responses between city and suburban residents. Much the same is found in response to all of the other offerings.

Although there is no set pattern of difference by place of residence within the metropolitan community, there is a marked pattern of difference by size of population. However, the striking finding here is that the effect of size on knowledge of high school offerings appear to operate in different ways as between central cities and suburbs. Almost without exception for each course offering, the proportion of "don't know" responses decreases with size among city residents, but among suburban residents the proportion tends to increase. The net effect is that the proportion of "don't know" responses tend to be highest in the large cities and in the medium-sized and small suburbs. This pattern of difference holds for every offering considered. The pattern by size class, as well as central city-suburban differences, becomes clear when an average percentage is computed for all of the offerings combined. Here we find that only in the large areas is the proportion of "don't know" responses higher in the city than in the suburbs. The lowest proportion of "don't know" responses is found in the suburbs of the large areas and in the cities in the small metropolitan areas. An equally high proportion is found in the large cities and in the medium and small suburban areas.

The higher proportion of "don't know" responses in the medium and small suburban areas take on added significance when it is recalled that these areas make more use of the schools than the cities in the same size class. Although not readily apparent, the higher proportion of such responses may be due to the size of school districts in these areas. Whereas in the city the size of school district declines as size of city decreases, the opposite may be the case among the suburban areas. The size of the school districts in the smaller suburban areas may exceed those in the large suburbs. Even though the latter areas have a much larger total population, it may be divided into a much larger number of separate and smaller districts. Thus, what appears to be an inverse relationship with size in the suburbs, when size is based on size of metropolitan area, might represent in actual fact a direct relationship when size of school district is considered. Still another factor, as noted earlier, which may account for the high proportion of "don't know" responses in the suburbs, is that some of the suburban districts, in the medium and small metropolitan areas, may not have a high school of their own and must send their children to a high school in another district. Consequently they are less familiar with the school and the type of program offered.

Level of Knowledge Scale Scores

In order to obtain some overall measure of the level of knowledge of schools, we combined the responses to several questions, assigning numerical weights.[2] This provided us with a rather crude scale representing the level of knowledge of each respondent. These data are shown in Table 3-4. If we consider only the totals, we find that there is a slight tendency for the average level of knowledge to be somewhat higher in the suburbs, and it also tends to vary inversely by size of metropolitan area. Differences in the level of knowledge

[2] The scale is based on the answers to the following five questions: (1) Do you know any member of the school board? (2) Who is the chairman of the board? (3) How is the chairman selected? (4) Who is the superintendent? (5) How does the superintendent obtain his position? The "yes" or "correct" responses were incorporated into a weight scale as follows: If all responses were "yes" or "correct," a score of five was assigned; if four responses were "yes" or "correct," a score of four was given. This was continued until none of the responses were "yes" or "correct," where a value of zero was assigned. Thus the scale ran from zero through five. The higher the score, the higher the level of knowledge.

TABLE 3-4

KNOWLEDGE OF SCHOOL SCALE BY CHILDREN IN SCHOOL BY PLACE
OF RESIDENCE AND SIZE OF METROPOLITAN AREA

Knowledge Scale and Size of Metropolitan Area	Central City			Suburbs		
	Children in School	None in School	Total*	Children in School	None in School	Total*
Large						
Total Number	157	317	477	216	278	495
	%	%	%	%	%	%
0	43.3	59.0	54.1	52.8	62.9	58.6
1	35.0	28.1	30.2	18.1	18.3	18.2
2–3	18.5	11.1	13.4	22.7	15.4	18.6
4–5	3.2	1.9	2.3	6.5	3.2	4.6
Total	100.0	100.0	100.0	100.0	100.0	100.0
Mean	0.9	0.6	0.7	1.0	0.7	0.8
Medium						
Total Number	160	295	457	245	248	493
	%	%	%	%	%	%
0	39.4	63.7	55.1	46.1	56.0	51.1
1	21.9	14.9	17.3	18.0	19.0	18.5
2–3	28.8	17.6	21.6	25.7	18.9	22.3
4–5	10.0	3.7	5.9	10.2	6.0	8.1
Total	100.0	100.0	100.0	100.0	100.0	100.0
Mean	1.4	0.7	1.0	1.3	0.9	1.1
Small						
Total Number	212	275	488	270	222	492
	%	%	%	%	%	%
0	42.9	48.4	46.1	35.2	55.8	44.5
1	25.5	22.9	24.0	29.6	23.0	26.6
2–3	24.0	21.4	22.6	29.3	15.8	23.1
4–5	7.6	7.3	7.3	5.9	5.4	5.7
Total	100.0	100.0	100.0	100.0	100.0	100.0
Mean	1.2	1.1	1.1	1.3	0.8	1.1

* Difference between total and the two columns added is due to "no answer" to
Children in School.

tend to vary more by size of community than between central city and suburbs. For example, the average scale values in the small metropolitan areas exceed the values in the large metropolitan areas by nearly 20 percent, with the difference being slightly larger in cities than in the suburbs. However, in none of the areas do the average scores in the suburbs exceed the city scores by more than 6 percent. The differences between central city and suburbs do not vary by size of community.

The most striking and socially significant observation here is the very high proportion of residents in all areas who have no knowledge of any of the five questions posed. More than half of the residents in both segments of the community in both large and small metropolitan areas had no knowledge of any of the questions included in this scale. In the small metropolitan areas, the proportion is only slightly lower.

Level of knowledge tends to vary more by whether households have children in school than by either place of residence or size of community. In all areas, residents with children in school have a higher score on the knowledge scale than those who do not have such contacts with the schools. The major differences tend to be found in the extremes of the scale. For example, in the large cities 43 percent of the households with children in school have no knowledge of these questions, but the proportion jumps to 59 percent among those with no children in school. In the suburbs the proportions are 53 percent and 63 percent, respectively. While 22 percent of the households with children in school in the large cities have a score of three or more, this declines to only 13 percent among those that do not have any children in school. In the suburbs the proportion declines from 29 percent to 19 percent. The same general pattern is observed in all areas except for the cities in the small metropolitan areas, where the distribution of scores tends to be approximately the same whether or not the household has children in school. However, in the small area suburbs the level of knowledge is not only higher than in the cities but there are marked differences according to whether the households have children in school. More than one-third (35 percent) of those with children in school were able to answer two or more questions correctly, while an equal proportion had no knowledge of any of the questions. Among the other households, the comparable proportions were 56 percent in the no knowledge category and only 20 percent in the most knowledgeable categories. Although there tends to be a rather low level of knowledge among the households in all parts of the metropolitan area, it is lowest among those who are not currently using the schools. This tends to hold within each place of residence and size of community category. To the extent that other differences are found, they are in favor of the suburbs and more particularly the suburbs of the smaller metropolitan areas. Knowledge of these questions tends to follow the same pattern as use of the schools, but the size of the differences is much less marked.

What are the factors other than having children in school that account for variations in level of knowledge of the schools among the residents of the metropolitan population? It is to this question that we now turn. First, we will examine the effects of selected personal characteristics of the residents, and second, we will consider the influence of previous residential experiences.

An inspection of the data presented in Table 3-5, indicates a rather wide variation in level of knowledge of the schools by a number of selected personal characteristics. Within each control variable, differences by place of residence do not appear to follow any specific pattern. To the extent that differences do occur, they tend to favor the city households; that at least is the case in the higher status categories. If we consider only the two top categories for education, income, and occupation, we have eighteen sets of score comparisons between central cities and suburbs. Among these scores in eleven comparisons (61 percent), the scores are higher in the city than in the suburbs. In only three cases (17 percent) do the suburban scores exceed the city scores, and in the remaining four sets of comparisons the scores are identical in both areas. The same pattern of difference is found if we consider only the percentage of households that have no knowledge of any of the questions. The proportion with no knowledge tends to be higher in the suburbs, particularly among those who have graduated from high school and those with some college training. This may be due to recency of arrival in the suburbs.

Among those with a high school diploma, the highest proportion with no knowledge of the schools is found in the large metropolitan suburbs. Here we find that 59 percent of the households with twelve years of education have no knowledge of the schools, as compared

TABLE 3-5

KNOWLEDGE OF SCHOOL SCALE SCORES* BY SELECTED
DEMOGRAPHIC VARIABLES BY PLACE OF RESIDENCE
AND SIZE OF METROPOLITAN AREA

Selected Demographic Variables	Large		Medium		Small	
	City	Suburb	City	Suburb	City	Suburb
Total	0.7	0.8	1.0	1.1	1.1	1.1
Age						
Under 25 years	0.4	1.2	1.0	0.3	0.6	0.6
25–34	0.7	0.7	0.9	0.8	0.9	0.9
35–44	0.7	1.0	1.1	1.3	1.3	1.3
45–54	0.9	1.0	1.2	1.3	1.4	1.2
55 years plus	0.7	0.6	0.7	1.1	1.4	1.0
*Sex***						
Male	0.9	1.0	1.3	1.2	1.4	1.0
Female	0.7	0.7	1.0	1.0	1.4	1.1
Education						
Grade school	0.4	0.6	0.5	0.6	0.5	0.7
9–11	0.8	0.6	1.4	0.7	0.7	1.0
12	0.8	0.8	1.2	1.0	1.4	1.2
College	1.0	1.1	1.7	1.7	2.5	1.7
Income (weekly)						
Not working	0.6	0.5	0.5	0.8	0.7	0.7
Under $75	0.6	0.9	0.7	0.6	0.8	1.1
$75–$99	0.7	0.7	1.0	1.0	1.2	1.0
$100–$149	0.9	0.8	1.2	1.1	1.3	1.0
$150 plus	1.3	1.2	1.6	1.6	2.0	1.6
Occupation						
Other	0.6	0.6	0.7	0.8	0.8	0.8
Craftsmen	0.6	0.7	0.9	0.7	1.3	1.0
Clerical-Sales	0.7	1.0	1.1	1.0	1.5	1.1
Prof.-Managerial	1.0	1.0	1.3	1.5	1.9	1.5

* Scores range from 0 to 5.
** Limited only to complete family units.

with 44 percent in the city at the same educational level. In both
residential areas, the proportion of such responses decreases with
size. The lowest proportion is found in the small metropolitan areas,
where we find 45 percent of the suburban households in this education category, as compared with 33 percent of those in the city. The
same pattern of difference is found at the college level also. Among

the college trained, the proportion with no knowledge of the schools ranges from a low of only 9 percent in the small cities to a high of 50 percent in the large suburbs. In each size class the proportion of such responses is higher in the suburbs than in the city, but within each zone the proportion of no knowledge scores declines as size of metropolitan area decreases. Differences by place of residence are not as clearly evident at the lower levels of education except at the grade school level, where the above patterns are reversed. At this level the central cities in each size class tend to have the highest proportion of households with no knowledge of the schools.

Similar differences in favor of the central city residents are found among the higher income and those in the higher occupational positions. Here, too, the proportion of households with no knowledge of the schools tends to be larger in the suburbs than in the cities. Again, in each sub-area, within each income and occupational category, the proportion of no knowledge responses decreases by size of community. The disproportionate number of higher scores in the city takes on added significance when it is recalled that the city has a disproportionate number of incomplete families and households that are less likely to have children in school. The importance of the latter is evident when we look at the scores for the age group with the largest proportion of households with children in school, that is, 35 to 44 years. Here the level of knowledge is higher among suburban residents in both large and medium-sized metropolitan areas. In the small metropolitan area no differences are found. In each residential area, level of knowledge increases with age. The scores reach a high point between 35 and 54 years of age and then decline. Level of knowledge is lowest among those under 25 and those 55 years of age and over. It is in these ages that households are least likely to have children in school; consequently, it is to be expected that they would be less concerned and aware of what is going on in the schools.

When we look at the sex differences, we find that males have higher scores than females. These scores are limited only to respondents living in complete households. The single, widowed, and divorced have been omitted, since we were interested primarily in how husbands and wives might differ in knowledge of schools. These data provide only indirect evidence, since we have a random sample of husbands and a comparable sample of wives, but each have been selected from separate households. At any rate, males exceed the females in each size class and in each area, with the single exception of the small area suburbs. Within each sex group knowledge scores in both cities and suburbs tend to increase as size of area declines.

The role of education is clearly evident. In all areas, the lowest scores are found among those in the grade school category while the highest scores are found in the college category. Generally speaking, the scores increase directly by education. The same pattern is found in each area and in each size class. Overall the scores range from a low of 0.4 in the grade school group in large cities to a high of 2.5 in the college educated in small cities. There tends to be more variation in level of knowledge by educational attainment than by either size of area or place of residence. However, the tendency is for the scores at the higher educational levels to be higher in the cities than in the suburbs; and within each educational level, scores tend to vary directly by population size in both segments of the metropolitan area.

The same pattern of difference is found by both income and occupation. As the status of the respondent increases, so does the level of knowledge of schools. In short, the highest scores are found among the college trained, high income, and those in the professional-managerial positions in the small cities. The lowest level of knowledge tends to be found among those low in education, income, and occupation in the large cities.

Thus, while the overall level of knowledge tends to be somewhat higher in the suburbs than in the central cities, these data suggest that the higher scores are more a function of the composition of the population than of place of residence or size of population. At any rate, when persons of comparable characteristics are compared, the overall suburban advantage is lost, and central city residents with high status characteristics seem to have a higher level of knowledge than is found among those living in suburbs.

Residential experience is also an important factor in accounting for variations in level of knowledge, as is evident from the data presented in Table 3-6. In general, the highest scores are found among households which have not lived in the opposite part of the metropolitan area. Those who have moved to their present residence from the opposite part of the metropolitan area within the last five years tend to have the lowest scores. The only exception to this is

TABLE 3-6

KNOWLEDGE OF SCHOOL SCALE BY RESIDENTIAL EXPERIENCE VARIABLES
BY PLACE OF RESIDENCE AND SIZE OF METROPOLITAN AREA

Selected Variables	Large		Medium		Small	
	City	Suburb	City	Suburb	City	Suburb
Total	0.7	0.8	1.0	1.1	1.1	1.1
Area Mobility						
Non-movers	0.7	1.1	1.0	1.5	1.2	0.9
Moved over 5 yrs.	0.9	0.8	1.1	1.0	1.2	1.1
Moved under 5 yrs.	0.5	0.5	0.5	0.9	0.6	1.2
Length of Time in Metropolitan Area						
Natives	0.8	0.9	1.2	1.2	1.3	1.2
15 years plus	0.7	0.8	0.9	1.0	1.2	1.2
5–15 years	0.4	0.9	0.8	1.0	0.9	0.8
Under 5 years	0.3	0.4	0.8	0.9	0.8	0.6
Where Respondent Attended High School						
In district	0.9	1.5	1.5	1.8	1.5	1.1
In same county	1.0	0.8	0.9	1.0	1.0	1.6
In different county	0.7	0.7	1.1	1.1	1.3	1.1
Did not attend	0.4	0.6	0.5	0.6	0.5	0.7

found in the small suburbs. Almost without exception, scores within each area mobility category in both residential zones increase as one goes from large to small metropolitan areas.

Knowledge of schools varies directly by length of time lived in the metropolitan community. Natives tend to have the highest scores, whereas the lowest scores are found among those who have moved into the community within the last five years. The same pattern of difference is found within each segment of the community and in each size class. The highest score is found among the natives in the small cities, while the recent migrants in the large cities have the lowest scores. Variations are more marked and follow a more consistent pattern by length of time in the metropolitan area than by either size of metropolitan area or place of residence. Scores range from a low of only 1.3 among the recent migrants in large cities to a high of 2.3 among natives in small cities. In these categories, the proportion with no knowledge of the schools ranges from a high of 74 percent to a low of only 20 percent, respectively.

Where the respondent attended high school is still another measure of residential experience. In general we find that those who attended high school in the present district of residence have the highest scores. The only exceptions to this are found in the large central cities and the small area suburbs. Among the residents in these areas, the highest scores are found among those who attended high school in the same county but in a different district. Of particular interest here are the disproportionately high scores found in the large and medium-sized suburbs among those who attended high school in the same suburban district, as compared with those who moved in from a different district either within the same county or from outside the metropolitan area. In all instances, the lowest scores are found among those who did not attend high school. This is further evidence of the importance of education, since these scores are even lower than those found among households with high school attendance outside of the metropolitan area. The higher scores among residents who attended high school in the district are a function of both high education and familiarity with the local setting.

Participation in School-Related Activities

Let us turn now from knowledge to actual participation in school affairs. Perhaps the most accessible avenue of participation is through the parents-teachers organizations. The criterion we have at our disposal for this purpose is rather gross; it consists in responses to the question: "Have you attended a PTA meeting at any time during the past two years?" The time spread is a less important defect than is the failure to assess the extent or fullness of participation. Nevertheless, the data in Table 3-7, are interesting on two counts. First, there is no appreciable variation in attendance at such meetings either by size of metropolitan area or as between central cities and suburban zones. Second, 40 percent or more of the respondents who have children in schools have not attended PTA meetings at any time during the past two years. How many of those who have attended have done so more than once or twice is not known. In any case, in view of the importance of education in the modern world, the frequency of participation in this form of school activity is not impressive. It would be interesting to know what lies at the roots of the apathy of so large a part of the population. The

TABLE 3-7

ATTENDANCE AT PTA BY CHILDREN IN SCHOOL BY PLACE OF
RESIDENCE AND SIZE OF METROPOLITAN AREA

Attendance and Size of Metropolitan Area	Central City			Suburbs		
	Children in School	None in School	Total	Children in School	None in School	Total
Large						
Total Number	157	317	477	216	278	495
	%	%	%	%	%	%
Attend	51.0	3.2	19.1	58.3	4.3	28.1
Not attend	49.0	96.8	80.7	41.7	95.0	71.5
No answer	—	—	0.2	—	0.7	0.4
Total	100.0	100.0	100.0	100.0	100.0	100.0
Medium						
Total Number	160	295	457	245	248	493
	%	%	%	%	%	%
Attend	55.6	5.1	23.0	60.0	7.3	33.5
Not attend	42.5	91.2	74.0	39.6	92.7	66.3
No answer	1.9	3.7	3.0	0.4	—	0.2
Total	100.0	100.0	100.0	100.0	100.0	100.0
Small						
Total Number	212	275	488	270	222	492
	%	%	%	%	%	%
Attend	57.5	4.7	27.7	57.0	6.8	34.3
Not attend	42.5	94.5	71.9	42.6	93.2	65.4
No answer	—	0.7	0.4	0.4	—	0.2
Total	100.0	100.00	100.0	100.0	100.0	100.0

small percentages of respondents without children in schools who
state that they have attended meetings may represent parents whose
children have left the schools some time during the two-year interval.

Attendance at meetings of school boards is quite a different matter. The content of school board meetings—questions of general
policy, of administrative organization, of finance—normally im-
pinges upon the pupil indirectly and often remotely. Hence, those
meetings are apt to elicit citizen attendance only when critical issues
appear on the agendas. In other words, the frequency of attendance
should be considerably less than that observed for PTA meetings.

Furthermore, the issues confronting school board meetings might be expected to touch the interests of persons who have no children in school as much or more often than is usually the case with matters treated in PTA meetings. Attendance by that group, therefore, should be larger at the one than at the other type of meeting.

As expected, the data in Table 3-8, indicate a much lower level of attendance at school board meetings. The frequency of attend-

TABLE 3-8

ATTEND SCHOOL BOARD MEETINGS BY CHILDREN IN SCHOOL BY
PLACE OF RESIDENCE AND SIZE OF METROPOLITAN AREA

Attend Meetings and Size of Metropolitan Area	Central City			Suburbs		
	Children in School	None in School	Total*	Children in School	None in School	Total*
Large						
Total Number	157	317	477	216	278	495
	%	%	%	%	%	%
Attend	8.3	1.3	3.6	14.4	3.6	8.3
Not attend	91.1	98.7	96.0	85.6	95.8	91.1
No answer	0.6	—	0.4	—	1.1	0.6
Total	100.0	100.0	100.0	100.0	100.0	100.0
Medium						
Total Number	160	295	457	245	248	493
	%	%	%	%	%	%
Attend	5.6	1.0	2.8	10.6	4.4	7.5
Not attend	92.5	95.3	94.1	89.4	95.6	92.5
No answer	1.9	3.7	3.1	—	—	—
Total	100.0	100.0	100.0	100.0	100.0	100.0
Small						
Total Number	212	275	488	270	222	492
	%	%	%	%	%	%
Attend	8.5	2.5	5.1	15.6	3.2	10.0
Not attend	91.5	96.7	94.5	84.4	96.4	89.8
No answer	—	0.7	0.4	—	0.5	0.2
Total	100.0	100.0	100.0	100.0	100.0	100.0

* Difference between total and column 1 and 2 added is due to "no answer" to Children in School.

ance is also considerably less on the part of residents with no children in school, though the gap between persons with and without children in schools is greatly reduced. Where there is no systematic association of attendance at school board meetings with size of metropolitan area in any of the categories of residents represented in Table 3-8, there is a substantial difference as between central city and suburban residents. The proportions of suburban residents who attend school board meetings are in general double the comparable proportions among central city residents. The implication would seem to be that the issues facing suburban school boards are more critical and thus attract a wider participation from the electorate than is the case in central cities. Conceivably, in the latter school districts boards are more concerned with routine administrative matters than with developmental problems. The difference in attendance frequencies may, of course, reflect differences in the educational levels and of the civic interests in the respective populations.

In all areas, residents are more likely to discuss school problems with a member of the school board than with the superintendent of schools. Contacts with the person in the latter position are limited but they tend to increase in the smaller areas. The range, however, is small. In the cities the proportion that have discussed school problems with the superintendent ranges from less than 4 percent to 7 percent. In the suburbs the comparable range is from 8 percent in the large areas to 14 percent in the small areas. Although not shown here, households with children in school would be more likely to have discussed school problems with the superintendent as well as with members of the board. But again it is emphasized that only a very small segment of the population have contacts with persons in these positions. Although contacts tend to occur more frequently in the smaller suburban districts such contacts are enjoyed by only a small minority. While people may argue that in small districts officials are more accessible and one can have a greater voice in how things are done, in actual practice this is little used, at least not in terms of the questions posed here. Yet we find that when residents do discuss school issues with members of the board they tend to do so in private rather than during a public meeting. For example, in the suburbs less than 2 percent report that they have discussed school problems with board members at a meeting while more than three times this proportion have done so in private. Even in the cities residents are more likely to discuss issues in private with members of the board. But it is noted that never more than 15 percent in any area ever discuss school issues with members of the board.

Still another index of participation in school-related activities, but certainly much less direct, is the frequency of voting in local school elections. One cannot assume however, that those persons who most frequently vote in such elections are the ones most interested and concerned about the schools, since, for example, some property owners may vote to oppose a bond issue for tax reasons without regard for what effect this might have on the quality of schools. In these instances, high participation may mean consistent opposition to any proposal that would improve the schools. On the other hand many who vote frequently could consistently support such issues. Thus the meaning of voting is not at all clear. Nonetheless, it is a dimension of participation in the schools regardless of the intent of the involvement. It will thus be reported. Later this dimension of participation will be assessed as a factor in resistance to change.

An inspection of the data presented in Table 3-9 indicates that frequency of voting is highest among households that are most likely to be concerned about the quality of schools, since they have children in attendance. Thus, for example, in the large central cities, 70 percent of those with children in school vote in nearly every election, as compared with 49 percent of those with no children in school. Comparable differences are found in all areas, though in the small metropolitan areas the differences are much less marked. There seems to be little variation in the frequency of voting by place of residence. Although suburban residents in both medium and large metropolitan areas have larger proportions voting in nearly every election than is found among city residents, the differences are very slight.

The significant observation here is that households with children in school are the ones most likely to vote in school elections, particularly in the larger areas. In viewing our data, we find that the differences within each area are larger between those with children in school and those without children in school than are the differences between places of residence within the metropolitan area. Thus the important factor seems to be not where one lives within

TABLE 3-9

HOW FREQUENTLY VOTE IN SCHOOL ELECTIONS BY CHILDREN
IN SCHOOL BY PLACE OF RESIDENCE AND
SIZE OF METROPOLITAN AREA

Frequency of Voting & Size of Metropolitan Area	Central City			Suburbs		
	Children in School	None in School	Total	Children in School	None in School	Total
Large						
Total Number	157	317	477	216	278	495
	%	%	%	%	%	%
Regularly	70.1	49.5	56.6	71.3	57.2	63.2
Occasionally	17.8	24.6	22.2	17.6	19.1	18.4
Never	9.6	17.7	14.9	6.9	16.9	12.5
Not applicable	2.5	8.2	6.3	4.2	6.8	5.8
Total	100.0	100.0	100.0	100.0	100.0	100.0
Medium						
Total Number	160	295	457	245	248	493
	%	%	%	%	%	%
Regularly	72.5	56.3	62.1	72.2	62.5	67.3
Occasionally	15.7	22.6	20.2	17.2	19.0	18.0
Never	10.6	15.3	13.6	9.0	13.7	11.4
Not applicable	1.3	5.8	4.2	1.6	4.8	3.2
Total	100.0	100.0	100.0	100.0	100.0	100.0
Small						
Total Number	212	275	488	270	222	492
	%	%	%	%	%	%
Regularly	58.5	57.1	57.8	56.7	50.9	54.1
Occasionally	24.6	20.3	22.1	23.3	26.1	24.6
Never	12.3	19.3	16.2	18.9	20.7	19.7
Not applicable	4.7	3.3	3.9	1.1	2.3	1.6
Total	100.0	100.0	100.0	100.0	100.0	100.0

the metropolitan community, but whether or not the residents are currently using the schools.

Contrary to expectations, frequency of voting does not increase as size of community declines. Quite the opposite is found among those with children in school; the proportion who vote in nearly every election declines with size. Almost identical findings are also observed in the suburbs. Among those who do not have children in school, no consistent pattern is found by size of community. It is of particular interest to note that there is little variation in frequency of voting, in the small metropolitan areas, by either place of residence or contact with the schools. Residents tend to vote less frequently than in the larger communities, but the proportions voting are approximately equal regardless of where they live or whether or not they have children in school.

The proportion of the population voting in nearly every school election is in large part dependent on the composition of the population. Actually, the differences by the characteristics of the population are more marked than those found by either size of community or place of residence within the metropolitan area. Looking first at age, we find that those most likely to vote in nearly every election are between 35 and 54 years of age. In general, the proportion of regular voters increases consistently with age up to the oldest age group, where the proportion declines slightly. The same pattern is found in all areas and in each size class.

Frequency of voting also varies markedly by socioeconomic status, whether measured in terms of education or occupation. Within each of these status categories, however, there is no consistent pattern of difference by place of residence within the metropolitan area. In short, frequency of voting is approximately the same among those with similar personal characteristics regardless of whether they live in the city or the suburbs; nor are any consistent differences found by size of community. But within each area, we find a wide range of differences by level of education. The proportion at the college level who vote in nearly every election exceeds the proportion at the grade school level by 50 percent or more in all areas except the large suburbs; in the latter, the difference is only 25 percent. By way of comparison, the college group exceeds the grade school group by 70 percent in the medium-size areas and by more than 100 percent in the small suburbs. In all of the cities, the college group exceeds the grade school group by 50 percent or more. Thus the importance of education in frequency of voting is apparent. In general, in all areas the proportion voting regularly increases with each increase in education. Whereas less than half of those in the grade school category vote in nearly every election, the proportion exceeds 70 percent at the college level. A very similar pattern of difference is found by occupation. Those in the lower occupation categories have the lowest proportion who vote frequently, while the highest proportion is found among those at the professional-managerial level. Within occupational categories, frequency of voting does not vary by place of residence. Similarly, the amount of income is much more important than place of residence within the metropolitan area. Again, size of community seems to have little effect on frequency of voting.

Length of residence in the metropolitan area is also an important factor in the frequency of voting. Natives tend to have the most frequent voting record. The lowest proportion of frequent voters is found among those who have lived in the metropolitan area for less than five years. This low proportion is likely due in part to age; but more importantly, many have not been in the community long enough to have had an opportunity to register and to vote in a school election. We find that between one-fourth and one-half of the more recent migrants have never voted in a local school election. And even among those who have been in the community from five to fifteen years, a disproportionately high percentage have never voted. In the cities, from 20 to 30 percent have never voted in the local area, and in the suburbs the proportion ranges from a low of 12 percent to a high of 33 percent. Even among those who have been in the community from five to fifteen years, a disproportionately low number vote in nearly every election. Thus it would seem that migrants play a less active role in school issues than non-migrants. At any rate, these data suggest that the effects of migration are not easily overcome. Seemingly, not until after fifteen years of residence do migrants become similar to the natives in voting behavior.[3]

Level of Participation Scale Scores

In order to obtain an overall index of participation in the community, we have combined the several indicators of participation in a single value. In doing so, we have assumed that each is of

[3] In an earlier study of voter registration in a single community, it was reported that "Migration has the effect of decreasing participation in the political life of the community, but this is only temporary. . . . It takes the farm and the rural non-farm migrants ten or more years in the community before they equal or exceed the natives in the proportion registered, whereas the urban migrants exceed the natives after they have lived in the community for only five years or more." B. G. Zimmer, "Participation of Migrants in Urban Structures," *American Sociological Review*, XX, No. 2 (April, 1955), pp. 218–224.

equal weight, and have averaged their frequencies of occurrence.[4] The result yields a somewhat rough, though useful, score for participation in school affairs. The outcome of this operation is shown in Table 3-10. When the accumulative effect of all of the activities is shown, the central city-suburban differences become much more marked than when each activity is considered separately. In each size class, suburban residents have a higher average score. For example, in the large areas the average score in the city is 0.9 as compared with 1.1 in the suburbs. Looking at the distribution of scores, we find that 41 percent of the central city residents do not participate in any of the activities covered, as compared with 30 percent of the suburban residents. On the other hand, only 18 percent of the former participate in two or more activities (a score of two or more), while 28 percent of the latter do so. Thus the suburban households exceed the participation of city residents at this level by more than 50 percent. A similar pattern of difference is also found in the other size classes.

But again we find that the level of participation varies more by whether or not there are children in school than by place of residence. For example, in the large metropolitan areas where the average participation of suburban residents exceeds the city rate by approximately 20 percent (1.1 vs. 0.9), those with children in school exceed those with no children in school by more than 100 percent in both areas. The average scores in the city are 1.4 and 0.6 respectively. The comparable scores in the suburbs are 1.7 and 0.7. Similar differences are found in both medium and small metropolitan areas.

Even when we control for children in school, the average level of participation remains higher among suburban than city households. Although there seems to be no consistent pattern of difference in average participation scores by size of community, the proportion of residents in the highest score category increases steadily with size

[4] The participation score is based on combined answers to the following five questions: (1) Have you attended a meeting of the PTA during the past year or two? (2) Have you attended school board meetings? (3) Have you ever discussed school problems with the superintendent of schools? (4) Have you ever discussed school problems with any member of the board of education? (5) Did you vote in the last local government or school election? Score values were assigned according to the number of "yes" answers. If all five questions were answered "yes," a score of five was assigned. If all were answered "no," a score of zero was given. Thus, scale values run from zero through five.

TABLE 3-10

PARTICIPATION IN SCHOOL SCALE BY CHILDREN IN
SCHOOL BY PLACE OF RESIDENCE AND
SIZE OF METROPOLITAN AREA

Scale and Size of Metropolitan Area	Central City			Suburbs		
	Children in School	None in School	Total	Children in School	None in School	Total
Large						
Total Number	157	317	477	216	278	495
	%	%	%	%	%	%
0	19.7	51.1	40.5	13.0	43.9	30.3
1	34.4	44.2	41.1	37.5	44.6	41.6
2	33.1	3.8	13.6	31.0	7.6	17.8
3+	12.8	0.9	4.7	18.5	3.9	10.3
Total	100.0	100.0	100.0	100.0	100.0	100.0
Mean	1.4	0.6	0.9	1.7	0.7	1.1
Medium						
Total Number	160	295	457	245	248	493
	%	%	%	%	%	%
0	15.0	39.3	30.6	15.5	32.7	24.1
1	31.3	54.6	46.4	30.6	51.2	41.0
2	40.6	3.7	16.6	33.5	9.3	21.3
3+	13.2	2.4	6.3	20.4	6.8	13.6
Total	100.0	100.0	100.0	100.0	100.0	100.0
Mean	1.6	0.7	1.0	1.7	0.9	1.3
Small						
Total Number	212	275	488	270	222	492
	%	%	%	%	%	%
0	21.7	45.5	35.0	24.4	53.6	37.6
1	31.1	45.1	39.1	27.0	35.6	30.9
2	31.1	6.2	17.0	21.5	7.2	15.0
3+	16.2	3.3	8.8	27.0	3.7	16.5
Total	100.0	100.0	100.0	100.0	100.0	100.0
Mean	1.5	0.7	1.0	1.7	0.6	1.2

of community. But no such pattern is found for any of the other scale values. And while the proportion with high scores is larger in the suburbs than in the city, we find the same increase as we move from the large to the small metropolitan areas. In each size class, the proportion of suburban households in the top score category is at least double the proportion of city respondents; and even among those with children in school, the proportion of high scores in the suburbs exceeds the city proportion by 50 percent or more. It is in the large cities that we find the smallest proportion in the high score category, while the largest proportion is found among the residents in the small suburbs—that is, the proportion with high scores ranges from 13 percent in the large cities to 27 percent in the small suburbs. The average participation score ranges only from 1.4 to 1.7 for the same areas.

A further and more detailed analysis of participation in school-related activities indicates the importance of composition of the population. This is evident from the marked differences in scores by the personal characteristics of the respondents, as shown in Table 3-11. Participation rates vary markedly by age, education, income, and occupation. These characteristics play an equally important role in level of participation in both cities and suburbs and in each size class. Although participation rates differ between cities and suburbs as well as by size of community, the differences are less marked than those found within each area according to the personal characteristics of the respondent or the household.

Participation scores tend to follow a very clear and distinct pattern of difference by place of residence as well as by the characteristics of the residents in both parts of the metropolitan area. In both cities and suburbs, participation rates increase with age, reach a high point among those 35 to 44 years of age, and then decline. The lowest participation rates are found in the youngest age group. For the most part, these households are in the early stage of the life cycle and have not yet reached the age where they would have children in school. The next lowest scores tend to be found among those 55 years of age and over. This age group is also less likely to have children in school, in that their youngest child, in most instances, would be beyond secondary school age.

For the total population, suburban participation rates tend to exceed those in the city by 15 percent in the medium-sized metro-

TABLE 3-11

PARTICIPATION IN SCHOOL-RELATED ACTIVITIES* BY
SELECTED VARIABLES BY PLACE OF RESIDENCE
AND SIZE OF METROPOLITAN AREA

Selected Variables	Large		Medium		Small	
	City	Suburb	City	Suburb	City	Suburb
Total	0.9	1.1	1.0	1.3	1.0	1.2
Age						
Under 25 years	0.2	0.6	0.4	0.4	0.3	0.3
25–34	0.7	0.9	0.9	1.1	1.0	1.1
35–44	1.3	1.7	1.4	1.8	1.5	1.7
45–54	1.1	1.3	1.2	1.4	1.3	1.4
55 years plus	0.7	0.8	0.8	1.1	0.8	0.8
Sex						
Male	0.9	1.2	1.0	1.4	1.2	1.2
Female	0.9	1.2	1.2	1.4	1.1	1.2
Education						
Grade school	0.7	0.8	0.6	0.7	0.7	0.7
9–11	0.9	0.8	1.1	1.1	0.8	1.1
12	0.9	1.3	1.2	1.4	1.2	1.4
College	1.3	1.5	1.5	1.7	1.9	2.0
Income (weekly)						
Not working	0.6	0.8	0.8	1.0	0.8	0.6
Under $75	0.7	0.6	0.7	0.8	0.8	0.9
$75–$99	0.8	0.6	1.0	1.1	0.9	1.1
$100–$149	1.1	1.3	1.3	1.4	1.3	1.3
$150 plus	1.7	1.7	1.5	1.8	1.8	1.9
Occupation						
Other	0.7	0.8	0.9	1.1	0.9	0.9
Craftsmen	0.9	1.1	1.1	1.2	0.9	1.2
Clerical-Sales	0.8	1.3	1.0	1.3	1.4	1.6
Prof.-Managerial	1.2	1.5	1.1	1.5	1.2	1.2

* Scores range from 0 to 5.

politan area, but by only 10 percent in both the small and large
areas. However, significantly larger differences are found among age
groupings in both segments of the metropolitan community. The
most active age group, 35 to 44 years, exceeds the least active, that
is those under 25 years of age, by more than 60 percent in the large
suburbs and by 100 percent or more in the two other size classes.
Similarly, in both small and large cities scores vary by more than

100 percent in both small and large cities and by more than 70 percent in the medium-sized cities, where the variation by age is least. Viewed differently, it is in the suburbs and among persons 35 to 44 years of age that we find the lowest proportion of non-participants in the school-related activities considered. Here the proportion reaches a low of only 13 percent in both the large and medium-sized areas and 25 percent in the small suburbs. Among city residents in the same age group, the proportion who do not participate in any activity is slightly less than 25 percent and does not vary by size of city. The rate of participation does not vary by sex.

A very distinct pattern of differences is found by education. Not only does the participation score increase by level of education, but within each educational category the suburban residents continue to have the highest scores. Except at the lower educational levels, the average scores tend to increase in both cities and suburbs as size of the metropolitan community declines. The latter pattern of difference is, however, less marked and less consistent than differences by place of residence or by educational level. Here too we find much larger differences by education than by place of residence. The importance of the latter is evident from the range in scores among the college trained. In this group the participation scores increased gradually and consistently from a low of 1.3 in the large cities to a high of 2.0 in the small suburban districts.

Participation in school-related activities also varies directly with income and occupational status. Here too we find that the range of scores among income and occupational categories exceeds the differences observed by place of residence. The lowest scores are found among those not working and in the lowest income group as well as among those in the "other" occupational category. The latter is made up of operatives, service workers, and other unskilled occupations. Scores increase consistently by income. The top income group has the highest scores in all areas, but within each size class, suburban scores tend to be higher than central city scores. Also there is a tendency for the scores to increase as size of area declines. Among occupational groups the same pattern of increase is found, as well as similar city-suburban differences. The only exception occurs in the small metropolitan areas, where the participation rate of clerical and sales workers exceeds the rate of those in the professional and managerial category.

Residential experience of the population adds a further source of variation. The highest scores occur among residents who have moved from the opposite area more than five years previously. These people have even higher scores than those who have not moved from either the city or the suburbs to the opposite area. The lowest scores are found among the recent arrivals, that is, those who moved to their present residence from the opposite part of the metropolitan area within the past five years. Within each mobility category, the participation scores tend to be higher in the suburbs than in the city. The same pattern of difference is found in all areas, regardless of size. Of particular significance here are the disproportionately low scores found among those who have recently moved to the central city from the neighboring suburbs. This group differs more from their counterpart in the suburbs, in each size class, than any other mobility status group. Recent arrivals in the suburbs have much higher scores than are found among those who moved in the opposite direction.

These differences are due, in large part, to differences in the composition of the population in the opposite streams of movement. Those moving into the city are much less likely to have children in school. For example, in the large metropolitan area more than two-thirds of the households that had moved into the city from the suburbs within the past five years had no children in school. In contrast, less than half of those that moved in the opposite direction, that is, from the central city to the suburbs, during the same time period had no children in school. Similar differences are found in the other two areas.

In each area, the lower scores among the non-movers as compared with those who moved more than five years ago is also due in part to differences in the use of the schools. In all areas, the non-movers have a larger proportion of households with no children in school than is found among those who moved into the area more than five years ago. This is illustrated also by the differences found in the large metropolitan areas. In the city, 69 percent of the non-movers do not have children in school, as compared with 53 percent of those who moved in from the suburbs more than five years ago.

In the suburbs, the differences are in the same direction, but less marked. Here we find that 63 percent of the non-movers and 55 percent of the movers do not have children in school. Undoubtedly residential moves do influence the rate of participation in school-related activities—but, as these data suggest, much of the differences found among mobility status groups can be attributed to differences in the use of the schools. Participation scores by mobility status tend to follow the same pattern as use of the schools.

There is a very marked and consistent relationship between participation scores and length of time lived in the metropolitan area. But within each length of residence category, the participation scores are higher in the suburbs than in the cities. Natives tend to have the highest rates, while the recent arrivals in the community have the lowest scores. The same pattern is found in the suburbs as in the cities. Closely related to these differences are those found by where the respondent attended high school. In general, those who attended within the district have the highest scores, while those who attended outside of the metropolitan area have the lowest scores. This, of course, excludes those who did not attend high school. The latter have lower scores than is found within any residential experience category, except among those who have lived in the metropolitan area less than five years. This, of course, indicates that movement, even migration, unless it took place only recently, has less effect on participation than a lack of education. Stated differently, lack of education is more of a handicap than lack of familiarity with the local setting.

Summary

In the above discussion we have found that the overall level of knowledge of the schools tends to be somewhat higher in the suburbs than in the city. However, when persons of comparable characteristics are compared, the suburban advantage is largely lost. Level of knowledge, for example, tends to vary more by education than by either size of area or place of residence. Suburban residents also have a higher overall participation rate in school-related affairs than those living in central cities. Participation rates vary much more by place of residence than by size of community. But regardless of area of residence, the major influence is whether or not the family has children in school. Also, the personal characteristics of the residents appear to be of more importance than either place of residence or size of community.

4

Evaluation of Schools—City and Suburb

IN THE PRESENT CHAPTER we are concerned with three general questions. Attention first will be concerned with an evaluation of the schools, or, more exactly, the extent to which the residents are satisfied with them. Second, we shall call attention to what the residents of the areas feel should be done in order to improve their schools. Where there is dissatisfaction, we shall be concerned about the reasons for that appraisal. The third major question pertains to how the residents evaluate the schools in the central city as compared with those in suburbs, and how they view the present organization of school districts within the metropolitan area. Specifically we have asked whether they view the present system of multiple school districts in the metropolitan area as being wasteful. The responses to the above questions have merit for their descriptive value, but more particularly we are concerned with the role of each as a factor in resistance to change in the organization of school districts.

Satisfaction with Schools

When the residents were asked how satisfied they were with the schools in their area, a substantial majority in all areas either stated that they were "very" or at least "somewhat" satisfied. Even though the residents in all areas are relatively satisfied with the schools, we find some rather interesting differences by place of residence and size of community, but the largest differences in all areas are found between those who have and do not have children in school at the present time. Households with no children in school were much more likely to withhold a judgment and report that they were "uncertain" about the schools. Nonetheless, it must be kept in mind that, if a proposal for change were presented for popular approval, this segment of the population would also be in a position to cast a vote in a general election. Thus it is important to know the level of satisfaction of the total population. However, since those with children in school are more likely to vote on school issues than the general population, attention will be addressed primarily to this segment of the population.

For the total population of each residential zone, we find that the relationship between size of community and satisfaction with schools is different for cities than for suburban areas. Among the cities, the proportion satisfied varies inversely with size. The range is from 72 percent in the large cities to 81 percent in the small areas. However, the opposite is found in the suburbs, where the proportion increases from 76 percent in the small suburbs to 85 percent in the suburbs of the large metropolitan areas. Consequently, central city-suburban differences tend to decrease with size—that is, the residents become more similar in their level of satisfaction as size of community decreases. Not only do central city and suburban areas become more similar, but the direction of difference changes. In the large metropolitan areas, the proportion satisfied in the suburbs exceeds the proportion in the city by some 20 percent; in the small areas, the proportion satisfied in the suburbs is 6 percent less than is found in the cities. The same pattern is found even when we limit the analysis only to those households with children in school. Among such households, the proportion satisfied ranges from 84 percent in the large cities to a high of 90 percent in the small central cities. For the same size groups in the suburbs, the proportion satisfied declines from 94 percent to 84 percent, respectively.

Of particular interest is the very low proportion of residents who report that they are dissatisfied with the schools. It is only in the small suburbs and in medium-sized central cities that the proportion exceeds 10 percent of all respondents. Yet when asked how the schools could be improved, only a minority of the residents reported that "no improvements" were needed. Satisfaction, in other words, does not exclude some criticism. Central city-suburban differences in the proportions who believed no improvements were necessary are particularly marked in the large metropolitan areas. As is shown in Table 4-1, only 16 percent of the central city residents reported that no improvements were needed, as compared with nearly 40 percent of those in the suburbs. Thus, residents in the latter zones were not only more satisfied than city residents, but they were also more likely to feel that the schools do not need to be improved. Here, too, the responses tend to converge in the smaller metropolitan areas, but in all size classes suburban residents were more likely

TABLE 4-1

PROPORTION OF RESIDENTS REPORTING HOW SCHOOLS
COULD BE IMPROVED BY PLACE OF RESIDENCE
AND SIZE OF METROPOLITAN AREA

Improvements Needed	Large		Medium		Small	
	City	Suburb	City	Suburb	City	Suburb
Total Number	477	495	457	493	488	492
	%	%	%	%	%	%
More schools— classrooms	21.7	15.6	18.2	17.6	21.4	16.3
More and better teachers—higher pay	20.2	10.5	19.8	12.2	9.6	11.4
School old—need remodeling	12.2	1.6	3.3	1.2	4.7	1.2
Strengthen academic— higher standards	1.9	4.8	5.8	4.0	4.7	3.2
Smaller classes	2.1	0.8	3.1	2.2	2.3	1.0
Use facilities full year	1.1	2.0	1.1	5.3	4.5	4.7
Less frills (recreation & social)	0.6	3.0	4.0	4.5	6.6	2.4
Better recreational facilities	5.7	2.4	4.2	2.2	4.1	3.5
Other	10.2	8.4	11.0	8.6	10.0	12.7
No improvements needed	15.6	38.9	16.3	30.2	26.3	34.1
Don't know	24.5	18.8	25.5	22.5	20.1	16.3
No answer	2.5	2.2	2.6	4.3	2.7	4.9
Total*	100.0	100.0	100.0	100.0	100.0	100.0

* Does not add to 100 percent because multiple responses were given.

than central city residents to feel that no school improvements were needed. While central city residents were less likely to feel that no improvements were needed, they were also less likely to know the specific improvements that could be made, as is evident from the high proportion of "don't know" responses. But such responses were frequent in all areas; at least one-fifth of the households either stated that they "don't know" or did not answer the question. Thus, it is apparent that a substantial number of the residents are uncertain as to the type of improvements that could be made in their schools at the local level.

The most frequent improvement mentioned was the need for more schools and classrooms. There is a slight tendency for this to be reported more frequently by city than suburban residents. A substantial proportion of the residents also felt that the schools need more and better teachers as well as higher pay for teachers. Central city residents in the larger metropolitan areas were much more likely to emphasize this than suburban residents. But from 10 percent to 20 percent of the respondents in every area reported this as an improvement that could be made in their schools. Central city residents, particularly those living in the large cities, felt that the old schools should be remodeled. But that improvement was rarely ever mentioned in the suburbs. The need for smaller classes was rarely mentioned as a needed improvement, but to the extent that this is needed, it is reported more frequently by central city than suburban residents. The latter were more likely to emphasize more efficient use of existing facilities, such as a full year program, and less attention to frills in the schools. Central city residents were more likely to see a need for better recreational facilities, though the proportion of such responses declines by size of city. Thus, while residents tend to be generally satisfied with their schools, many seem to be aware that they could be improved. And the most frequently mentioned improvements pertain to basic facilities—that is, more classrooms, more and better teachers, as well as the need for higher salaries for teachers.

Satisfaction with High School Training

In a more specific question which was asked pertaining only to the high school, the responses were very similar to those given for schools in general. When asked if they were satisfied with the type of training provided by the high school, we again find that a substantial majority reported that they were satisfied.[1] Here too, we find that residents in all areas were less likely to report that they are dissatisfied with the training in the high school than that they "don't know." Residents in the large suburbs appear to be most satisfied, whereas those in the large cities are least satisfied. The gap between central city and the suburbs is most marked in the large metropolitan areas, where the proportion satisfied is 25 percent higher in the suburbs (74 percent) than in the city (59 percent). It is noteworthy that in the small metropolitan areas the proportion satisfied with the training offered in the high school is 12 percent less in the suburbs than in the city. This is the same pattern of differences already noted above in the responses concerning schools in general. The significant point here is the large proportion in all areas who are satisfied with the training offered. Thus, it is evident that any proposal for change will encounter populations that are, or were, generally satisfied with what they already have in their local areas. Only a small minority explicitly stated that they were dissatisfied.

In all areas, the proportion dissatisfied was highest among those with the most education. The relationship tends to be rather consistent with each increase in level of education. In the large central cities, for example, the proportion not satisfied with the high school training increases from only 5 percent among those with only a grade school education, to 8 percent among those with some high school, and to 15 percent among those who completed high school. Among the college group, the proportion increases to 23 percent. Thus the college trained were nearly five times as likely to express dissatisfaction as those who have not attended high school. In the suburbs, the proportion ranges from less than 4 percent to more than 9 percent. The same pattern of difference by education is found in all of the other areas. But within each educational category, we find less dissatisfaction among suburban than among central city households.

The most common complaints concerning the high schools seem to be directed at the type of program offered. Residents who are

---

[1] Obviously, lack of knowledge of the specific courses offered did not prevent the respondents from expressing an evaluation of the training offered (see Table 3-3).

dissatisfied appeared to be most concerned about the lack of emphasis on essentials, the poor quality of teaching, and the need for curriculum improvement. They also complain that children are not being properly trained for college. Although the differences by place of residence are not large, these complaints were somewhat more frequent in the suburbs than in the cities. The only exception is found in the small metropolitan area, where the opposite is found. In all areas, except the large central cities, a substantial number of those dissatisfied felt that too much emphasis is placed on sports and that too many extra, useless things go on in the high schools. In all areas, except the small central cities, from one-sixth to one-fourth of those who are dissatisfied report that more emphasis should be placed on practical subjects and that attention should also be focused on the needs of special groups. These data suggest that most of those who have expressed dissatisfaction with the high schools in their area have based their judgment on what they perceive to be specific shortcomings of the programs of study. The only exception to this is found in the small suburbs, where a substantial number did not specify their source of dissatisfaction. It may be that their dissatisfaction did not stem so much from the type of training offered, but rather was due to the fact that, in some areas, they have to send their children outside of their own district in order to attend a high school.

Central City and Suburban Schools Compared

Although the general level of satisfaction with schools appears to be high, it may be that the local residents would evaluate their schools differently when they thought about how their schools compared with those in the opposite part of the metropolitan area. Certainly we would expect that their perception of the relative quality of the schools in the other areas would have an important bearing on how they would feel about a reorganization of school districts on a community-wide basis. It is evident from our data that residents tend disproportionately to rate their own schools as being better than those in the opposite part of the metropolitan area. The only exception is found in the small area suburbs. Some rather substantial differences are found by size of metropolitan area. An inspection of the data presented in Table 4-2, shows that the propor-

TABLE 4-2

HOW CITY AND SUBURBAN SCHOOLS COMPARE
BY PLACE OF RESIDENCE AND SIZE
OF METROPOLITAN AREA

How Schools Compare	Large		Medium		Small	
	City	Suburb	City	Suburb	City	Suburb
Total Number	477	495	457	493	488	492
	%	%	%	%	%	%
Better in city	30.6	7.1	31.7	11.6	47.3	27.4
Better in suburbs	21.2	43.8	17.1	35.9	8.6	18.1
Same in both areas	29.6	38.2	31.1	39.1	32.2	47.2
Don't know	18.2	10.7	19.7	13.2	11.9	7.3
Total	100.0	100.0	100.0	100.0	100.0	100.0

tion rating the central city schools as better than those in the suburbs increases as one moves from the large to the small metropolitan areas. The same type of variation is found in the suburbs as in the central cities. The disparities between central city and suburban judgments relative to the superiority of central city schools decreases as size of metropolitan area declines. Conversely, the belief that suburban schools are better becomes markedly less prominent in each smaller metropolitan area, both in central cities and in suburbs. Of particular interest is the sharp decline in the suburbs, where the proportion falls from 44 percent in the large to only 18 percent in the small area suburbs. Among the cities, the decline is from 21 percent to less than 9 percent in the same areas.

In a further and more detailed analysis, we find that central city residents tended to evaluate the schools about the same whether or not they have children in school. But in the suburbs, substantial differences are found. In all of the latter areas, families with children in school were much more likely to rate the suburban schools as superior to those in the city. Again we find the same pattern of difference by size. Among families currently using the schools, the proportion rating the suburban schools above those in the central city ranges from a high of 51 percent in the large areas to a low of 24 percent in the small suburbs. Among suburban families which do not have children in school, the proportions of such responses ranges from 39 percent to 10 percent in the same areas.

Similarly, when we view the responses by age, we find the suburban residents between 25 and 44 years were most likely to rate the suburban schools above those in the city. It will be recalled that this was the age group with the highest frequency of children in school. The same differences by age are also found among central city residents—that is, those between 25 and 44 years of age are most likely to report that city schools are better than schools in the suburbs. However, differences by age are less marked in the central city than in the suburbs. It is noted that the same pattern of difference is found by place of residence and size of area even when we control for use of the schools and age of the respondent. Only the size of the difference is affected.

The influence of size of metropolitan area continues to be evident when we introduce as controls a number of selected socioeconomic and residential experience variables.[2] In regard to education, we find that among both central city and suburban residents the proportion rating the central city schools as better varies inversely by size. A similar pattern of difference is found among the suburban residents at both levels of education. These data are shown in Table 4-3. Again it is noteworthy that in the small metropolitan areas a substantial proportion of the suburban residents rate the city schools above their own. In short, the smaller the area the greater is the agreement as to the superiority of central city schools.

Similar differences are found by both place of residence and size of area within each occupational category and among both low- and high-income households. In the small metropolitan areas, city schools tend to be rated above suburban schools. And in this evaluation there is substantial agreement among both central city and suburban residents. But in the large metropolitan areas, suburban schools are more likely to be rated above city schools. It is noteworthy that it is only in large metropolitan area suburbs, among persons with high status characteristics, that a majority rate suburban schools above those in the city. On the other hand, it is only in the small area suburbs that a substantial number of the suburban residents rate city schools as better in quality than their own. This tends to hold regardless of the characteristics of the households, though the higher status residents in the small suburbs are most

[2] Because of space limitations we have presented, in Table 4-3, data only for extremes of education, occupation, and income.

TABLE 4-3

EVALUATION OF SCHOOLS BY SELECTED SOCIOECONOMIC
CHARACTERISTICS* BY PLACE OF RESIDENCE
AND SIZE OF METROPOLITAN AREA

Socioeconomic Characteristics	Percentage Reporting					
	Better in City			Better in Suburbs		
	Large	Medium	Small	Large	Medium	Small
	%	%	%	%	%	%
Education						
(Grade School)						
City	27.0	28.8	40.4	12.6	11.6	9.2
Suburbs	7.8	9.3	23.8	30.4	25.3	17.0
(College)						
City	31.1	33.7	54.5	28.4	18.1	7.6
Suburbs	6.2	9.8	35.9	60.0	43.8	14.1
Occupation						
(Below skilled)						
City	28.2	29.7	46.2	22.0	18.0	11.0
Suburbs	10.5	8.6	23.0	32.6	32.4	18.5
(Prof.-Managerial)						
City	32.5	30.0	55.3	24.1	24.4	6.4
Suburbs	5.8	11.3	23.8	54.4	39.0	24.8
Income (*weekly*)						
(Under $75)						
City	31.4	31.7	40.3	20.6	16.8	10.1
Suburbs	4.3	13.5	22.3	36.2	26.9	20.9
($150 plus)						
City	45.2	33.3	57.1	22.6	16.7	6.1
Suburbs	4.3	14.9	31.6	52.1	41.6	23.7

* Only extreme values shown for illustrative purposes.

likely to view central city schools more favorably than those in their own area.

Neither migration status nor area mobility has any effect on the pattern of difference already noted in the evaluation of the schools by place of residence and size of metropolitan area. However, the size of the difference does vary with the residential experience of the population. Although the proportion of recent migrants who rate the central city schools as superior increases inversely with size, as is also found among the natives, we find that within each size class natives are slightly more likely to rate the city schools favorably. Only in the large cities do recent migrants differ markedly from the natives in their evaluation of the central city schools. Here we find that only 17 percent of the recent migrants report city schools as better than those in the suburbs, but among natives the proportion increases to 35 percent. On the other hand, recent migrants in the large cities are more likely than natives to rate suburban schools above those in their own area. This pattern of difference is not, however, found in the suburbs.

On the other hand, movement within the metropolitan area appears to be an important factor in how residents evaluate the schools. Although we continue to find the same pattern of difference by size as well as place of residence within each mobility category, it is noted that central city residents who have never lived in the suburbs are more likely to rate their own schools as superior than are those who had previously lived in the suburbs before moving to the central city. Among suburban residents, those who have moved from the central city are most likely to rate the suburban schools as superior. This is particularly true in the large metropolitan areas where nearly half of those who have moved from the central city report that the suburban schools are superior, as compared with only one-third of those who have lived only in the suburbs. Similar differences are found in both the medium and small suburbs, but the size of the difference is less marked. Previous residence in the city appears to have little effect on the proportion of suburban householders who rate the central city schools as better than those in their own area. Although within each residential experience category, the proportion rating central city schools as better increases inversely by size of community, no differences are found between those who have lived only in the central city and those who formerly lived in the suburbs.

Male respondents tend to place a somewhat different evaluation on the schools than do females.[3] But again, within each sex category we continue to find a repetition of the pattern of difference already noted for a number of characteristics—that is, substantial differences are found in the evaluation of schools by both size of area and place of residence within the metropolitan community. Among cen-

---

[3] It will be recalled that this discussion applies only to those respondents in complete family units—that is, married and living with spouse.

tral city residents, males are more likely than are females to rate the central city schools as better than those in the suburbs. The same differences are found in each size class. But no differences are found by sex among those in the suburbs who rate the central city schools as better than their own. However, among the central city residents who report the suburban schools as better, we find that the females are more numerous. But again, among suburban residents, men and women are approximately the same in the proportion who state that their own schools are better.

The now familiar pattern of difference by size of area and place of residence persists even when we control for level of participation in school-related activities, as is done in Table 4-4. However, we

TABLE 4-4

EVALUATION OF SCHOOLS BY LEVEL OF PARTICIPATION IN
SCHOOL-RELATED FUNCTIONS BY PLACE OF RESIDENCE
AND SIZE OF METROPOLITAN AREA

Participation Level	Percent Reporting					
	Better in City			Better in Suburbs		
	Large	Medium	Small	Large	Medium	Small
	%	%	%	%	%	%
Low						
Central city	30.6	28.6	38.6	17.1	21.4	10.5
Suburbs	10.0	14.3	26.5	34.0	28.6	11.9
Medium						
Central city	27.6	31.6	49.7	23.0	11.8	7.3
Suburbs	6.8	8.9	23.0	46.1	34.2	18.4
High						
Central city	37.5	36.2	55.6	26.1	21.9	7.9
Suburbs	4.3	12.8	32.9	51.1	43.0	25.2

do find that the comparative evaluation of the schools depends, in part, on the extent to which residents are active in school-related functions. In general, the higher the participation rate the higher the proportion who rate their own schools as being superior to those in the opposite area. This relationship is found among both central city and suburban residents in all size classes, but the size of the difference varies inversely by size of metropolitan area.

The range of difference by level of participation is more marked among suburban than central city residents. For example, in the large metropolitan areas, the proportion of city residents who rate their schools above those in the suburbs varies from 31 percent among the least active participants to 38 percent among the most active. But among suburban residents, the proportion rating their own schools as superior varies by the same levels of participation from 34 percent to 51 percent.

It is of particular interest to note the evaluations in the different size classes, expressed by the high participants in the suburbs. While only 4 percent in the large area suburbs rate city schools as better than their own, this proportion increases to one-third in the small metropolitan suburbs. By way of contrast, more than half of the former, but only one-fourth of the latter, evaluate their own schools above those in the city. At all participation levels in both the large and medium-sized areas, residents rate their own schools above those in the opposite area. But in the small suburbs the pattern of difference is again reversed. Here at all participation levels residents are more likely to rate city schools above those in the suburbs, regardless of place of residence. Within each level of participation category in both cities and suburbs, the proportion rating city schools as better increases as size of metropolitan area declines, while the proportion rating suburban schools as better declines directly with size. However, within each size class the proportion of suburban residents who rate their own schools above those in the city increases as level of participation in schools increases.

Among suburban residents, it is only in the small metropolitan area suburbs that the evaluation of the schools favors the city. Noteworthy in these data is the general lack of any clear-cut consensus among the residents in how they evaluate the schools. While central city and suburban residents differ substantially in their evaluations and, except in the small metropolitan areas, tend to rate their own schools as superior, it is only in a few selected categories that we find a majority of the residents in agreement. For example, it is only among the higher-status residents in the small central cities and in the large suburbs that a majority of the residents agree on their evaluation of the schools. In both areas, such residents rate their own schools as superior to those found in the opposite part of the metropolitan community.

Views Concerning Multiple School Districts

In concluding this chapter, we turn to a consideration of the question of whether residents feel that having multiple school districts in the area is wasteful. The specific question asked was stated thusly: "Do you feel that having a number of separate school districts in the area is wasteful?" The attitudes concerning this issue vary not only by place of residence but also by size of metropolitan area. Among both central city and suburban residents, the proportion of affirmative responses tends to increase in each smaller size of metropolitan area, ranging from 37 to 44 percent in the central cities and from 30 to 40 percent in the suburban areas. The size of the difference is small but consistent. Also, in each size class, central city residents are more likely than suburban residents to report that the present system of school district organization is wasteful. However, there is less difference between central city and suburbs in the proportion holding this view in the small than in the large metropolitan areas.

It is significant that while a substantial proportion of the residents in both parts of the metropolitan area feel that multiple districts are wasteful, the largest proportions of residents, ranging from 49 percent in the small area suburbs to 57 percent in the large area suburbs, do not agree that efficiency is lost in multiplicity. There was, however, a larger degree of uncertainty among central city residents on the matter, as revealed by the proportions of "don't know" responses. Such responses tend to increase directly by size of area. At any rate, our data suggest that to the extent that residents might accept change to avoid the wastefulness of multiple districts, we would expect less resistance to change in the small than in the large metropolitan areas. Also, we would expect more similarity between city and suburban residents in views regarding change in the small than in the larger metropolitan areas.

Views of the present system of multiple school districts vary substantially among different age groups of the population. In all areas, the proportion who feel that multiple districts are wasteful increases directly with age up to a high among those 45 to 54 years, then declines rather sharply among those 55 years of age and over. However, part of the difference is due to the high proportion of "don't know" responses in the older age groups; one-fifth or more of the older residents in all areas were unable to pass a judgment on this issue. If we view the data differently, we find that the age groups most likely to view multiple districts as not being wasteful are those between 35 years and 44 years of age, while the proportions are lowest among those over 55 years of age and, to a lesser extent, those under 25 years of age. Again the "don't know" responses are an important factor here. This pattern of variation is particularly marked among suburban residents, but almost negligible in the central cities. Thus, it is the families with children in school that are least likely to report the current system of organization of school districts as not being wasteful, whereas those in the age groups least likely to have children in school, regardless of place of residence, are more likely to see multiple districts as being wasteful. This is clearly the case in the suburbs where, among those 35 to 44 years of age, more than half of the residents in the small suburbs and more than three-fifths of those in both medium and large suburbs report that multiple district organization is not wasteful. But again the influence of size of area is obvious. Only in the large and medium-sized suburbs do a majority of the residents in most age groups feel that having multiple districts is not wasteful.

There appears to be a rather consistent and direct relationship between socioeconomic status and the feeling that multiple districts are wasteful. These data are shown in Table 4-5. The same pattern of difference by these characteristics is found among both city and suburban residents. But at all status levels, central city residents are more likely than suburban residents to view multiple districts as wasteful. Moreover, the divergence among socioeconomic status seems to be more marked in the central cities than in the suburbs. Actually, in the large suburbs the proportion reporting that multiple districts are wasteful tends to be approximately the same at all status levels, whereas in the large cities the responses vary substantially among different segments of the population. A similar but less marked difference is found among occupational groups. But no such pattern of difference is found in the large suburbs. The range as well as the pattern of difference by socioeconomic status in the small suburbs is very similar to that observed in the large cities. Here we find that the higher the status of the residents, the more likely they are to view multiple districts as being wasteful.

The proportion of residents within each status category who feel

TABLE 4-5

PROPORTION REPORTING THAT MULTIPLE DISTRICTS ARE WASTEFUL
BY SOCIOECONOMIC STATUS AND SEX BY PLACE OF RESIDENCE
AND SIZE OF METROPOLITAN AREA

Socioeconomic Status and Sex	Large		Medium		Small	
	City	Suburb	City	Suburb	City	Suburb
	%	%	%	%	%	%
Total	37.1	30.3	42.0	35.7	43.9	40.0
Education						
Grade school	30.8	31.4	37.0	29.3	32.6	34.0
9–11	40.8	27.9	45.4	35.7	46.0	41.0
12	37.9	29.6	38.0	35.5	44.9	40.6
College	43.2	32.3	53.0	39.2	62.1	48.7
Occupation						
Other	31.1	31.6	38.3	24.8	44.1	37.0
Craftsmen	44.7	31.8	45.0	41.1	36.6	37.6
Clerical-sales	42.2	25.6	45.6	35.8	45.3	50.7
Prof.-managerial	43.4	32.2	44.4	39.5	57.4	45.7
Income (weekly)						
Under $75	34.3	25.5	46.5	26.9	37.8	29.9
$75–$99	37.5	33.7	41.5	33.6	50.0	38.5
$100–$149	43.4	34.8	45.5	42.6	44.4	41.6
$150 plus	58.1	26.6	47.6	37.6	59.2	55.3
Sex						
Male	43.2	33.3	46.4	43.3	53.6	47.3
Female	34.5	29.0	38.0	27.3	38.5	33.3

that multiple districts are wasteful tends to increase, particularly among suburban residents, as the size of the area declines. The same pattern of increase is found in the cities also, among those in the higher-status positions. Thus, for example, among the college trained the proportion reporting that multiple districts are wasteful increases from a low of 43 percent in the large cities to a high of 62 percent in the small cities. A similar but less marked difference is also found among the high school graduates, but the variations by size of city tend to disappear at the lower levels of education. Much the same kind of pattern is found within occupational groupings. In the suburbs, the same pattern of difference by size of area is also found, but the range of difference is less marked.

The influence of size of area is particularly important among suburban residents. Almost without exception, the proportion within each status grouping that report multiple districts as wasteful increases inversely by size of area. The size of the difference is particularly marked at the high status levels. Thus, for example, among the college trained the proportion reporting multiple districts as wasteful increases from 32 percent in the large suburbs to a high of 49 percent in the small suburbs. The comparable range for those in the highest occupational level is from 32 percent to 57 percent. And at the top income level, the range of such responses is from 27 percent to 59 percent. Thus the latter exceeds the former by more than 200 percent. A similar pattern of difference is also found at the lower socioeconomic levels, but the size of the difference is much less marked. There seems to be much more variation in the responses by size of area than is found among different segments of the population. But consistent variations by socioeconomic status are noted regardless of the variable used as an index of status.

In the larger metropolitan suburbs, particularly among the higher-status residents, a distinct majority—for example, two-thirds of the top income group—feel that multiple districts are not wasteful, but the proportion of such responses declines to approximately two-fifths of the residents of the same status in the small suburbs. Thus, it is quite apparent that residents in the larger metropolitan areas view the present organization of school districts quite differently from those living in the small areas. This pattern of difference holds regardless of the control variables introduced. At each status level, suburban residents are much less likely than city residents to view multiple districts as wasteful, but the size of the difference is less in the smaller metropolitan areas.

Males in all areas are more likely to see the wastefulness of multiple school districts than are female respondents. Regardless of size of area, city residents of both sexes are more likely than suburban residents to view multiple districts as wasteful, but in every case the males have a higher proportion who do so. It is among males in particular that the proportion of such responses increases as size of area declines.

Summary

It is evident that most of the residents in all of the areas are quite satisfied with their schools; however, this does not exclude some criticism. Many residents, particularly those in the city, have specific opinions as to the type of improvements that are needed. Both central city and suburban residents show a marked tendency to rate their own schools as being superior to those in the opposite part of the metropolitan area. The only exception to this pattern occurs in the small area suburbs. The relative evaluations attached to city and suburban schools vary consistently with a number of indices of socioeconomic status. Our data show that city residents are more likely than suburban residents to view the present system of multiple school district organization as being wasteful. While in all residential zones this view varies substantially by social status, there is even more variation by size of area than among different segments of the population. The influence of size is particularly important among suburban residents. In short, as the size of the area declines, the views held by central city and suburban residents tend to become more similar.

5

The Taxation Issue

ONE OF THE PERENNIAL problems faced by residents in local communities, as far as schools are concerned, is the issue of taxation. Essentially education is a commodity to be purchased.[1] Schools need adequate financing in order to maximize the type of program offered, but the amount of funds available necessarily depends in part on the taxes paid by local residents. Communities vary markedly in their abilities to produce the funds with which to upgrade the level of education that can be provided. The quality of education in any district depends in large part on the ability as well as the willingness of the population to devote funds for these purposes. It is quite likely that part of the resistance to reorganizing school districts in the metropolitan community is due to the tax issue. It may be that change is viewed with apprehension because of the uncertainty as to what would happen to taxes in the area. This is, of course, an empirical question, and it is one dimension of the problem that we intend to investigate. But before doing so we need to know how the residents in different parts of the metropolitan community view the present tax structure as far as the schools are concerned.

The present chapter is devoted to an analysis of the attitudes residents express concerning the taxes that they pay in support of the local educational system. Here, too, the major thrust of the dis-

[1] As one observer notes, "All of the problems of the schools lead us back sooner or later to one basic problem—financing." Rockefeller Brothers Fund, *The Pursuit of Excellence: Education and the Future of America* (N. Y.: Doubleday, 1958), p. 33.

cussion will be focused on central city-suburban differences as well as on size of metropolitan area. Of particular interest also is how taxes are viewed by various segments of the population and how residents feel about the amount of money that is being spent on education in their areas. Two other related questions pertain to the preferences of residents for better schools or reduced taxes and the extent to which residents would be willing to pay more in order to improve the quality of their schools. The latter questions will provide some notion of the extent to which the residents feel that they have either already overburdened themselves for the schools or have at least assumed as much of a burden as they are willing to accept.

Views Concerning Present Taxes

Our data indicate that while a majority of the residents in all areas feel that the amount of taxes paid for their school is "about the right amount," a substantial minority feel that school taxes are too high. Rarely do we find residents reporting that taxes are lower than they should be. It is noteworthy that the attitudes concerning taxes are quite different in the suburbs than in the central cities. Although the suburbs are usually portrayed as areas that place a great deal of importance on their schools, we nonetheless find that suburban residents are more likely than those in the city to report that taxes are too high. This difference is found regardless of size of metropolitan area. And while only a small proportion of the residents in every area report that taxes are too low, such responses are much more common among central city residents in each size class than among residents of the suburbs. Central city residents, particularly in the large and medium-sized areas, are also more likely not to express an opinion regarding local taxes—that is, they "do not know" how they feel about school taxes in their area. This might be due, in large part, to the much higher proportion of renters in these areas. The higher home ownership rate may also account, in part, for the higher proportion of suburban residents who report that taxes are too high. But that this is of only limited importance is suggested by the similarity of responses among both central city and suburban residents in all three size classes, even though the proportion of renters varies substantially by size of area. In the central cities, the proportion of renters ranges from a low of 34 percent in the small to a high of 54 percent in the large metropolitan areas. In the contiguous suburbs, the proportions are 16 percent and 27 percent, respectively. At any rate, taxes are paid, at least indirectly, and central city residents tend to be somewhat less critical than those in the suburbs about the taxes that must be paid. These views vary little by size of area.

Since attitudes toward taxes are likely to vary among population subgroups, and since the composition of the populations of the city and the suburbs differs, we turn our attention now to a discussion of how various segments of the population in each area view the current school tax situation. These data are shown in Table 5-1.

TABLE 5-1

PROPORTION OF RESIDENTS REPORTING THAT SCHOOL TAXES ARE TOO HIGH
BY SELECTED CHARACTERISTICS BY PLACE OF RESIDENCE
AND SIZE OF METROPOLITAN AREA

Selected Characteristics	Large		Medium		Small	
	City	Suburb	City	Suburb	City	Suburb
	%	%	%	%	%	%
Total	29.6	35.1	21.9	32.3	30.5	38.2
Age						
Under 25 years	31.1	24.0	17.9	19.2	23.5	35.1
25–34	21.7	33.3	15.4	25.6	20.8	26.3
35–44	27.9	35.9	21.3	31.0	25.0	38.3
45–54	29.2	34.0	24.7	28.6	33.0	34.1
55 years plus	34.3	40.7	25.0	50.0	41.0	58.6
Education						
Grade School	38.4	42.2	28.8	38.7	38.3	46.3
9–11	24.2	38.7	20.4	39.8	32.7	36.6
12	28.2	34.3	21.6	33.7	29.3	37.6
College	21.6	27.7	13.3	22.2	13.6	26.9
Occupation						
Other	29.4	43.2	24.2	34.3	29.7	31.1
Craftsmen	35.9	38.3	22.5	41.1	38.8	39.0
Clerical-sales	29.7	31.4	16.2	26.9	24.0	37.3
Prof.-managerial	24.1	29.8	23.3	25.6	20.2	38.1
Income (weekly)						
Under $75	37.4	31.9	23.8	46.2	30.3	40.3
$75–$99	26.7	41.6	21.3	28.3	28.7	33.3
$100–$149	24.5	32.3	20.0	34.2	27.4	38.7
$150 plus	29.0	30.9	14.3	21.8	22.4	31.6

Due to space limitations, we are reporting only on those who feel that taxes are a little or much too high. Almost without exception, in every subgroup suburban residents are more likely than those in the central city to feel that school taxes are too high. The proportion ranges as high as 59 percent among those 55 years of age and over in the small suburbs; in the large and medium-sized suburbs, the proportion of such responses exceeds two-fifths of those 55 years of age and over. Central city-suburban differences are marked as well as consistent in all areas within each age category, except for those under 25 years of age in the large metropolitan areas.

Within each population size class, there seems to be much more variation by socioeconomic status within each zone of the metropolitan area than that between central city and suburban residents. In every residential zone, the lower the status the higher is the proportion of residents who feel that school taxes are too high. And at every status level, suburban residents are even more likely than central city residents to report that taxes are too high regardless of the size of the metropolitan area. Size of area does not seem to be important as far as attitudes toward taxes are concerned, in that there is no consistent pattern of difference by size among either central cities or suburban areas. Social status, however, is a significant factor in how residents view school taxes. In all residential zones, particularly within educational and income groups, we find a marked inverse relationship with the proportion reporting that taxes are too high. And at each status level, the proportion of such responses tends to be higher in the suburbs than in the city. Inconsistency in this respect occurs only in the relationship to occupation in the suburbs of small areas.

Length of residence in the metropolitan area also appears to be an important factor in how residents view the present tax structure. Part of the differences are probably due to age, but again, within each length-of-time-in-the-community category, the proportion of residents reporting that taxes are too high continues to be higher in the suburbs than in the central city. This pattern of difference is found regardless of the size of the metropolitan area. But of particular interest is the direct relationship between the proportion reporting that taxes are too high and the length of residence in the metropolitan area. Either the natives, or those who have lived in the community for more than fifteen years, are the ones most likely to feel that taxes are too high. These are the residents who would be least likely to have some basis for comparison of the tax burden faced by other communities. It is, however, noted that, at least in the suburbs, the old-time residents have experienced substantial changes in their areas in recent years, due to a rapid growth in population, with all of the problems of physical expansion of the schools and the need for additional tax monies that accompanied such growth. This concern over high taxes is probably a reaction to the marked changes that have occurred in their areas.

Recent migrants—that is, those who have been in the community for less than five years—are least likely to feel that taxes are too high. But much of this difference is due to the high proportion who "do not know" how they feel about taxes in the area. Even if these latter responses are dropped from the analysis, recent migrants are less likely than other segments of the population to feel that taxes are too high, and in most areas they are most likely to feel that taxes are too low. In short, the evidence suggests that many of the recent migrants are still uncertain as to how they feel about the local tax structure. The "don't know" responses are more frequent in central cities than in the suburbs.

Views regarding school taxes vary substantially by whether or not residents have children in school and by the type of school that their children attend. These data are shown in Table 5-2. The proportion of residents who report that taxes are "about right" is highest among those with children in public schools and is lowest among those with no children in school, except in the medium-size metropolitan areas, where the proportion is lowest among those with children in non-public schools which, in nearly all instances, are Catholic parochial schools. The difference is particularly marked in the suburbs of medium-sized areas, where only 40 percent with children in non-public schools report taxes to be "about right," as compared with 49 percent of those with no children in school and 66 percent of those with children in public schools. This difference is not observed in the suburbs of either large or small areas.

The major difference, particularly in the suburbs, is a difference between stating that taxes are "much too high" as compared with reporting that they are a "little too high." Residents with children in non-public schools are much more likely to report that taxes are "much too high," whereas those with children in public schools or

TABLE 5-2

ATTITUDE TOWARD SCHOOL TAXES IN AREA BY TYPE OF SCHOOL
CHILDREN ATTEND BY PLACE OF RESIDENCE
AND SIZE OF METROPOLITAN AREA

Attitude Toward Taxes and Size of Metropolitan Area	Central City			Suburban Area		
	Public	Non-Public	None in School	Public	Non-Public	None in School
	%	%	%	%	%	%
Total	100.0	100.0	100.0	100.0	100.0	100.0
Large						
Much too high	8.6	15.6	17.3	9.4	20.9	14.4
Little too high	11.8	9.4	16.1	24.8	9.0	22.7
About right	62.4	51.6	41.3	56.4	62.7	49.3
Lower than should be	9.7	9.4	5.0	4.0	1.5	3.6
Don't know	6.5	12.5	18.9	5.4	6.0	9.7
No answer	1.1	1.6	7.3	—	—	0.4
Medium						
Much too high	6.6	12.8	8.5	2.5	35.4	16.1
Little too high	14.0	12.8	13.6	18.8	16.7	21.0
About right	62.0	53.8	55.6	66.0	39.6	49.2
Lower than should be	7.4	12.8	5.1	6.9	2.1	3.6
Don't know	9.9	7.7	16.9	6.6	6.3	10.1
No answer	—	—	0.3	—	—	—
Small						
Much too high	5.6	9.6	18.5	9.9	24.3	16.7
Little too high	15.6	26.9	16.0	19.3	18.9	30.2
About right	66.9	50.0	50.2	59.7	56.8	45.9
Lower than should be	8.8	7.7	4.4	4.3	—	0.5
Don't know	3.1	5.8	9.8	6.9	—	6.3
No answer	—	—	1.1	—	—	0.5

with no children in school are more likely to report that taxes are "a little too high." In each of these categories, central city residents are less likely to report that taxes are "much too high."

In both residential zones there tends to be more similarity in the responses regarding taxes between those with children in non-public schools and those with no children in school than between either of these groups and those with children attending public schools. Householders with children in public schools are least critical of the taxes that they must pay in support of the schools. This is to be expected, in that the other residents are not currently receiving any direct personal benefits from the taxes paid and view the burden on them accordingly. But the significant observation here is that, except in the medium-size suburbs, a distinct majority of those whose children attend non-public schools report that the school taxes paid are "about right." A lesser proportion, but still nearly half of those with no children in school, concur with this view. Thus, while there are substantial differences in views by whether or not residents are currently using the schools, we nonetheless find that a substantial number of those who are not using the schools are not overly critical concerning the school taxes that they must pay. When complaints are reported, however, they tend to be found most frequently among suburban residents. These data suggest that willingness to support the local schools through taxation is most likely to come from that segment of the population with children attending public schools, and is least likely to be found among suburban residents who send their children to non-public schools. Although the latter constitute only a minority, the number is such that this segment of the population would represent a substantial block of votes in any general election. Consequently, their views are a dimension that needs to be assessed.

Views Concerning Present Expenditures

In light of the discussion regarding views on taxation, it is of interest to note how residents feel about the amount of money that is being spent on education in their areas. These data are shown in Table 5-3. We have already noted that a substantial number of residents feel that taxes are higher than they should be; however, we find that only a small proportion of the residents feel that too much money is being spent on education. And contrary to expectation, in each size class suburban residents are more likely than those in the central cities to feel that too much is being spent. The differences, although slight, are consistent. On the other hand, suburban residents are more likely than city residents to feel that the right amount is being spent, but the city-suburban difference declines in the smaller areas. Thus, while the proportion of suburban residents in the large metropolitan areas who feel that the right amount is being spent on education exceeds the proportion of such responses in the central city by 63 percent, the comparable difference is less than 7 percent in the small metropolitan areas. By way of contrast, central city residents are more likely to feel that not enough is being spent in their area, but the proportion sharing this view declines as size of city decreases. It is also in the cities that we find the largest proportion of residents who "do not know" how they feel about this issue.

TABLE 5-3

HOW RESIDENTS FEEL ABOUT AMOUNT OF MONEY SPENT ON
EDUCATION IN THEIR AREA BY PLACE OF RESIDENCE
AND SIZE OF METROPOLITAN AREA

Amount Spent on Education is:	Large		Medium		Small	
	City	Suburb	City	Suburb	City	Suburb
Total Number	477	495	457	493	488	492
	%	%	%	%	%	%
Too much	6.9	9.9	5.7	8.7	10.7	11.8
About right amount	40.9	66.9	49.7	66.9	53.7	57.3
Not enough	34.0	12.7	26.0	13.8	19.1	15.7
Don't know	17.6	10.5	18.2	10.3	16.4	14.8
No answer	0.6	—	0.4	0.2	0.2	0.4
Total	100.0	100.0	100.0	100.0	100.0	100.0

The data in Table 5-3 suggest that many residents want more from their schools than they are willing to pay for through taxes. For example, while 30 percent of the residents of large central cities reported that their taxes were too high, only 7 percent felt that too much money was being spent on their schools. Conversely, while only 7 percent thought taxes were lower than they should be, we find that nearly five times as many (34 percent) feel that not enough is being spent on education. Similar differences between what residents want to pay in taxes and the amount they want spent on education are found in all of the other areas. Apparently residents would like a well-financed school system, but they would rather not pay for it through taxation. We shall return to this topic in the next chapter where we look at the question of who should support the schools.

It is expected that various segments of the population would react differently to the amount of money that is being spent on education in their areas. It is to this question that we now turn our attention. The major emphasis of the discussion will center around age groupings and educational levels. We have already observed on several occasions that variations by income and occupation tend to follow the same general pattern of difference observed by variations in education. Consequently, detailed data are presented only for education, which will serve as an index to illustrate the importance of socioeconomic status. These data are shown in Table 5-4.

The importance of age is markedly evident, particularly among central city residents, though the same pattern is found also in the suburbs. There tends to be a consistent increase in the proportion who feel that too much money is being spent on education as age increases. The proportion reaches a high point among those 45 years of age and over. It is also apparent that within each size class and in most age categories, suburban residents are more likely to feel that too much money is being spent on education. The central city-suburban differences tend to be larger among the older residents—that is, those that are least likely to have children in school. Apparently these age groups are more sensitive to the costs of education in the suburban areas than are those who live in the city. At any rate, in each size class, it is the older residents in the suburbs who are most likely to feel that too much is being spent on education. It will be recalled that it was also those in the older ages in the suburbs who were most likely to feel that school taxes were too high and least likely to feel that taxes were lower than they should be.[2]

The influence of age is even more evident when we consider those who feel that not enough money is being spent on education in their respective areas. Here too, responses vary substantially both by place of residence and size of metropolitan area. Looking first at cities, we find that there is a marked decline in the proportion of residents who feel that not enough is being spent on education as age increases. Also we find a consistent and substantial decline in such responses in all age groups as size of metropolitan area declines. At all ages, the proportion of residents in the large cities who feel that not enough money is being spent on education is approximately double the pro-

[2] Again it is noted that the older suburban residents, in particular, would have experienced a period of rapid transition and expansion of school facilities in their areas in recent years. This would have substantially increased their taxes in order to provide the facilities needed because of the growth in population.

TABLE 5-4

HOW FEEL ABOUT AMOUNT OF MONEY SPENT ON EDUCATION IN AREA
BY AGE AND EDUCATION BY PLACE OF RESIDENCE
AND SIZE OF METROPOLITAN AREA

Age, Education and Place of Residence	Money Spent on Education is:								
	Too Much			About Right			Not Enough		
	Large	Medium	Small	Large	Medium	Small	Large	Medium	Small
	%	%	%	%	%	%	%	%	%
Age									
Central City									
Under 25 years	2.2	3.6	11.8	31.1	42.9	35.3	44.4	35.7	23.5
25–34	2.4	5.1	5.0	39.7	35.9	48.5	41.0	34.6	28.7
35–44	7.7	8.3	5.4	39.4	50.9	64.3	36.5	26.9	20.5
45–54	8.3	6.2	11.7	44.4	51.5	52.1	34.7	32.0	19.1
55 years plus	9.5	4.2	16.7	43.2	56.2	55.5	26.0	14.6	10.4
Suburban									
Under 25 years	8.0	3.8	10.8	68.0	50.0	54.1	8.0	11.5	24.3
25–34	8.7	6.0	2.3	65.9	70.7	54.1	11.9	15.0	24.8
35–44	11.1	7.7	13.5	70.1	69.7	59.4	15.4	14.1	13.5
45–54	8.7	11.0	18.2	67.0	60.4	59.1	16.5	19.8	11.4
55 years plus	11.0	13.0	17.2	65.3	68.0	58.6	7.6	7.0	7.1
Education									
Central City									
Grade school	9.4	6.2	16.3	40.9	51.4	48.9	23.9	17.1	13.5
9–11	5.8	8.3	7.1	45.0	51.9	49.6	33.3	25.0	21.2
12	6.5	6.0	9.0	37.1	43.1	59.3	46.8	31.9	19.2
College	4.1	1.2	9.1	40.5	54.2	57.6	35.1	33.7	27.3
Suburban									
Grade school	4.9	6.7	12.9	58.8	65.3	53.1	12.7	9.3	12.9
9–11	11.8	10.2	6.0	61.3	65.3	59.7	17.2	17.3	20.9
12	12.4	11.4	12.0	66.3	66.9	57.1	12.4	11.4	16.5

portion found in the small cities. The overall range in the proportion of such responses is from a low of only 10 percent among those over 55 years of age in the small cities to a high of 44 percent among those under 25 years of age in the large cities. Variations by age as well as size of city are not only consistent but marked.

Among those in the younger ages, small area suburban residents are more likely than those in the larger areas to feel that not enough is being spent on education. This is the opposite of the pattern found by size of city. Why this is so is suggested by our earlier observations concerning how suburban residents in each size class viewed their schools. It will be recalled that the level of satisfaction with schools was higher in the large and medium-sized suburbs than in the small suburbs. Also, residents in the latter area were much more likely to rate schools in the cities as better than their own, while residents in the larger suburbs were much more likely to rate their own schools as better than those found in the city. Thus the low proportion of residents in the larger suburbs who feel that not enough is being spent on education may represent a high degree of satisfaction with the schools as they are now functioning.

Residents in the small suburbs seem to be much less content with their schools, and they apparently express this discontent by more frequently reporting that not enough is being spent on education in their area. And it is the younger residents—that is, those with children in school or about to start school—that are most likely to feel that not enough is being spent on education in their area. In the cities, also, it is among the same age groups that we find the most concern about not enough being spent on education. The frequency of such responses, however, declines with size of city. The significant point here is that in the large and medium-sized cities, in particular, a substantial number of the residents feel that not enough money is being spent on education, whereas this judgment is rarely expressed by the residents in the contiguous suburbs. Such responses are reported much less frequently in the large cities than in the small ones, but more frequently in the small than in the larger suburbs. As a result, there is a convergence of opinion among the residents in both zones in the small metropolitan areas.

In general, suburban residents at all ages seem to be more content with what is being spent on education, whereas city residents are much more likely to feel that more should be spent. The only ex-

ception to this is found in the small metropolitan areas, where city
and suburban residents are quite similar in their evaluations. Thus,
to the extent that resistance to change has any roots in the content-
ment with the amount of money being spent on schools, little support
for change is to be expected among residents in either large or medium-sized suburbs.

In the lower panel of Table 5-4, it is only among those with a
grade school education that the proportion who feel that too much
is being spent is higher in the city than in the suburbs. At all other
educational levels, suburban residents are most likely to feel that too
much money is being spent on education in their area. However, the
pattern of variation is erratic by level of education. There is, however, more of a tendency for those in the small metropolitan areas,
at all educational levels, to report that too much is being spent, but
even in these areas such responses are infrequent. But then, nearly
the same proportion of residents feel that not enough is being spent,
whereas among city residents, particularly among those in large and
medium-sized areas, we find a substantial proportion who report
that not enough is being spent on the schools.

When we look at those who feel that not enough is being spent,
we find that in the suburbs such responses are unrelated to education, but education exerts considerable influence among city residents in all size areas. The proportion of city residents sharing this
view increases directly by education. The range of difference is
marked. At each level of education, least differences are found in
the small metropolitan areas, where the city and suburban responses
are very similar except among the college trained. Among the latter,
city residents are nearly three times as likely as those in the suburbs
to feel that not enough is being spent. By way of contrast, the college-
educated in the small suburbs are the ones most likely to report that
too much is being spent on the schools in their area. It may well be
that this segment of the population disproportionately complains
about the amount spent because of the quality of education that is
provided in their areas. It will be recalled that of all of the suburban
residents, the college group in the small area suburbs most frequently
reported that city schools were better than their own and that multiple districts were wasteful.

It would seem that in both large and medium-sized metropolitan
central cities, particularly among the younger and better-educated

groups, a substantial segment of the population expresses the view that the schools are not adequately supported and not enough is being spent on education in their areas. By way of comparison, suburban residents appear to be much more content with what they are doing for their schools. And this seems to hold generally for all segments of the population. At least no consistent or marked differences are found, either by age or education. Although not shown here, the above differences by place of residence and size of metropolitan area are also found, even when we control for occupational or income levels, as well as by length of residence and movement within the metropolitan area.

Let us now examine a somewhat different aspect of the tax issue. The next two questions, which will conclude the present chapter, are rather severe tests of interest in schools: the willingness of the residents to devote additional resources in order to improve their schools, and whether they would prefer cutting taxes rather than to improve their schools. It is the latter question that we will consider first.

Preferences for Better Schools or Lower Taxes

In response to the general query, "If you had the opportunity to choose only one, would you prefer getting better schools or cutting taxes?" we find that in all areas an overwhelming majority report that they would prefer better schools. But a substantial minority, particularly in the small and large metropolitan areas, are in favor of reduced taxes. Keeping in mind that this attitude is shared by only a small segment of the population, the question of interest here pertains to the type of residents who are most likely to prefer cutting taxes rather than having better schools. Thus the emphasis of the discussion is in terms of these responses.

This is an important segment of the population, for it may well be among such persons that resistance to change is strongest. On the other hand, it may be that these persons would disproportionately favor reorganization with the expectations that change would lead to a reduced tax burden. Even apart from this issue, however, these data have descriptive value, since a detailed analysis will help us to identify the type of residents most likely to favor reduced taxes over better schools in their area. That there are large and consistent differences among various segments of the population is readily evident from the data presented in Table 5-5. Here too, we have presented data in detail for only a few selected population characteristics, in order to demonstrate the kind of variations that are found within

TABLE 5-5

PROPORTION STATING PREFERENCE FOR CUTTING TAXES OVER BETTER
SCHOOLS BY TYPE OF SCHOOL CHILDREN ATTEND AND SELECTED
CHARACTERISTICS BY PLACE OF RESIDENCE
AND SIZE OF METROPOLITAN AREA

Type of School Attended and Selected Characteristics	Large		Medium		Small	
	City	Suburb	City	Suburb	City	Suburb
	%	%	%	%	%	%
Total	23.5	19.6	14.2	14.6	21.9	20.5
School Attended						
Public	17.2	13.4	9.9	8.6	11.9	16.7
Non-public	15.6	11.9	12.8	18.7	21.2	18.9
None in school	27.1	24.8	16.3	18.5	27.6	24.8
Age						
Under 25 years	13.3	8.0	7.1	15.4	8.8	13.5
25–34	20.5	9.5	5.1	11.3	12.9	18.0
35–44	17.3	18.8	14.8	8.5	12.5	19.5
45–54	18.1	17.5	11.3	15.4	28.7	19.3
55 years plus	33.7	35.6	22.2	27.0	34.0	28.3
Education						
Grade school	32.7	35.3	23.3	30.9	33.3	27.9
9–11	22.5	20.4	13.0	18.4	23.0	21.6
12	18.5	18.3	11.2	10.2	18.6	16.5
College	13.5	7.7	4.8	9.1	4.5	11.5
Length of Time in Metropolitan Area						
Under 5 years	19.0	8.6	7.3	6.7	9.3	12.3
5–15	20.0	6.0	8.9	8.5	17.6	19.1
15 years plus	18.0	24.0	15.3	17.4	26.9	24.5
Natives	28.1	22.3	17.5	17.4	21.7	20.7

the different residential areas. Much more variation is found among subgroups of the population within each area than by place of residence or size of metropolitan area. Within each of the control groups and in each size class, there is no consistent pattern of difference by place of residence, size of city, or size of suburban area. However, within each size class and in both residential zones, large and consistent differences are found by the type of school children attend and by variations in age and educational level, as well as by length of residence in the community.

Residents least likely to prefer a tax cut over better schools are those who currently have children attending public schools. Those whose children attend non-public schools are somewhat more likely to favor a tax cut, but the residents most likely to do so are those who had no children in school. This pattern of difference holds in every area, regardless of size. It is found in the suburbs as well as in the cities. But a point worthy of note is that even among residents who do not have any children in school, less than three out of ten would place more emphasis on reduced taxes than on getting better schools. Stated differently, regardless of whether or not they currently use the public schools, 70 percent or more of the residents in all areas would prefer better schools to reduced taxes. This represents a rather substantial commitment to the schools in the area. And of those who do have children in public schools, an even higher proportion would rather have better schools than reduced taxes. However, it is worthy of note that much more variation in responses is found by differences in the characteristics of the population than by whether or not residents are currently using the public schools.

There is a marked and consistent pattern by age. As age increases, the proportion of residents in all areas who would prefer a tax reduction increases also. It may be that this concern is a result of limited and fixed incomes in the face of rising costs, including higher taxes. Yet even among the older residents, a large majority favor better schools over a reduced tax burden. Thus, while there are marked variations in the proportion favoring a tax cut over better schools, the proportion of such responses never exceeds more than one-third in any age group.

Level of education is also an important factor in how residents feel about schools and taxes. The lower the level of educational attainment, the higher the proportion of residents who report that they would prefer a cut in taxes rather than having better schools. These responses overlap the variations already observed by age, because of the close relationship between age and education. Still, the variations found by education can only partly be attributed to the age factor. A substantial part of the difference is due to the influence of education alone. It is noteworthy that within each educational level there is no pattern of difference by place of residence or size of metropolitan area. As far as this particular issue is concerned, the reactions of the residents are much more dependent on their educational level than on the type or size of community in which they live.

The residents least likely to favor a tax cut are those who have only recently moved to the community, regardless of where they live within the metropolitan community. However, as length of residence in the community increases, so does the proportion who would favor a reduced tax burden. Among migrants, those who have lived in the community for fifteen years or more are the ones most likely to favor a tax cut. Recent migrants in the large area central cities are much more likely than those in the suburbs to favor a tax reduction. This is likely due to the population composition of the recent migrants to the large cities. As compared with those who have settled in the suburbs, recent migrants to the large cities are likely disproportionately made up of individuals and households who are currently not using the schools. Also, they are more likely to be in the lower socioeconomic levels. As a consequence of this combination of factors, this group is more likely to favor a tax cut than recent migrants in the suburbs.

In all areas, natives tend to be very similar to the long-time migrant residents. Thus it would seem that those who are most familiar with the community are the ones most likely to favor a tax reduction. It may well be that the long-time residents have witnessed a steady increase in school costs over the years, with a consequent increase in school taxes, and many may feel that they have been pushed to, if not beyond, a saturation point. They may feel that a disproportionate amount of the local resources have been devoted to the schools. At any rate, the natives are more likely than recent migrants to favor a tax cut. But again, it is noted that this view is shared only by a minority. For a majority of the residents, regardless of how long they have lived in the community, better schools are preferred over reduced taxes. And so it is, regardless of the characteristics of the population, place of residence, or size of the metropolitan community. The importance placed on having good schools in the community is thus readily apparent. Only a small minority, never exceeding one-third of any subgroup, would prefer reduced taxes over better schools. But how would the residents feel about increasing their taxes in order to improve their schools?

Willingness to Pay More in Taxes

While a very substantial majority of the residents in all areas stated a preference for better schools over a cut in taxes, we find that a much smaller proportion of the residents would be willing to pay more in order to improve their schools. Actually, a larger proportion of the residents would be opposed to any such increase, and another large segment of the population, ranging from 10 to 20 percent, is somewhat unclear as to how they feel about further support of the schools. That is, they either "don't know" whether they would pay more to improve their schools or they qualify their answer so much that it suggests that further support may be forthcoming only under very special and limited conditions. For purposes of this discussion, our attention shall be focused only on those who gave a clear-cut "yes" or "no" to the question, since this is the segment of the population that has established a clear-cut "position" as far as future support of the schools is concerned. It must be kept in mind, however, that in the case of an actual vote the outcome would be influenced by those in the "don't know" and "depends" categories. These data are shown by a number of selected characteristics of the population in Table 5-6.

Some rather interesting but not unexpected differences in willingness to support the schools are found among residents by use of the schools. Willingness to pay more in order to improve the schools is most frequently reported by residents who currently have children attending the public schools. A majority of such residents in all areas except in the large area suburbs report that they would be willing to pay more. But even in the suburbs of large areas, we find that 47 percent would be willing to do so; however, this is somewhat lower than the 56 percent who would be willing to do so in the large cities. On the other hand, approximately one-third of the residents with children in public schools report that they would not do so.

Residents least willing to pay more in order to improve the schools are those who do not have any children in school, whereas families with children in non-public schools seem to fall midway between those with and without children in school. This is clearly evident in

TABLE 5-6

PERCENT REPORTING THAT THEY WOULD PAY MORE TO IMPROVE
SCHOOLS BY SCHOOL CHILDREN ATTEND BY SELECTED
CHARACTERISTICS BY PLACE OF RESIDENCE
AND SIZE OF METROPOLITAN AREA

School Attended and Selected Characteristics	Large		Medium		Small	
	City	Suburb	City	Suburb	City	Suburb
	%	%	%	%	%	%
Total	46.1	41.2	50.5	44.1	46.1	47.4
School Children Attend						
Public	55.9	47.0	61.6	56.9	58.8	54.9
Non-public	43.8	37.3	43.6	25.0	44.2	45.9
None in school	43.5	33.8	46.8	37.9	39.3	39.6
Age						
Under 25 years	53.3	64.0	67.9	53.8	50.0	59.5
25–34	57.8	50.0	57.7	53.4	53.5	63.2
35–44	45.2	40.2	55.6	45.1	57.1	49.6
45–54	52.8	43.7	53.6	44.0	43.6	42.0
55 years plus	35.5	25.4	37.5	29.0	33.3	22.2
Education						
Grade school	35.2	28.4	43.8	30.7	29.8	41.5
9–11	45.8	41.9	51.9	50.6	41.6	49.2
12	55.6	43.2	50.0	42.8	53.3	49.6
College	54.1	48.5	61.4	51.6	71.2	51.3
Income (weekly)						
Under $75	47.1	27.7	48.5	34.6	42.9	35.8
$75–$99	51.7	39.6	55.3	40.7	49.1	53.0
$100–$149	53.8	46.8	51.8	45.8	50.4	54.0
$150 plus	48.4	52.1	59.5	55.4	59.2	52.6
Length of Residence in Metropolitan Area						
Under 5 years	57.1	54.3	68.3	53.3	58.1	63.2
5–15	56.4	46.3	58.2	52.4	44.6	57.4
15 years plus	43.2	37.2	45.8	41.9	43.1	44.8
Natives	43.3	40.1	47.5	40.0	46.8	39.9

both large and small metropolitan areas, but in the medium-sized
areas those with children in non-public schools are the ones least
willing to pay more in order to improve the schools. Why this group
would differ so much in the medium-sized areas, particularly in the
suburbs, is not readily clear. In the other areas, those with children
in non-public schools tend to be about 20 percent less likely to be
in favor of paying more in order to improve the schools than those

with children attending the public schools, whereas those with no children in school are about 30 percent less likely to be willing to pay more. The latter is also found in the medium-sized areas, but the public–non-public difference is larger than that found in the other areas, particularly among suburban residents, where only 25 percent of those with children in non-public schools would be willing to pay more, as compared with 57 percent of those with children attending the public schools.

Within each of the school attendance categories, central city residents are more likely than suburban residents to be willing to pay more in order to improve the schools, whereas the negative responses are more frequent in the suburbs. The only exception to this observation occurs in the small metropolitan areas, where the central city-suburban responses are very similar. There seems to be no significant difference in willingness to pay more by size of area. Much larger differences are found by the type of school children attend than by place of residence within the metropolitan area. Further support of the schools is most likely to come from those who currently have children attending the public schools, whereas those who do not have any children in school seem to be least willing to pay more in order to improve the schools; but even within this group such support would be forthcoming from one-third to nearly one-half of the residents. However, in most areas an even larger proportion would be opposed to paying more.

Marked differences are found in all areas among age, education, income, and length of time lived in the metropolitan area categories. In most areas, the pattern of difference is consistent and in the direction expected. Thus, in general, we find that the proportion willing to pay more to improve the schools decreases with age. Except for the younger residents in the small metropolitan areas, in each age group central city residents are more likely than suburban residents to report that they would pay more. These differences are illustrated by the residents in the large suburbs, where the proportion willing to pay more decreases from a high of 64 percent among those under 25 years of age to a low of only 25 percent of those 55 years of age and over. Conversely, those who would be opposed to paying more ranges from a low of 20 percent to a high of 64 percent for the same age categories.

A very similar pattern of difference by age is observed in all of the other areas. Here, as elsewhere, we find much more variation by age than by place of residence. Willingness to further support the schools is much more closely related to age than to either size of area or place of residence within the metropolitan community. Level of education and size of income are also both important factors in how people view the schools. The proportion willing to pay more in order to improve the schools increases directly with education as well as with size of income. The same pattern of difference is found in all areas. The range of the difference is large, and the variation is consistent. In both large and medium-sized areas, within each educational and income category, central city residents consistently show more willingness than suburban residents to pay more. But in the small metropolitan areas, central city-suburban differences show no such pattern. In general, the residents in both zones tend to be quite similar in their responses. The point we wish to emphasize here also is that we find much more variation in the responses by both educational and income levels than by place of residence. It is unlikely that those at the grade school level or in the lower income categories would approve any school proposal which would place a further tax burden on them, whereas the chances are quite good that those at the higher levels of education and income would be willing to devote further local resources to the support of the schools. And central city residents would be somewhat more likely to do so than those in the suburbs.

In the last panel in Table 5-6, we find that the proportion of residents willing to pay more in order to improve the schools varies inversely with the length of time lived in the community. In all areas, the recent migrants—that is, those who have lived in the community less than five years—are most likely to be willing to pay more. However, the proportion willing to do so declines in all areas and reaches a low point among the natives and those who have lived in the community fifteen years or longer. Much of this difference may be due to age differences, since the recent migrants are more likely to be younger. At any rate, support is more likely to come from short-term residents than from those who have lived in the community longer.

These data suggest that close to a majority of the residents in all areas would be willing to pay more in order to improve their schools, but there are certain segments of the population that are much less likely to do so. Any proposal seeking additional funds so as to improve the schools would have to obtain the support of at least a segment of the population which has not yet taken a set position on this issue, or from among those who already feel that they would not be willing to pay more. But the significant point here is that apparently further support would be readily forthcoming from a very large, though not a majority, segment of the population. While there seem to be few central city-suburban differences in the small metropolitan areas, the proportion who report that they would pay more in order to improve the schools is consistently higher among city residents in both the large and medium-sized metropolitan areas. This difference holds even when we control for a number of selected variables.

Summary

In this discussion we have noted that suburban residents are more likely than those in the city to feel that present school taxes are too high. Within each size class, there seems to be much more variation in the proportion holding this view by socioeconomic status than by place of residence. The lower the status, the higher the proportion who feel that taxes are too high. But regardless of socioeconomic status, this view is more frequently expressed by suburban than central city residents. In each residential zone, families with children attending public schools are least critical of the taxes that they must pay. While a substantial number of residents feel that taxes are too high, a much smaller proportion express the view that too much is being spent on education in their area. But in each size class, suburban residents are more likely to do so than those living in the city.

On the other hand, while city residents are more likely to feel that not enough is being spent in their areas, the proportion declines as size of area decreases. In most areas, residents appear to want much more from their schools than they are willing to support through their taxes. That is, residents in all areas appear to want a well-financed school system, but would prefer not to pay for it through taxation. The gap between city and suburban views tends to be least in the small metropolitan areas, where the views become quite similar. As compared with other suburbs, the residents in the small area suburbs more frequently report that not enough is being spent on education. In the large- and medium-sized cities, a sizable number of the residents, particularly among the younger and better educated, are of the opinion that the schools are not adequately supported and that not enough is being spent on education in their areas. By way of comparison, suburban residents in the same areas are much more content with what they are doing for their schools.

While most of the residents in all areas state a preference for better schools over lower taxes, a substantial number would rather reduce taxes. The latter view is held primarily by the older residents and those in the lower educational, occupational, and income categories. Residents least likely to prefer a tax cut are those who have children attending the public schools. This is also the group that most frequently reports a willingness to pay more in order to improve their schools. While central city residents are more willing than suburban residents to pay more in order to improve their schools, much larger differences are found by type of school children attend than by place of residence within the metropolitan area. Also, variations in such responses are more marked by socioeconomic status than by either place of residence or size of area.

6

Views of the Source of Support of Schools

IN THE LAST CHAPTER we were concerned about the attitudes of residents toward taxation and their willingness to support the local schools. The present discussion deals with a set of related but different questions. One is the general issue of who should support the schools. Another is how do residents view the responsibilities of families with no children or with many children as far as the support of the schools is concerned. A final question has to do with what do residents feel the ordinary citizen can do to influence the way school money is spent.

In the early history of this country, support of the schools was primarily a local responsibility. School district boundaries were drawn to reflect local community interest and to acknowledge the autonomy of local interest. With the passing of time and the urbanization of society, with its increased demands for a more uniform and more sophisticated educational system, there has been a concomitant change in the sources of support of the schools. Increasingly, support has come from sources outside of the local community.[1] However, outside support, which has come largely from the

[1] Every state in the union increased the amount of its contributions to education between 1890 and 1930. Many of the states made marked increases after 1915. For example, state and federal contributions to the support of education increased by more than 30 percent during the five-year period 1925 to 1930. These contributions were being paralleled by a large increase in expenditures for education. See Paul R. Mort, *State Support for Public Education* (N. Y.: American Council on Education, 1938), p. 23, and his discussion on "Evolution of the Fundamental Principles Underlying State School Support," pp. 32–44.

state, is intended to supplement rather than to replace local support. The purpose of outside aid is to improve and equalize educational opportunities, for changing conditions have caused enormous variation among school districts in their abilities to support adequate educational systems. Moreover, new sources of revenue to supplement the traditional property tax were found; sources which could best be captured by the state.[2] In more recent years the national government has begun to contribute in various ways to the support of schools in local districts throughout the nation.[3] These funds have generally been channeled through the state. The role that the federal government should play in the local school districts, however, is a controversial and as yet unresolved question.[4] In the present chapter, we will discuss how the residents living in metropolitan areas included in this study feel about the involvement of the federal government in the support of the schools in their areas.

Role of Federal Government

The first question to be considered is: "Would you be in favor of the federal government providing funds to help cover the cost of operations for local schools?" How the residents responded to this question is shown in Table 6-1. It is readily apparent that a distinct majority of the residents in all areas would be in favor of the federal government contributing funds to local school dis-

[2] The absolute amount of money involved is large, and the volume of grants has increased sharply in recent years. Local school districts receive approximately 40 percent of their revenues from the states. For a full discussion of this, see Benson, *op. cit.* note 22, chap. 1. For data on sources of revenue, see U. S. Bureau of the Census, Census of Governments, 1957, *Historical Summary of Governmental Finances in the United States,* IV, 3 (Washington: U. S. Department of Commerce, 1959), p. 15.

[3] In a recent report, *Schools for the Sixties,* the National Education Association recommended that the federal government should provide general financial assistance for the improvement of public education (N. Y.: McGraw-Hill, 1963; p. 123).

[4] For a discussion of the arguments in favor and opposed to federal aid, see *ibid.,* chap. 8, pp. 250–286. See also Hearings Before the Subcommittee on General Education of the Committee on Education and Labor, House of Representatives, 86th Congress, First Session, *School Support Act of 1959* (Washington: U. S. Government Printing Office, 1959); F. J. Seider, *Federal Support for Education* (Washington: Public Affairs Institute, 1959); and U. S. Commission on Intergovernmental Relations, *Federal Responsibility in the Field of Education* (Washington: U. S. Government Printing Office, 1955).

TABLE 6-1

ATTITUDES TOWARD FEDERAL FUNDS FOR OPERATIONS
BY PLACE OF RESIDENCE AND SIZE
OF METROPOLITAN AREA

Favor Federal Funds	Large		Medium		Small	
	City	Suburb	City	Suburb	City	Suburb
Total Number	477	495	457	493	488	492
	%	%	%	%	%	%
Yes	68.8	59.2	63.9	59.6	58.6	54.7
No	23.7	35.2	27.4	34.5	32.8	37.2
Don't know	6.5	5.7	7.9	5.5	8.0	7.7
No answer	1.0	—	0.9	0.4	0.6	0.4
Total	100.0	100.0	100.0	100.0	100.0	100.0

tricts to help cover the cost of operations. There is, however, a tendency for suburban residents to be somewhat more opposed to such support than central city residents. The difference is not large, but the consistency is noteworthy. The opposition to federal aid tends to increase slightly as size of metropolitan area declines, but the pattern of difference is meaningful only among the central cities, where the proportion opposed ranges from 24 percent in the large central cities to 33 percent in the small central cities.

Federal aid to education seems to be an issue on which residents have a clear-cut opinion, as is evidenced by the very small proportion of "don't know" and "no answer" responses. In all areas, more than nine out of every ten stated a definite preference either for or against federal aid. And as noted, most of the residents favored federal support. The proportion ranges from a high of 69 percent in the large central cities to a low of 55 percent in the small area suburbs. It may very well be that federal support is a less controversial issue than generally believed.[5] At any rate, there appears to be a general consensus that federal support would be viewed with favor. However, since this is an issue that is likely to become increasingly important in the future, we would like to pursue the analysis further, focusing our attention on the kinds of

[5] See Committee for Economic Development, *Paying for Better Public Schools* (New York, 1960). Also see John K. Norton, *Critical Issues in American Public Education* (Pittsburgh, Pa.: University of Pittsburgh Press, 1965).

people most likely to oppose such a program of support for the local schools.

That various segments of the population react to this issue differently is strikingly evident from the data presented in Table 6-2.

TABLE 6-2

PROPORTION OF RESIDENTS OPPOSED TO FEDERAL AID FOR OPERATIONS
OF LOCAL SCHOOLS BY SELECTED CHARACTERISTICS BY PLACE
OF RESIDENCE AND SIZE OF METROPOLITAN AREA

Selected Characteristics	Large		Medium		Small	
	City	Suburb	City	Suburb	City	Suburb
	%	%	%	%	%	%
Total	23.7	35.2	27.4	34.5	32.8	37.2
Age						
Under 25 years	24.4	40.0	17.9	26.9	26.5	18.9
25–34	32.5	41.3	26.9	31.6	27.7	30.8
35–44	21.2	35.0	31.5	36.6	33.9	40.6
45–54	15.3	29.1	25.8	39.6	35.1	42.0
55 years plus	24.9	33.9	27.1	32.0	35.4	43.4
Education						
Grade school	13.2	16.7	18.5	14.7	19.9	21.8
9–11	21.7	21.5	25.0	22.4	22.1	25.4
12	26.6	32.0	27.6	33.7	38.9	50.4
College	44.6	63.8	45.8	52.3	63.6	64.1
Occupation						
Other	20.3	16.8	15.6	21.9	16.6	23.0
Craftsmen	21.4	26.2	30.2	34.6	27.6	30.5
Clerical-sales	25.0	38.4	29.4	34.3	50.7	50.7
Prof.-Managerial	33.7	52.0	41.1	42.6	53.2	54.3
Income						
Under $75	16.7	23.4	20.8	19.2	26.1	23.9
$75–$99	22.5	30.7	30.9	29.2	24.1	26.5
$100–$149	33.0	31.0	30.0	34.8	38.5	45.3
$150 plus	35.5	59.6	42.9	55.4	55.1	56.6

Very marked and consistent differences are found among socioeconomic groups, but the pattern of difference among age groups is much less clear. How various age groups respond to this issue seems to be largely influenced by the size of metropolitan area in which they live. Thus, for example, in the large metropolitan areas, opposition tends to be highest among those in the younger ages and declines steadily up to the oldest age group, where the proportion again increases. The pattern is the same in both central city and suburban areas. But within each age group, the proportion opposed to federal aid is higher among suburban than central city residents. However, the opposite pattern of difference by age is found in the medium-sized and small metropolitan areas. Here too, though, opposition is more frequent in the suburbs, at each age level, than among city residents. And in both areas, opposition appears to increase with each increase in age. The most marked differences by age are found in the small area suburbs, where only 19 percent of those under 25 years of age oppose federal aid, as compared with 43 percent of those 55 years of age and over. The same pattern is found among residents in the small cities, but the range of difference is more limited.

In general, within each age group, opposition to federal aid tends to vary inversely by size of city. Although the amount of difference is not large, the pattern of differences shows a marked consistency. However, in the suburbs this pattern of difference by size is not the same at all ages. Actually, the differences among those under 35 years of age and those who are older run in opposite directions. Among the suburban residents, opposition to federal aid is highest in the large area suburbs and lowest in the small area suburbs. The differences are substantial. But in the older age groups, opposition tends to be inversely related to size. And here, too, the range of difference is sizable. It is not readily apparent why the younger residents in the large metropolitan areas, on the one hand, and the older age groups in the small metropolitan areas, on the other, should be most opposed to federal aid. Yet the size of the differences is such that they cannot be ignored.

Education, unlike age, shows a very distinct and consistent association with opposition to federal aid in all areas. Those with only a grade school education are least likely to be opposed to the federal government helping out the local schools, whereas most opposition comes from the college trained. In each area, with each increase in level of education, we find an increase in the proportion of residents who are opposed to federal support. But it is only among those who have attended college that nearly half or more report that they would be against federal aid. Opposition is substantially lower among those who have graduated from high school.

At each educational level, though, opposition to federal aid is most frequent in the small cities. Actually we find more opposition to federal aid among the high school graduates in the small area suburbs than among the college trained in any of the other areas. While most frequent opposition to federal aid comes from the college trained in all areas, the proportion opposed is particularly high in the large area suburbs and in both segments of the small metropolitan areas. In the latter areas, two out of every three who have attended college report that they would be opposed to the federal government providing funds to help cover the cost of operations of the local schools.

Even though we consistently find more opposition to federal aid among suburban than central city residents, the range of difference is substantially larger among educational levels, within each area, than by place of residence within the metropolitan community. However, both education and place of residence are important factors in how citizens view the role of the federal government in relationship to the local school system. It is noteworthy that within the large metropolitan area population, the range of opposition would vary from a low of only 13 percent of those at the grade school level in central cities to a high of 64 percent of the college trained in the suburbs. Thus the latter are five times as likely as the former to oppose federal aid. Similar differences are also found in the other metropolitan areas.

That support for federal aid to education comes largely from those at the lower socioeconomic levels, whereas opposition is most likely to be found among those more favorably placed, is further evident from an inspection of the responses by both occupational and income groups. These data are shown in the lower panels of Table 6-2. As the level of occupational status increases and as the size of income increases, we consistently find that opposition to federal aid also increases, regardless of place of residence or size of metropolitan area. The pattern of differences is substantial in all areas. The relatively greater opposition of suburban residents to federal aid is again apparent in these data. Here, too, we find much larger variations by occupational status and income than by place of residence. Those at the professional-managerial levels exceed those below the craftsmen level by 65 to 300 percent in all areas. Similar differences are found among income groups. But it is only in the top income group in the sub-urbs, and in the central cities of the small metropolitan areas, that a distinct majority would be opposed to the federal government providing funds to help support the local schools. In most sub-categories, opposition is rarely expressed by more than one-third of the residents.

Thus as far as support of the schools is concerned, we find sub-stantial approval of federal aid. However, we also find that a sizable minority would be opposed to the federal government get-ting involved in such a program. Opposition, or for that matter support, does not come equally from all segments of the population. The influence of age is rather unclear in that it seems to vary by size of area, but not so with socioeconomic status. There is no question but that opposition to federal aid comes disproportionately from those in the higher socioeconomic status groups. The college trained, the professional-managerial workers, and those with high incomes are most likely to oppose federal aid, whereas those in the lower socioeconomic status positions are most likely to favor a program by which the federal government would help support the local schools.

Distribution of Federal Funds

Given general support of federal aid, the next area of concern pertains to how residents feel the federal funds should be dis-tributed. That is, if federal funds were to be made available, on what basis should such monies be allocated to the local schools? What should be the criteria for determining the amount of funds that would be given to each local school system? This part of the analysis is limited only to that segment of the population reporting that they would be in favor of federal support.

There seems to be general agreement, at least among a majority of the residents in all areas, that federal funds should be distributed to the local school districts on the basis of need. There is a slight tendency for the residents of the smaller central cities to place somewhat more emphasis on need, while those in the large central cities tend disproportionately to report that funds should be dis-tributed on the basis of number of children in school. But among suburban residents, there is no pattern of difference by size of metropolitan area. In all suburban areas, approximately three-fifths of the residents who favor federal aid feel that funds should be distributed on the basis of need, while one-fourth feel that the distribution should be made on the basis of number of children in school. However, among central city residents, the proportion who feel that funds should be distributed on the basis of need increases from 55 percent in the large to 68 percent in the small metropolitan areas. On the other hand, the proportion who report that such funds should be distributed on the basis of number of children in school ranges from a high of 28 percent in the large cities to a low of 18 percent in the small cities. Thus the former exceeds the latter by more than 50 percent.

Only a small minority feel that federal funds should be distributed on the basis of the amount of taxes collected by the local school district. Those who would prefer this as the basis for distribution do not follow any pattern of difference, either by size of area or place of residence. Of particular interest here is the very small proportion of residents in the "other," "don't know," and "no answer" categories. This suggests that those who are in favor of federal aid have rather definite notions as to how the funds should be distributed. At any rate, when given an opportunity to select alternative ways of distributing funds, more than 95 percent made a choice.

Thus, in all metropolitan areas, a substantial majority of the residents would favor federal support for their schools; and further, there is general agreement that such funds should be distributed on the basis of need. This suggests that there is a high degree of congruence between practice and what the people want, since in the distribution of either federal or state funds to local school districts the general practice has been to allocate funds on the basis of need, with the poorer districts getting a disproportionate amount of the funds. However, as we pursue the analysis further, we find that residents are not really quite as willing to have federal funds distributed on the basis of need as would appear to be the case from the above responses.

After having determined how residents felt about federal aid and how they thought such funds should be distributed, we asked the following qualified question: "If the federal government did provide funds for education at the local level, people in this area would pay more in federal taxes than they would get in return, since other parts of the country are not as well off. Would you be in favor of such a program?" The responses to this question are shown in Table 6-3. It is readily evident that the views regarding federal aid in response to this question differ substantially from those observed in response to the more general question. Even though a distinct majority of the residents feel that federal funds should be distributed on the basis of need, a substantially smaller proportion of residents in all areas continued to favor federal aid when reminded that they might have to pay in more than they received in return, because their "need" may be less than that of school districts in other areas. In none of the areas do we find a majority of residents in favor of federal aid under these circumstances.

When we compare the responses in Table 6-3 with those reported in Table 6-1, and express these as a ratio, as we have done in

TABLE 6-3

ATTITUDES TOWARD FEDERAL AID IF AREA WOULD PAY
DISPROPORTIONATELY BY PLACE OF RESIDENCE
AND SIZE OF METROPOLITAN AREA

Favor Federal Funds	Large		Medium		Small	
	City	Suburb	City	Suburb	City	Suburb
Total Number	477	495	457	493	488	492
	%	%	%	%	%	%
Yes	42.6	43.0	49.9	48.9	35.0	30.7
No	35.0	39.8	33.5	43.0	46.7	47.0
Don't know	21.4	17.2	15.5	7.9	17.6	22.2
No answer	1.0	—	1.1	0.2	0.6	0.2
Total	100.0	100.0	100.0	100.0	100.0	100.0

Table 6-4, we find a sharp increase in the proportion opposed to federal aid, but an even more marked increase in the proportion of "don't know" responses. Those in favor of federal aid decline substantially. Thus, while residents appeared to have rather set notions concerning the desirability of federal aid to local school districts, as noted above, we find that when they are reminded of its relative costs for the residents of their districts, they become less certain of their views, as is evident from the sharp increase in the

TABLE 6-4

RATIO OF RESPONSES CONCERNING FEDERAL AID REPORTED IN
TABLE 6-3 TO THOSE IN TABLE 6-1 BY PLACE OF
RESIDENCE AND SIZE OF METROPOLITAN AREA

Size of Area and Place of Residence	Ratio of:		
	Yes	No	Don't Know
Large			
Central city	.62	1.48	3.29
Suburb	.73	1.13	3.02
Medium			
Central city	.78	1.22	1.96
Suburb	.82	1.25	1.44
Small			
Central city	.60	1.42	2.20
Suburb	.56	1.26	2.88

"don't know" responses. The proportion of residents opposed to federal aid also increases. These data suggest that people tend to view federal aid as a "gift" from outside, with little or no realization of the original source of funds. This, of course, is generally known, but these data so strikingly demonstrate different views regarding federal aid that they are worthy of note.

In all areas except the small area suburbs, a majority of those who originally reported that they were in favor of federal aid continued to support such aid even after told that the program would cost them more than they would receive in return. But the differences in responses are marked. The decline in support of federal aid is most substantial in the small metropolitan areas, where only 53 percent of the city-dwellers and 47 percent of the suburban residents who had previously stated they were in favor of federal aid continue to favor such a program, even though they would pay disproportionately.

Our concern now is whether these changes in views were distributed throughout the whole population, or were they disproportionately due to selected segments of the population? This question is readily answered from the data presented in Table 6-5. In general, the higher the socioeconomic status the more consistency

TABLE 6-5

PROPORTION FAVORING FEDERAL AID EVEN THOUGH AREA WOULD PAY
DISPROPORTIONATELY* BY SELECTED SOCIOECONOMIC
CHARACTERISTICS BY PLACE OF RESIDENCE
AND SIZE OF METROPOLITAN AREA

Socioeconomic Characteristics	Large		Medium		Small	
	City	Suburb	City	Suburb	City	Suburb
	%	%	%	%	%	%
Total	57.0	60.1	68.5	69.4	53.1	47.2
Education						
Grade school	44.7	42.7	61.6	55.4	41.9	40.2
9–11	61.4	57.8	64.8	75.7	53.3	52.9
12	58.0	63.9	72.7	67.3	57.9	44.3
College	81.6	84.4	83.3	77.6	81.0	62.5
Occupation						
Other	53.1	55.3	61.1	66.7	49.5	41.9
Craftsmen	49.4	53.6	66.7	70.7	55.3	46.1
Clerical-sales	59.1	63.3	63.6	70.0	60.0	60.7
Prof.-Managerial	75.0	72.4	80.4	72.5	65.9	50.0
Income						
Under $75	49.3	53.3	65.3	57.9	44.3	41.9
$75–$99	58.8	63.5	77.2	60.0	58.3	49.3
$100–$149	73.5	62.7	71.0	81.3	63.8	55.9
$150 plus	78.9	78.4	65.2	76.7	57.9	61.5

* Limited only to those who had earlier reported that they favored federal aid to local school systems. See Table 6-1.

we find in how residents answered the two questions. That is, when the question regarding federal aid was reworded in such a way as to indicate that the residents in the district would have to pay relatively more than they would receive in return, the responses changed least among those in the higher socioeconomic levels, who were originally least in favor of federal aid. The most marked changes tend to be found among those at the lowest levels of education, occupation, and income. It will be recalled that the latter groups were the ones most likely to favor federal aid in response to the more general question.

The data presented in Table 6-5 are limited to those who had earlier stated that they would favor federal aid to help support the local schools. And the proportions reported are those who con-

tinued to support federal aid even though they were told that they
would have to pay disproportionately. As is evident, very marked
differences are found by socioeconomic status. For example, in
the central cities of the large metropolitan areas, only 45 percent
of those at the grade school level continue to favor federal aid if
they would have to pay disproportionately, as compared with 82
percent among those at the college level. Among suburban residents, the proportions range from a low of 43 percent to a high of
84 percent, respectively.

In both the large central city and its suburbs, as in all the other
areas, the proportion continuing to favor federal aid tends to increase with each increase in education. Apparently the higher the
education, the more realistic the residents were in their original
position. That is, the better educated were already aware that if
funds were allocated to local school districts, they would not get
their proportionate share of the federal funds distributed. Thus,
when they were reminded of this, they were less likely to change
their views, whereas many of those at the lower levels of education
may not have realized that they would have to pay disproportionately. It is noted, however, that the shift to opposition to federal
aid is substantially less than the decrease in favor of such support.
This is due to the high proportion of responses that shifted to the
"don't know" category. And the "don't knows" tend to be substantially higher among those at the lower levels of education,
where the proportionate decline in favor of federal aid is largest.
Similarly, within occupational and income groups, we find that
the proportion who continue to favor federal aid varies directly
with socioeconomic status. And the same pattern is found in all
areas.

Since such marked changes are found in the responses to the
more specific question among the different segments of the population, it becomes necessary to take a further look at the views concerning federal aid to local school districts. In Table 6-6, we have
shown the proportion of residents at each educational level who
remained in favor of federal aid to local school districts even after
they were told that their district would not receive a proportionate
share of the federal funds, since they were better off than districts
in other parts of the country. For purposes of comparison, we
have also included the proportion of residents at each educational

TABLE 6-6

PROPORTION FAVORING FEDERAL AID ACCORDING TO TYPE OF
QUESTION ASKED BY EDUCATION BY PLACE OF RESIDENCE
AND SIZE OF METROPOLITAN AREA

Education of Respondent	Large		Medium		Small	
	City	Suburb	City	Suburb	City	Suburb

Would you be in favor of the federal government providing funds to help cover the cost of operations for local schools?

	%	%	%	%	%	%
Grade school	71.7	73.5	67.8	74.7	66.0	66.0
9–11	73.3	68.8	65.7	71.4	68.1	64.9
12	71.0	63.9	66.4	60.8	56.9	45.9
College	51.4	34.6	50.6	43.8	31.8	30.8

If the federal government did provide funds for education at the local level, people in this area would pay more in federal taxes than they would get in return since other parts of the country are not as well off. Would you be in favor of such a program?

	%	%	%	%	%	%
Grade school	32.1	31.4	41.8	41.3	27.7	26.5
9–11	45.0	39.8	42.3	54.1	36.3	34.3
12	41.1	40.8	48.3	41.0	32.9	20.3
College	42.0	29.2	42.2	34.0	25.8	19.2

level originally favoring federal aid, in response to the more general question. The marked differences in the responses to the two questions we have already noted. Here attention will be focused only on the relationship between socioeconomic status, as measured by education, and views regarding federal aid to local schools.

In terms of the more general question, a substantial majority of the residents favored federal aid. Support for such a program comes disproportionately from those at the lower levels of education, and as the level of education increases the proportion of residents favoring such aid declines. And in all areas the decrease is substantial. It is only among the college trained in all of the suburban areas and in the small cities that less than a majority favor providing federal funds to help cover the cost of operations of local schools. In short, in all areas the differences by level of education are marked and consistent. However, this is not the case in respect to the responses to the more specific question, as is

shown in the lower portion of Table 6-6. Support for federal aid
at all educational levels declines sharply. There is an almost complete lack of a majority, in any of the residential areas, at any level
of education. The only exception is found among those who attended high school, but did not graduate, in the medium-sized
area suburbs. The residents in medium-sized metropolitan areas
generally, in both residential zones, show slightly more support
for federal aid than those in either the large or small metropolitan
areas.

The striking point about the responses to the more specific
question, in the lower portion of the table, is the general lack of a
clear-cut pattern of difference by level of education. Differences
do exist, but the pattern no longer varies consistently as level of
education increases. Least support for federal aid, under these
conditions, seems to come from those at the extremes of education
—that is, those at the grade school and at the college level. But
the range of difference is small as compared to the range observed
earlier in the responses to the more general question. Level of
education appears to be much less of a factor in the responses to
the more specific question. However, the latter question involves
several dimensions which makes interpretation of the responses
difficult. Apparently there are at work here several cross pressures
which should be noted.

Implicit in the question, first of all, is the very general but significant issue of whether the federal government should become involved in contributing funds to local schools. The responses to
this general policy issue would vary among educational groups.
That is, one would expect resistance to this policy to increase
directly by level of education. But the more specific question also
covers a second issue, which is that of funds being distributed according to "need and ability to pay," regardless of the amount of
revenue collected by the federal government from the local area.
Consequently, these areas would pay in more than they would
get in return. This, of course, raises the further basic issue of
whether the federal government should take from the "haves"
and give to the "have-nots." The more specific question, as stated,
thus includes the very practical issue of whether the residents in
these areas would favor a program of federal aid which would,
in effect, result in their contributing to the support of less well-to-do
districts.

One would expect those at the lower levels of education to take a more parochial, or perhaps provincial, view of this than the better educated; thus they would be less likely to favor such a program. On the other hand, those at the higher educational levels would tend to favor a proposal which would equalize educational opportunities among districts; but, at the same time, they would be opposed to federal aid. Clearly, the question involves at least two basic issues, regarding which various educational groups would respond in opposite ways. Consequently, in the responses to this question, we do not find any clear-cut pattern of difference by level of education. At any rate, the responses do clearly indicate that only a minority of the residents of these metropolitan areas would be in favor of a federal aid program if they knew that they would not get their proportionate share of the funds that were being collected and distributed.

But we can also infer, from the responses to the earlier and more general question, that a substantial majority of the residents, and particularly those at the lower socioeconomic level, would be in favor of the federal government providing funds for the local schools because it is viewed as a "gift" from the outside, with little or no attention paid to the source of such funds. It would seem that any proposed program of federal aid to education at the local level would find ready support from the population, except among those in the higher socioeconomic positions. That is, only the college trained, those in the professional and managerial occupational categories, and those in the top income groups would not favor such a proposal. But then, these segments of the population account for only a relatively small minority. In short, our data suggest that a substantial majority of the population would be in favor of federal aid to education, regardless of their place of residence or size of metropolitan area. But people would not want this to be the primary source of support. Evidence concerning this will be presented below.

We now turn our attention to the reasons people give for either being in favor of or opposed to federal aid after they were told that residents in their area would have to pay disproportionately. It is worthy of note that even when this qualification is specifically stated, a sizable minority of the residents still report that they would favor federal support for local schools. Another sizable, but somewhat smaller, proportion report that they would be opposed to federal aid if they had to pay in more than they would receive in return. After residents stated a definite view regarding federal aid, they were asked: "Why do you feel that way?" It was felt that this question would not apply to those who reported that they "didn't know" whether or not they would favor federal aid in terms of the qualifications stated. Nor was the question asked of those who did not give an answer as to their views. The reasons given to support their views, for those who did take a specific position concerning this issue, are shown in Table 6-7.

Focusing first on those who are in favor of federal aid, we find that the most frequently mentioned reasons seem to be cast in terms of the overall needs of the larger society: that everyone deserves equal access to a good education, and that in order to achieve that end some areas need help from the outside. Differences do not seem to follow any distinct pattern, either by place of residence or size of metropolitan area, although in some instances both variables seem to exert a limited amount of influence. Approximately one-fifth of those who favored federal aid reported that there was a general need for better schools and that the country needed educated people. In both large and medium-sized metropolitan areas, this response was more frequent among suburban than central city residents. A somewhat smaller proportion of the residents reported that "education is everyone's responsibility" and that federal aid would "raise the educational standards." Thus it is apparent that nearly all of those who favor federal aid even though they would pay disproportionately, do so because they see the problem of education as being much larger in scope than their local districts. Implicit in their responses is a broad societal orientation. They seem to be concerned with the general quality of education throughout the nation, and they seem to feel that youths, regardless of where they live, should all have equal access to the same quality of education. That they would have to pay disproportionately did not cause them to change their views on the need for federal aid. Only a very small minority did not have a specific reason for favoring such a program.

Among the residents who are opposed to federal aid to local schools, the most frequent objection is that such a program "would raise taxes, which are already too high." Although this is the most common objection in all areas, it is reported most frequently

TABLE 6-7

REASONS FOR FAVORING OR OPPOSING FEDERAL AID IF DISTRICT
WOULD PAY DISPROPORTIONATELY BY PLACE OF RESIDENCE
AND SIZE OF METROPOLITAN AREA

Reason for Favoring or Opposing Federal Aid	Large		Medium		Small	
	City	Suburb	City	Suburb	City	Suburb
Total Number	203	212	228	241	171	151
	%	%	%	%	%	%
Favor Federal Aid						
Need better schools—country needs educated people	18.2	27.4	15.8	20.3	17.5	13.2
Provide equal opportunity for all	36.5	43.4	38.6	44.0	26.9	37.7
Some areas really need help	23.6	19.8	24.1	27.0	26.3	27.2
Education is everyone's responsibility	5.9	6.6	6.6	5.8	8.2	6.6
Would raise the educational standards	9.4	5.7	10.5	6.6	6.4	7.9
Other	4.5	3.7	3.1	2.1	8.2	5.3
No answer	5.4	5.7	7.9	7.1	12.3	5.3
Total*	100.0	100.0	100.0	100.0	100.0	100.0
Total Number	167	197	152	212	228	231
	%	%	%	%	%	%
Opposed to Federal Aid						
Would raise taxes—already too high	39.5	32.0	26.3	23.6	26.3	20.8
Federal control—don't want federal govt. in education	16.2	22.3	26.3	22.6	23.2	23.8
Too much waste in federal govt.	6.0	8.1	8.6	11.3	11.8	12.1
Education is local responsibility	15.6	21.8	17.1	19.3	13.6	19.9
Not interested in paying someone else's taxes, keep money in district	21.6	31.5	21.7	25.0	20.2	22.5
Would lower our standards	0.6	2.5	0.7	0.5	0.9	0.9
Other	2.4	1.0	4.6	5.7	6.2	2.6
No answer	9.0	3.0	7.9	4.2	8.3	5.6
Total*	100.0	100.0	100.0	100.0	100.0	100.0

* Percent adds to more than 100 because multiple reasons were given.

by those in the larger metropolitan areas, and somewhat more frequently in the cities than in the suburbs. Another reason, mentioned almost as frequently, is that they are "not interested in paying someone else's taxes and that money should be kept within their own districts." This type response tends to be somewhat more frequent among suburban residents in each size class. Less frequent, but still quite common, is the objection to federal aid that is stated thusly: "Federal control—don't want federal government in education"; and still another frequent response is that "education is a local responsibility." Occasionally there is a concern over "too much waste in the federal government," but this accounts for only a very small proportion of the reasons given for being opposed to federal aid. A point worthy of note is that only rarely did anyone claim that federal aid "would lower our standards." Thus, for the most part, the tax issue was the main basis for opposition. Clearly, fear of higher taxes, or objections to paying someone else's taxes, are the most frequent concerns of those who opposed federal aid. Fear of federal control is a frequent concern also. A small minority are opposed to such an aid program because they feel that education is a local responsibility, and thus the federal government should "stay out."

Both those who favor and those who are opposed seem to have rather set reasons for their position, as is suggested by the small proportion of responses in the "none" or "no answer" category. There is no question but that their views of education and their responsibilities regarding education are markedly different. Those who favor federal aid are much less parochial, in that their concerns seem to be society-wide in scope, whereas those opposed to federal aid are much less concerned with "quality of education" and "equal opportunities for all" and more concerned about what such a program would mean to them personally as far as taxes are concerned.

Level of Government with Primary Responsibility for Support of Schools

To this point we have been primarily concerned with the general issue of federal aid to local school districts. Let us now look at the question of "primary responsibility." That is, what level of government do the people feel should assume primary responsibility for the cost of buildings and the cost of operations at the local school level? Although we have found considerable support for federal aid to local schools, this clearly is not desired as the major source of funds. As is shown in Table 6-8, the largest pro-

TABLE 6-8

LEVEL OF GOVERNMENT THAT SHOULD HAVE PRIMARY RESPONSIBILITY
FOR BUILDINGS AND OPERATIONS BY PLACE OF RESIDENCE
AND SIZE OF METROPOLITAN AREA

Level of Government	Large		Medium		Small	
	City	Suburb	City	Suburb	City	Suburb
Total Number	477	495	457	493	488	492
BUILDINGS						
Total	% 100.0	% 100.0	% 100.0	% 100.0	% 100.0	% 100.0
District	31.0	42.8	28.9	38.7	35.7	42.1
County	17.4	10.7	10.5	9.5	11.1	13.8
State	25.8	24.8	32.2	28.8	24.4	25.8
Federal	15.1	13.1	14.9	11.8	15.4	10.0
Don't know	7.5	7.3	10.3	8.1	9.2	6.5
No answer	3.1	1.2	3.3	3.0	4.3	1.8
OPERATIONS						
Total	% 100.0	% 100.0	% 100.0	% 100.0	% 100.0	% 100.0
District	29.6	43.0	31.5	47.1	36.9	37.8
County	21.6	10.5	14.7	12.8	13.5	20.3
State	27.5	30.1	32.4	24.7	28.9	24.8
Federal	10.7	8.7	9.2	5.1	8.8	8.7
Don't know	8.2	5.3	10.1	8.1	8.4	6.1
No answer	2.5	2.4	2.2	2.2	3.5	2.2

portion of respondents feel that the residents of the local school district should be primarily responsible for both buildings and the cost of operations at the local level. However, it is noted that in none of the areas do we find a majority in agreement as to what level of local government should have primary responsibility.

Where the primary responsibility for either buildings or the cost of operations is not viewed as belonging to the local district, residents then tend to look to the state, but rarely do they look to the federal government. It is noted, however, that the federal government is more frequently reported regarding buildings than in respect to the cost of operations. But in no instance is it mentioned by more than 15 percent of the total as being the level of government that should be responsible for buildings, nor by more than 10 percent regarding operations.

Suburban residents are more likely than those in the central cities to view these as primarily local district responsibilities, but there doesn't seem to be any consistent pattern of difference by size of area. Size of area, however, does seem to be an important factor in the extent to which residents would look to the county for primary support, particularly in respect to the cost of operations. But an opposite pattern of difference is found in the suburbs, as compared with central cities. For example, while only 10 percent of the residents in the large area suburbs would look to the county as the level of government that should assume primary responsibility for the cost of operations, we find that 20 percent in the small area suburbs would do so. In the central cities, the proportion of such responses declines from 22 percent in the large to 14 percent in the small cities. Central city residents are also more likely to report that the federal government should assume these responsibilities; but as already noted, in none of the areas is this reported by more than a small minority.

For the most part, respondents feel that the primary responsibility for financing the local schools rests in the hands of the local residents, and, if not a local responsibility, it should be assumed by the state. A much smaller proportion of the residents would look either to the county or to the federal government as the primary source of support.

After residents had made their first choice as to the level of government they felt should have primary responsibility for providing funds for school buildings in local school districts, they were asked to state a second choice. When we relate the responses to the two questions, it becomes increasingly clear that the predominant second choice is the next level of government. The pattern is identical in both central city and suburban areas in each size class. Thus, those whose first choice was that the residents of the district should be primarily responsible, disproportionately gave the county as their second choice. And those who gave the county as first choice next turned to the state, while those who felt that buildings should be a state responsibility next turned to the county or to the federal government.

This varied by both size and place of residence. Among large metropolitan residents and those in medium-sized cities, the second choice was the county. Residents in medium-sized and small suburban areas were more likely to turn to the federal government as a second choice, whereas those in small central cities were about equally divided between the county and the federal government. Rarely did the residents in any of the areas allocate this responsibility to the local district residents, even as a second choice. Those who felt that the federal government should provide these funds overwhelmingly turned to the state as their second choice. The same pattern of difference is also found regarding the cost of operations. Thus, while the most frequent view is that funds for buildings and for the cost of operations should be the primary responsibility of the residents in the local school district, a majority of the residents feel that such funds should come from a level of government beyond the local district. For the most part they seem to feel that the funds should come from the state—but, if not from the state, then they should come from the county. The federal government is the least frequent choice. Even as a second choice it is taken by only a small minority. Again it is noted that while residents seem to favor federal aid to help support the schools, they rarely view this as being the level of government that should have the primary responsibility for the schools.

Since the most frequent choice is that the residents in the local district should be primarily responsible for providing funds for school buildings (as well as operations), it seems appropriate to ask what kinds of people are most likely to share this view. Accordingly, we have presented in Table 6-9, the proportion of residents in each subcategory who report that the local residents should be primarily responsible. That central city and suburban residents differ in their views regarding this issue continues to be observed within each status category,[6] but even more marked differences are found by socioeconomic status. Although the size of

___

[6] Although not discussed here, the same observation would obtain regarding funds for operations. The latter data are omitted because of the marked similarity with the responses regarding buildings.

TABLE 6-9

PROPORTION OF RESIDENTS WHO FEEL THAT LOCAL DISTRICT SHOULD
BE PRIMARILY RESPONSIBLE FOR PROVIDING FUNDS FOR SCHOOL
BUILDINGS BY SELECTED CHARACTERISTICS BY PLACE OF
RESIDENCE AND SIZE OF METROPOLITAN AREA

Selected Characteristics	Large		Medium		Small	
	City	Suburb	City	Suburb	City	Suburb
	%	%	%	%	%	%
Total	31.0	42.8	28.9	38.7	35.7	42.1
Age						
Under 25 years	33.3	36.0	25.0	30.8	26.5	40.5
25–34	38.6	48.4	23.1	30.1	36.6	35.3
35–44	38.5	47.9	29.6	46.5	42.0	47.4
45–54	30.6	35.9	28.9	39.6	34.0	39.8
55 years plus	23.1	40.7	32.6	40.0	34.0	46.5
Education						
Grade school	23.3	23.5	20.5	21.3	26.2	30.6
9–11	24.2	32.3	28.7	30.6	22.1	32.1
12	36.3	43.8	32.8	40.4	45.5	52.6
College	50.0	63.8	39.8	50.3	54.5	62.8
Occupation						
Other	28.8	30.5	24.2	26.7	22.8	31.1
Craftsmen	24.3	37.4	35.7	41.1	27.6	39.7
Clerical-sales	34.4	44.2	27.9	43.3	58.7	46.3
Prof.-Managerial	42.2	55.6	32.2	43.6	52.1	58.1
Income						
Under $75	25.5	31.9	28.7	32.7	28.6	35.8
$75–$99	26.7	34.7	28.7	30.1	29.6	35.0
$100–$149	38.7	47.5	31.8	37.4	40.2	49.6
$150 plus	41.9	58.5	31.0	60.4	57.1	57.9

the differences is not large nor is it always consistent, there is a tendency in most residential zones for the proportion holding this view to increase up to 45 years of age, and then decline. That is, the middle age groups are the ones most likely to view this as primarily a local responsibility. The same general pattern is found in both central city and suburban areas in each size class.

It is of particular significance to note the marked differences in how residents at various socioeconomic levels view the responsibilities of the local district. Regardless of the socioeconomic variable used, we find with each increase in socioeconomic status a substantial increase in the proportion who view this function as primarily a local responsibility. The range is substantial in both areas, but the difference tends to be somewhat larger among suburban than central city residents. Thus, for example, in the large metropolitan areas the proportion who feel that local residents should have the primary responsibility for providing funds for school buildings increases from only 23 percent of those in the grade school category to 50 percent among the college trained. In the suburbs, the proportion increases from 24 percent to 64 percent. The same pattern of difference is also found in both the medium-sized and small metropolitan areas. Similarly, differences are found by variations in occupation and income. Clearly, differences are much more marked by variations in socioeconomic status than by either place of residence or size of metropolitan area. While only a minority of the residents feel that support of the schools should come primarily from the local residents, this view is shared by a majority of those in the highest socioeconomic status categories in most areas.

Residents in the lower socioeconomic status categories are much more likely to look to a level of government outside the local district, and beyond the area in which they are directly taxed, for the support of their schools. This is illustrated by the data shown in Table 6-10 on educational attainment. As the level of education increases, the proportion reporting either that the state or national government should assume this responsibility declines. It is evident at all educational levels that the least frequently reported alternative is the federal government. But only among the college trained is the proportion consistently below 10 percent. Further, it is noted that the proportion reporting that the federal government should have this responsibility does not exceed 20 percent at any educational level in any of the areas. Approximately one-fifth to one-third of the residents feel that the state should provide these funds. And, as already noted, it is at the lower educational levels that we find the highest proportion holding this view. But even among the college trained we find a substantial minority who feel that the state government should be primarily responsible for providing these funds.

These data clearly show that various segments of the population hold different views as to the level of government that should

TABLE 6-10

PROPORTION OF RESIDENTS REPORTING THAT THE STATE OR FEDERAL
GOVERNMENT SHOULD BE PRIMARILY RESPONSIBLE FOR PROVIDING
FUNDS FOR SCHOOL BUILDINGS BY EDUCATION BY PLACE OF
RESIDENCE AND SIZE OF METROPOLITAN AREA

Level of Gov-ernment and Education	Large		Medium		Small	
	City	Suburb	City	Suburb	City	Suburb
STATE GOVERNMENT						
	%	%	%	%	%	%
Grade school	28.9	26.5	26.0	29.3	23.4	27.9
9–11	29.2	30.1	34.3	30.6	31.0	34.3
12	23.4	27.2	38.8	31.3	23.4	21.1
College	17.6	16.9	31.3	24.8	18.2	15.4
FEDERAL GOVERNMENT						
	%	%	%	%	%	%
Grade school	16.4	20.6	16.4	14.7	20.6	15.0
9–11	15.0	16.1	17.6	17.3	19.5	11.2
12	17.7	11.2	13.8	11.4	12.6	6.0
College	8.1	7.7	10.8	7.2	4.5	5.1

have primary responsibility for providing funds for the local
schools. There is a marked tendency for those at the lower socioeconomic levels to look outside the district for such support, while
those at the higher status levels disproportionately view support of
the schools as primarily the responsibility of the residents living
within the school district.

Taxation in Relationship to Children in Family

We turn now to still another dimension of the issue as to who
should support the schools. At this point we are concerned with
the relative tax burden that residents feel should be the responsibility of families with no children or with many children in school.
Essentially, the point at issue here is whether such families should
pay the same or a different tax than the other segments of the
population.

A distinct majority of the residents make no distinction in
terms of the taxes that should be paid, whether or not the family
has any or many children in school. Thus, most of the residents

see the schools as a community-wide responsibility, the support of which should be shared equally by all of the residents. Yet a sizable minority hold a different view. Approximately 10 percent of the residents in all areas feel that families with many children should have to pay a higher school tax than others in the community. This proportion tends to be only slightly higher in the large and medium-sized central cities than in the suburbs. The proportion declines continuously by size of central city, ranging from 14 percent to 9 percent, but does not vary by size in suburban areas. The important point is that more than eight out of ten residents report that families with many children in school should pay the same tax as others.

But they are much less agreed that families with no children in school should pay the same tax as others. In nearly all areas, less than 70 percent feel that such families should pay the same tax as others. Approximately one-fifth, or slightly more, feel that such families should pay a lower tax, and from 8 to 10 percent of the residents feel that such families should not be taxed at all for the support of the schools. Thus there seems to be a considerable sentiment that families with no children in school should not carry the same tax burden as others in the community. While only a very small proportion of the residents would favor a higher tax for families with many children in school, a substantial minority (nearly one-third in most areas) feel that families with no children in school should be taxed less or not at all for the support of the schools. From this we can infer that many residents feel that the schools should be the responsibility largely of those who are currently using them. It is not at all surprising that such a view should be reported disproportionately by those who do not have any children in school. They are at least 50 percent more likely to respond thusly than are those who do have children in school. But much larger differences are found by socioeconomic status, as illustrated by level of education, than by place of residence, size of area, or even whether or not the residents are currently using the schools. These data are shown in Table 6-11.

There is a very consistent tendency for the proportion who feel that the same tax should be paid by everyone to increase directly by level of education. The same general pattern of difference is found in all residential zones in each size class. But the range of

TABLE 6-11

PROPORTION OF RESIDENTS WHO REPORT THAT FAMILIES WITH NO CHILDREN
IN SCHOOL SHOULD PAY SAME TAX, LESS TAX, OR NO TAXES
BY LEVEL OF EDUCATION BY PLACE OF RESIDENCE
AND SIZE OF METROPOLITAN AREA

Relative Tax and Education	Large		Medium		Small	
	City	Suburb	City	Suburb	City	Suburb
	%	%	%	%	%	%
Same Tax as Others:						
Grade school	54.7	64.7	58.2	68.9	49.6	56.5
9–11	65.0	60.2	70.4	72.4	66.4	61.2
12	71.7	65.7	70.7	74.7	70.1	74.4
College	71.6	82.3	88.0	86.3	84.5	79.5
Less Taxes than Others:						
Grade school	25.2	23.5	24.7	24.3	29.8	29.3
9–11	22.5	28.0	17.6	16.3	19.5	20.1
12	17.7	24.9	21.6	22.9	22.8	18.8
College	21.6	16.2	7.2	11.1	12.1	12.8
No Tax:						
Grade school	12.6	11.8	4.8	2.7	16.3	10.9
9–11	8.3	9.7	1.9	3.1	11.5	16.4
12	9.7	7.1	3.4	2.4	6.0	3.8
College	5.4	1.5	3.6	2.0	1.5	7.7

difference is particularly marked in the small metropolitan areas, for it is in these areas, among those at the grade school level, that we find the smallest proportion who feel that families with no children should pay the same tax as others. Rather, they feel that such families should either pay less school taxes or none at all. In all areas, it is the grade school group that is most likely to report that families with no children should either pay less tax or no tax at all. The proportion sharing this view declines as level of education increases. Consequently, it is largely at the college level that we find residents who are least likely to feel that there should be a tax differential for such families. Thus, while a majority of the residents in all areas would not make a distinction in the taxes that should be paid by families with no children in school, as compared with the rest of the population, a sizable minority would do so. And the ones most likely to make such a distinction are those at the lower levels of education. Although the data are not presented here, the same pattern of difference was also found in a detailed analysis by occupation and income groups. It is those at the lower socioeconomic levels who are most likely to favor less tax burden on families who do not have children in school. No doubt some of the differences by socioeconomic status can be attributed to age, and to differences in the proportion of families with children in school, but as already noted, the largest differences are found by socioeconomic status.

Role of Citizens in How School Funds Are Spent

The last topic to be considered in the present discussion is only peripherally related to the main theme of the chapter. Yet it is likely an important factor in how residents would respond to a proposal regarding reorganization of school districts. We turn now to the general question of the extent to which residents feel that the ordinary citizen in their area can have a say about how school money is spent. These data are shown in Table 6-12. It is

TABLE 6-12

PROPORTION OF RESIDENTS WHO FEEL THAT THE ORDINARY CITIZEN
CAN DO QUITE A BIT ABOUT HOW SCHOOL FUNDS ARE SPENT
BY EDUCATION BY PLACE OF RESIDENCE
AND SIZE OF METROPOLITAN AREA

Education	Large		Medium		Small	
	City	Suburb	City	Suburb	City	Suburb
	%	%	%	%	%	%
Total	43.4	57.4	40.0	51.5	42.0	55.1
Grade school	34.6	47.1	24.0	37.3	34.8	40.1
9–11	42.5	52.7	39.8	48.0	39.8	57.5
12	47.6	56.8	48.3	47.6	46.1	63.9
College	56.8	70.0	56.6	65.4	51.5	64.1

readily evident that suburban residents are more likely to feel that the ordinary citizen does have a say about how school funds are spent. It is noted further that the central city-suburban differences tend to be approximately the same in each size class. But perhaps the most significant point here is the large proportion of residents in all areas who feel that the ordinary citizen "can't do much." Although not shown here, this attitude is expressed by 40 percent or more of the suburban residents and by slightly more than half of the central city residents. Again it is noted that size of area is unimportant in respect to this issue.

When we employ education as an index of socioeconomic status, as we have done in Table 6-12, it is evident that there are marked and consistent differences among subgroups of the population. Although we continue to find the same pattern of central city-suburban differences within each educational level, the point to be emphasized is that larger differences are found by variations in education than by place of residence. As the level of education increases, so does the proportion of residents, in all areas, who feel that the ordinary citizen can have a voice in how school funds are spent. Clearly, city-suburban differences are not due to the higher level of education found in the suburbs, since at each level of education the suburban residents are more likely to express this view than those in the city. For example, in the large metropolitan areas only 35 percent of the central city residents, at the grade school level, feel that the ordinary citizen can do quite a bit about how school money is spent, whereas this increases to 47 percent among those at the same educational level in the suburbs. Among the college trained, the proportions are much higher in both residential zones, but the range is from 57 percent of the city residents to 70 percent among suburban residents. Similar differences obtain in the other metropolitan areas also, by both education and place of residence. In short, suburban residents are more likely than those in the city to feel that the ordinary citizen can have a say in how school funds are used. And this belief, among suburban residents, is likely a factor in their resistance to change, for many would feel that this advantage would be lost if they lived in a larger district. We shall return to this issue in Chapter 8.

Summary

Residents generally favor federal aid to the local school districts. To the limited extent that there is opposition, it is more frequent in the suburbs and among the high socioeconomic groups. Views vary much more by socioeconomic status than by place of residence. It is noteworthy that support for federal aid declined sharply when residents were told that their district would likely pay in more than they would receive in return. The largest decline occurred in the lower socioeconomic groups. Those who supported federal aid under these circumstances did so on the grounds that all youths deserve equal access to the same quality education, regardless of where they live; whereas those who were opposed claimed that they did not want to pay other people's taxes. Residents tend to view the support of the school as primarily the responsibility of the local district residents, and suburban people are even more likely to do so than those in the city. The proportion sharing this view increases with each increase in socioeconomic status. Actually, larger differences are found by socioeconomic status than by place of residence. The number of children in school is not seen as an important factor in the amount of school taxes that a family should pay; however, there are frequent exceptions to this view, particularly among those at the lower socioeconomic levels. But here too no differences are found either by place of residence or size of metropolitan area.

Lastly, suburban residents are more likely than those in the city to feel that the ordinary citizen does have a say in how school funds are distributed, but again views regarding this issue vary more by socioeconomic status than by place of residence. In short, while we do find rather consistent differences in the attitudes expressed by central city and suburban residents, even larger and more consistent differences are found among different segments of the population, regardless of place of residence within the metropolitan community. We turn now to a discussion of the views residents have concerning the reorganization of school districts on an area-wide basis.

7

Views on Reorganization of School Districts

WE TURN NOW TO a discussion of how the residents of the metropolitan community would view changes in the organization of
local school districts. Specifically, we are interested in the extent
to which residents would favor a reorganization of school districts
on an area-wide basis. This is offered as an alternative to the present
organization of multiple school districts throughout the larger
community. In each of the areas included in the study, the community is divided into a number of independent school districts
varying widely in respect to size, as well as in ability to support a
school system. Consequently, the quality of the programs provided
varies substantially. The question to be considered here pertains
to the willingness of the residents throughout the metropolitan
area to support a proposal for change which would result in a
single school district for the larger community. Accordingly, the
residents were asked whether they would vote for or against a
proposal to set up a single school district which would combine
the city and the suburban districts.[1]

In the present discussion, we are primarily concerned with how
the views held by residents regarding this proposed change vary

[1] It is interesting to note that in a recent report prepared by a national committee
of the National Education Association whose self-appointed task was to "identify
critical concerns in American education and formulate recommendations about
them," not a single word was said about the problem of school district organization. *Op. cit.* note 3, chap. 6.

by place of residence within the metropolitan community, and by size of metropolitan area. It is our expectation that suburban residents are much more likely than central city residents to be opposed to such a proposal, and further we would expect opposition, particularly among suburban residents, to vary directly by size of metropolitan area.

TABLE 7-1

HOW VOTE ON SETTING UP SINGLE SCHOOL DISTRICT BY PLACE
OF RESIDENCE AND SIZE OF METROPOLITAN AREA

How Vote on Single District	Large		Medium		Small	
	City	Suburb	City	Suburb	City	Suburb
Total Number	477	495	457	493	488	492
	%	%	%	%	%	%
For	46.5	22.0	44.4	29.0	44.9	35.8
Against	36.3	68.9	34.8	60.6	37.5	49.8
Don't know	15.9	8.7	18.8	10.2	15.6	12.8
No answer	1.3	0.4	2.0	0.2	2.0	1.6
Total	100.0	100.0	100.0	100.0	100.0	100.0

How residents responded to this proposal is shown in Table 7-1. It is readily apparent that support for change comes disproportionately from central city residents.[2] The same pattern of difference is found in each size class, though the size of the difference between central city and suburban residents declines as size of metropolitan area decreases. This is due to variations in responses among suburban residents by size of metropolitan area. Among suburban residents, we find increased support for reorganization of school districts as the size of metropolitan area declines; however, no comparable differences are found among central city residents. Quite the contrary, size appears to be unimportant for central city residents; we find almost identical distributions of responses in each size of metropolitan area. In each size of central city, slightly less than a majority of the residents report that they would vote for a proposal which would combine all of the separate school

[2] The specific question asked was stated thusly: "If you had a chance to vote on a proposal to set up a single school district which would combine (name of central city) and the suburban districts, would you vote for it or against it?"

districts into a single system. Approximately one-third of the city residents would vote against such a proposal, and another one-fifth report that they are "uncertain" as to how they would vote on this issue.

By way of comparison, suburban residents differ markedly in their responses to this proposed change. The proportion who would vote for such a change ranges from a low of only 22 percent in the suburbs of the large metropolitan areas to a high of 36 percent in the small area suburbs. On the other hand, while opposition to such a proposal is expressed by nearly 70 percent of the large area suburban residents, the proportion declines consistently by size of area. In the small area suburbs, we find that only half of the residents express opposition to the proposal.

It is worthy of note that in all areas suburban residents are much less likely than city residents to be "uncertain" as to how they would vote on such a proposal. This tends to vary inversely by size, and ranges from only 9 percent in the large area suburbs to 13 percent in the small area suburbs. By way of contrast, nearly one-fifth of the central city residents in each size class report that they "don't know" how they would vote. This, of course, means that a firm position on this issue has more likely already been taken by suburban residents. Thus we can infer from this that in case of an actual issue being presented to the voters, there is only a very small segment of the suburban population who have not already decided how they would vote on such a proposal. Since, in all suburban areas, half or more of the residents have taken the position that they would vote against a reorganization proposal which would combine the city and the suburban districts, this poses a much more difficult problem in bringing about change than if a large segment of the population were uncertain as to how they would vote.

As a rough index of the most that one could expect in an actual vote on such an issue, the apparent opposition is such that even if all of the "don't know" responses in the suburban areas voted in support of such a proposal, a favorable majority vote would still be lacking in all areas. Even under these conditions, the vote would be close only in the small area suburbs. If this admittedly unlikely pattern of voting occurred—that is, if all "don't know" responses voted in support of a proposed reorganization—we would find clear majorities in all of the cities, but a substantially negative vote would still be registered at least in the suburbs of both large and medium-sized metropolitan areas. In short, there seems to be very little likelihood that any such proposed change in the organization of existing school districts would find support from suburban residents, with the possible exception of the residents in the small metropolitan areas.[3]

When attention is focused on the perception residents have of how others in the community would respond to a proposal for combining central city and suburban districts into a single system, it is quite evident that in none of the areas can the residents accurately assess the climate of opinion that is expressed in any of the city areas. Contrary to expectation, residents in all areas tend to consistently underestimate the willingness of others in the community to support a proposal for change. And in all instances the differences are substantial. Thus, for example, while nearly half of the residents of the large cities reported that they would vote for such a proposal, less than one-third of the residents in both parts of the metropolitan areas were of the opinion that the city residents would favor such a change. In this response central city and suburban residents agreed. On the other hand, suburban residents were slightly more likely than central city residents to report that those in the city would be opposed to such a proposal and would vote against it. Thus, while 43 percent of the suburban residents felt that those in the city would vote against such a proposal, only 36 percent of the residents of the central cities, as we have already noted, reported that they would do so.

It is apparent that in the large metropolitan area suburbs residents tend to overestimate the amount of opposition that would be forthcoming from the central city. The same pattern of difference is also found in the medium-sized and small metropolitan areas. Here too we find that suburban residents tend to expect more opposition than is actually reported by the residents of the city. Con-

---

[3] It is interesting to note that there is more opposition to reorganization of school districts on a metropolitan scope than to a proposal for the reorganization of government for the same area. For example, while 69 percent in the large suburbs would vote against school district reorganization, only 47 percent reported that they would vote against a proposal to set up a single government for the city and the suburban areas. In other words, retaining local control of the school system appears to be more important than retaining local control of the municipal government.

versely, they are less likely to expect the amount of support for combining school districts that is reported by those living in the city. But central city residents are even less realistic in their appraisal of how others in the city would vote regarding such a proposal. For example, while approximately 45 percent of the central city residents in both medium and small metropolitan areas reported that they would vote for such a proposal, less than one-fourth of the city residents felt that others in the central city would vote in favor of reorganization. Thus, how people say they would vote exceeds how others in the community think they would vote by some 90 percent or more. It is noted, however, that a very large proportion of the residents "do not know" how others would vote. And such responses are more frequent in the cities than in the suburban areas. This, in part, accounts for the marked tendency to underestimate the amount of support that would be found for a reorganizational proposal.

Suburban residents also underestimate the central city vote in favor of change, and they tend to consistently overestimate the amount of opposition that would be found. A point worthy of emphasis is the high proportion of residents in all areas who have no opinion as to how city residents would respond to such a proposal. While this tends to decline by size of area, the proportion of such responses never falls below 20 percent. In each size class, the proportion of "don't know" responses, as to how city people would vote on setting up a single district for the area, is higher among city than suburban residents. With the exception of the residents in the small area suburbs, nearly one-third report that they "do not know" how the people in the city would vote on such a proposal. Thus, while a general consensus as to how city residents would respond to such an issue is lacking, the most frequent response is that city residents would not vote for reorganization. This is directly opposite to how residents of the city say they would vote, since the most frequent response in all cities was that the residents would vote in favor of such a change.

When we examine how residents view the expected reaction of those living in the suburbs, we find that city residents tend to overestimate the amount of support that would be forthcoming from suburban residents in the large metropolitan areas, while they tend to underestimate the proportion that would vote for such a proposal in both the medium and small area suburbs. It is noteworthy that while central city residents in the large areas tend to overestimate by some 37 percent the willingness of the residents in the contiguous suburbs to vote for reorganization, small central city residents tend to underestimate by 52 percent the proportion of residents in their suburban areas who would support reorganization of school districts. Certainly these data would support the notion that city residents have little accurate knowledge as to how the suburban residents would respond to such an issue.

If we focus on expected opposition, we find that central city residents in both large and medium-sized metropolitan areas substantially err in their estimation of how suburban residents would respond. This is illustrated in the large metropolitan areas, where nearly 70 percent of the suburban residents reported that they would vote against the reorganization of school districts, but only 43 percent of the city residents were of the opinion that suburban residents would do so. In the medium-sized metropolitan areas, only 35 percent of the city residents would expect a negative vote, but 61 percent of the suburban residents reported that they would vote against such a proposal. While the same pattern of difference is found in the small metropolitan areas also, the size of the difference is substantially less.

Suburban residents tend to be much more accurate in their estimation of what proportion of the residents in their area would be opposed to setting up a single district. In both large and medium-sized areas, their expectations as to the proportions who would vote against change are almost identical to the responses on how people say they would vote. In the small metropolitan areas, the suburban residents tend to overestimate the amount of opposition, but even here the difference is less than 10 percent. However, in all areas, suburban residents substantially underestimate the amount of support for change that is found in the suburbs. While the actual support for change ranges from 22 percent in the large to 36 percent in the small area suburbs, the expected favorable vote ranges only from 14 percent to 24 percent in the same areas. Thus support for change among suburban residents exceeds what suburban residents would expect in their own areas by 50 percent or more in each size class.

Again we find a high proportion of "don't know" responses. And such responses tend to be more frequent among central city than suburban residents. At least one-fourth or more of the central city residents report that they do not know how suburban residents would respond to a proposed reorganization, but less than one-fifth of the suburban residents are uncertain as to how others in the suburbs would vote. A distinct majority feel that the residents in their areas would be opposed to such a change. Thus they can find ready support for their opposition in the expectation that a majority of those living in their area share their views and would vote accordingly. Their opposition is thus reinforced. The likelihood of an area-wide approach to the schools seems at best remote. Not only do a majority of the suburban residents oppose combining the city and the suburban districts into a single district, but they also feel that this is the consensus of opinion among those living in their zones.

Views on Combining Only Suburban Districts

We have already observed that a majority of suburban residents, particularly in medium-sized and large metropolitan areas, reported that they would vote against a proposal for combining central city and suburban districts, and also that a distinct majority felt that others in the suburbs would do likewise. However, another way in which reorganization of existing school districts might be approached is through combining only the suburban districts into a single system independent from the city. How suburban residents respond to this alternative is shown in response to the question: "How would you feel about joining into a single school district with neighboring suburban districts only? If such a proposal came up for a vote in the near future, would you vote for or against it?"

This is a much more acceptable alternative. We find more who would vote for combining suburban districts only than who would be in favor of joining an area-wide system which would include the central city. The largest difference is found among the large area suburban residents. While only 22 percent reported that they would vote for a single district including the city, the proportion who would favor joining only with other suburban districts increases to 36 percent. The same pattern is also found in both medium-sized and small area suburbs, but the size of the difference is substantially less. In the latter areas, the proportion who would vote to combine with other suburban districts exceeds the proportion who would vote for an area-wide district by approximately 20 percent, but in the large area suburbs the size of the difference amounts to 65 percent.

Opposition to joining with other suburban school districts declines by size of area. It is worthy of note that in none of the areas do we find a clear-cut majority opposed to reorganization, as long as the change does not include the central city. But even here, nearly half of the residents in both large and medium-sized suburbs report that they would vote against joining with other suburban districts. In both areas, the negative vote exceeds the proportion who would vote in favor of reorganization of suburban districts by 30 percent or more. The opposite is found in the small area suburbs, where 43 percent favor change, while 35 percent would vote against .this proposal. Although we do not find a majority in any response category, it is noteworthy that more people in the small area suburbs have stated that they would vote for than would vote against such a proposal. Support exceeds opposition by more than 20 percent. This is the only area in which this occurs. Although this pattern was not found in response to a proposal to join into a single school district with the central city, most support for change in the suburbs did come from the small areas. But even in the small suburban areas, opposition exceeded support by some 40 percent. By way of contrast, in the large and medium-sized area suburbs, the proportion opposed to a single district for the whole area was more than double the proportion who reported that they would vote in favor of a proposal to reorganize school districts on an area-wide basis.

Even when the proposed reorganization of school districts is limited only to the suburban areas, residents generally are not very accurate in their appraisal of how others in their area would respond to such a proposed change. Here too we find a marked tendency for residents to underestimate the proportion in their area who would likely vote in favor of reorganization of school districts. The gap between how people would vote and how they think others would vote is greater in the large and medium-sized area suburbs than in the small areas. Residents seem to be more accurate in estimating the amount of opposition to change than in evaluating the proportion who would favor reorganization. For example, while 36 percent of the residents report that they would vote for change, only 20 percent feel that most others in the area would vote in this way. On the other hand, while 50 percent would vote against a proposal to combine suburban districts into a single system, only a slightly smaller proportion, 44 percent, feel that most others in the suburbs would do likewise. Very similar differences are found in medium-sized and small area suburbs also. Thus a substantial segment of the residents, particularly in the larger areas, would be opposed to change, and a nearly equal proportion feel that most others in their area would also vote against such a reorganization proposal. But perhaps the most significant point here is that approximately one-third of the suburban residents were so unaware of how others in their area would feel about such an issue that they were unable to express an opinion.

Anticipated Reaction from School Board

An inspection of the data presented in Table 7-2 would indicate that suburban residents, particularly in the medium-sized and large

TABLE 7–2

RESIDENTS' EVALUATION OF HOW SCHOOL BOARD WOULD FEEL ABOUT
A SINGLE DISTRICT BY PLACE OF RESIDENCE
AND SIZE OF METROPOLITAN AREA

How School Board Would Feel	Large		Medium		Small	
	City	Suburb	City	Suburb	City	Suburb
Total Number	477	495	457	493	488	492
	%	%	%	%	%	%
Favor	23.1	9.3	20.8	9.7	27.0	18.7
Oppose	24.9	55.2	28.2	47.3	27.9	37.4
Don't know	50.1	35.2	49.5	42.8	42.8	43.1
No answer	1.9	0.4	1.5	0.2	2.3	0.8
Total	100.0	100.0	100.0	100.0	100.0	100.0

metropolitan areas, who are opposed to setting up a single school district for the city-suburban area, would find ready support for their position in terms of how they feel their own school board would react to such a proposal. Less than 10 percent in both large and medium-sized area suburbs feel that the members of the school board in their district would be in favor of the reorganization proposal. Even in the small suburbs, where most support for change is found, less than one-fifth of the residents think that the school board would favor reorganization on an area-wide scale. In all areas, only a very small minority of the residents feel that their school board would be in favor of reorganizing school districts on an area-wide basis, but city residents are much more likely than suburban residents to feel that their school board would favor such a proposal.

It is of particular interest here to note the high proportion of "don't know" responses. A substantial proportion of the residents in all areas, ranging from 35 percent to 50 percent, report that they do not know how their school board would feel about the proposed change. These data are a striking commentary on residents' lack of touch with school board opinion. Nonetheless, a rather large proportion of the suburban residents feel that their school board would be opposed to change. The proportion of such responses increases from a low of 37 percent in the small area suburbs to a high of 55 percent in the large area suburbs. This is, of course, consistent with how residents in the area would vote on such a proposal.

Actually there is a very close relationship between how residents think their school board would react to the proposed change and how the residents themselves would vote on the issue. In all of the suburban areas, as shown in Table 7-3, half or more of those who feel that the school board would favor change would vote in favor of reorganization. It will be recalled that only 22 percent of the residents in the large area suburbs reported that they would vote in favor of a single district, but the proportion of such votes increases to 50 percent among those who feel that the suburban school board members would favor such a change. Of those who feel that the school board would be opposed to such a proposal, only 18 percent would support change. The proportion who would vote against reorganization ranges from only 44 percent of those who think the school board would favor to 80 percent of those who feel that the school board would be opposed to the proposed change. A very similar pattern of difference is also found in both medium-sized and small suburban areas.

There is a danger that this is a superficial relationship, in that the residents may merely be projecting their feelings to the school board. Nonetheless, one might at least tentatively infer from these data that community-wide support for change would more likely be

TABLE 7-3

HOW VOTE ON SINGLE SCHOOL DISTRICT BY HOW RESIDENTS THINK SCHOOL BOARD
WOULD FEEL BY PLACE OF RESIDENCE AND SIZE OF METROPOLITAN AREA

School Board Position & Size of Metropolitan Area	Central City					Suburban Area				
	Number	Favor	Oppose	Other	Total	Number	Favor	Oppose	Other	Total
		%	%	%	%		%	%	%	%
Large										
Favor	110	68.2	22.7	9.1	100.0	46	50.0	43.5	6.5	100.0
Oppose	119	48.7	43.7	7.6	100.0	273	18.3	79.9	1.8	100.0
Don't know	239	35.1	40.2	24.6	100.0	174	20.7	58.0	21.2	100.0
Medium										
Favor	95	57.9	34.7	7.4	100.0	48	50.0	45.8	4.2	100.0
Oppose	129	42.6	47.3	10.1	100.0	233	23.2	70.4	6.4	100.0
Don't know	226	40.7	27.9	31.4	100.0	211	30.2	53.6	16.1	100.0
Small										
Favor	132	59.8	34.1	6.1	100.0	92	59.8	37.0	3.3	100.0
Oppose	136	47.1	47.1	5.9	100.0	184	31.0	63.0	5.9	100.0
Don't know	209	34.4	34.9	30.6	100.0	212	30.2	43.4	26.5	100.0

forthcoming if the members of the local school boards favored reorganization. At any rate, their opposition to change likely serves as a substantial obstacle. It would seem to encourage resistance to change among residents also.[4]

School district reorganization would involve some very basic changes in the community. A much more conservative type of change would be to retain the existing school districts as separate political and administrative organizations, but establish the high schools on an area-wide basis. Accordingly, residents were asked how they would feel about handling high schools on an area-wide basis rather than have each local area provide them separately. The responses to this question are shown in Table 7-4.

TABLE 7-4

HOW FEEL ABOUT HIGH SCHOOL ON AN AREA-WIDE BASIS BY PLACE
OF RESIDENCE AND SIZE OF METROPOLITAN AREA

Attitude Toward Area-Wide High School	Large		Medium		Small	
	City	Suburb	City	Suburb	City	Suburb
Total Number	477	495	457	493	488	492
	%	%	%	%	%	%
Favor	53.2	23.2	45.3	30.6	56.4	51.8
Indifferent	5.9	2.4	7.4	5.7	8.0	5.5
Oppose	32.5	70.3	36.1	59.6	28.3	37.0
Don't know	7.5	3.6	10.1	3.9	6.1	4.9
No answer	0.8	0.4	1.1	0.2	1.2	0.8
Total	100.0	100.0	100.0	100.0	100.0	100.0

High Schools on Area-Wide Basis

There is a marked similarity between how residents feel about having high schools on an area-wide basis and how they would vote on setting up a single school district for the area. The responses tend to follow the same pattern by size of area and place of residence within the metropolitan community. The only exception is found in the small area suburbs. And this difference is worthy of note. Whereas only about one-third of the residents, in the small area suburbs, would vote in favor of a single school district for the city

[4] How school officials would react to change is discussed in Chapter 10.

and suburban areas, a slight majority (52 percent) would favor area-wide high schools. Only slightly more than one-third of the residents of the small area suburbs would be opposed to an area-wide high school, whereas half reported that they would vote against a single school district for the area. Thus it is clearly evident that a proposal to set up an area-wide high school would find much more support from the residents in the small area suburbs than would a proposal to reorganize the local school districts into a single system. This difference, however, does not hold in either medium-sized or large area suburbs, where there tends to be comparable opposition to both proposals. Clearly a distinct majority of the residents would resist such changes. Stated differently, a majority of the residents in both large and medium-sized area suburbs are opposed to any proposal to change the existing structure of the local school systems.

These data suggest that to the extent "reform" in school district organization is at all possible, it can occur only in small metropolitan areas. Resistance to change is likely so widespread in the larger metropolitan areas that it could not be successfully overcome. Nonetheless, there is a substantial minority of residents—that is, from 20 to 30 percent—who would favor change. This, of course, provides the basis for the analysis that appears in succeeding chapters, which attempts to get at the roots of the resistance to change. By a careful comparative analysis of those who favor and those who oppose reorganization, we will have a better understanding of the factors that account for resistance to change.

Costs as a Factor in Reorganization

However, before pursuing this analysis, attention will be focused on another dimension of how residents view the reorganization of school districts in the area. In this discussion the factor of cost is introduced, to determine how this would influence the views of residents regarding school district reorganization. Specifically the question was asked: "If you had to choose between paying higher taxes to your present local school district, or paying lower taxes in a single school district for the whole area, including the city and the suburbs, which would you choose?" It is noted that one of the major shortcomings of the question as stated is that it is not unidimensional, in that the issues of both reorganization and taxation are involved. The question, however, was deliberately stated in this way so as to emphasize the cost factor, to see how this would change the responses to the issue of reorganization.

TABLE 7-5

PREFERENCE FOR PRESENT DISTRICT WITH HIGHER TAXES OR
A SINGLE DISTRICT WITH LOWER TAXES BY PLACE OF
RESIDENCE AND SIZE OF METROPOLITAN AREA

Preference for:	Large		Medium		Small	
	City	Suburb	City	Suburb	City	Suburb
Total Number	477	495	457	493	488	492
Present district	%	%	%	%	%	%
with higher taxes	23.1	47.9	23.4	39.1	22.5	28.7
Single district						
with lower taxes	62.1	41.0	60.4	46.9	63.5	57.3
Don't know	18.4	10.5	14.7	13.6	11.5	13.0
No answer	1.5	0.6	1.5	0.4	2.5	1.0
Total	100.0	100.0	100.0	100.0	100.0	100.0

How the residents responded to this question is shown in Table 7-5. We continue to find marked central city and suburban differences. In all areas, suburban residents are more likely than central city residents to prefer their present local school district, even though it would mean paying higher taxes. Among city residents, size of metropolitan area seems unimportant. The responses are approximately the same in each size class. And in all central cities, a distinct majority of the residents state a preference for a single district for the whole area, with lower taxes. Only a minority, less than one-fourth, report that they would prefer to remain a separate district and pay the higher taxes. But size of area in the suburbs is an important factor in how the residents respond to these alternatives. Even with the added costs, a substantial number in all suburban areas, but not a majority, would still prefer to hold on to their present local school district. The proportion who share this conviction declines markedly by size of area, ranging from a high of 48 percent among the residents in the large area suburbs to a low of 29 percent in the small areas. On the other hand, the proportion who would favor a single district with lower taxes increases consistently in the opposite direction. Whereas only slightly more than two-fifths of the residents of the large area suburbs prefer a single district for the whole area, with lower taxes, nearly three-fifths of the residents in the small area suburbs state such a preference. These data certainly reinforce our earlier interpretation that resistance to change in the suburbs tends to increase directly as size of metropolitan area increases. Less than a majority of the residents in both medium-sized and large suburban areas would favor a single school district for the whole area, even though this would mean lower taxes. Although the threat of higher taxes does seem to increase the amount of support for reorganization, resistance to change nonetheless continues to be substantial, particularly in the larger areas.

It is noted that while only 22 percent of the residents of the large area suburbs reported that they would vote in favor of setting up a single district for the whole area, the proportion of residents who would favor a single district with lower taxes is nearly twice as large—that is, 41 percent state this as a preference over retaining their present district with higher taxes. And while 69 percent reported that they would vote against setting up a single district, we find that only 48 percent would choose to maintain their present district, with higher taxes, rather than to have a single district with lower taxes.

In all areas the proportion of residents who state a preference for their present district with higher taxes is much lower than the proportion who earlier had stated that they would vote against setting up a single district. The difference is particularly marked in the suburbs. The proportion favoring the present district with higher taxes, as compared with the proportion who earlier had stated that they would vote against reorganization, declines by 30 percent in the large suburbs and by 42 percent in the small suburban areas. Apparently the cost factor is much more important in the small than in the larger areas. It is noted also that among suburban residents, those living in small metropolitan areas were the ones who most frequently viewed reorganization favorably. Calling attention to the cost differentials merely attenuates this pattern of difference by size of area. But in all areas, city and suburban, the proportion who would prefer a single district with lower taxes is higher than the proportion who reported that they would vote in favor of setting up a single district for the whole area. The pattern already noted in the large area suburbs obtains in all of the other areas also.

It would seem from the data presented in Table 7-5, that the chances for reorganization of school districts are much better than we would have expected on the basis of the responses reported in Table 7-1. Clearly when the cost factor is introduced as an integral part of the reorganizational proposal, the amount of support for change increases substantially. In the central cities, a sizable majority state a preference for a single district with lower taxes. The proportion does not vary by size of central city, and in all instances it exceeds 60 percent. But the significant point here is the much larger proportion of residents in the suburbs who state a preference for a single school district for the whole area when lower taxes are offered as part of the proposal, and the amount of support increases consistently by size of area. The proportion stating such a preference increases consistently from a low of 41 percent in the large area suburbs to a high of 57 percent in the small area suburbs. Thus, in the latter areas, there is a distinct majority who appear to favor change under these conditions.

The highly significant role that the promise of lower taxes plays in the responses of suburban residents becomes increasingly evident when we take a more careful look at the relationship between these responses and the responses to the earlier question (Table 7-1) as to how they would vote on setting up a single district for the whole area. When we focus only on those who stated a preference for a single district with lower taxes, we find that from one-third in the small area suburbs to two-fifths in the large suburban areas had earlier stated that they would vote against a proposal to set up a single school district. On the other hand, nearly all of those who stated a preference for their present district with higher taxes had previously reported that they would be opposed to reorganization of school districts on an area-wide basis. There seems to be little question but that the latter represent the hard-core opposition to change. The added cost factor through higher taxes does not deter them in their choice.

It would seem safe to infer from the above findings that there is a substantial segment of the population in the suburbs who would be opposed to the reorganization of school districts in principle, but they are not sufficiently firm in their position to pay increased taxes in order to retain their separate systems. And this segment of the population is of such a size that if it could be effectively reached, and convincingly informed that it is more costly to maintain separate systems, the chances of bringing about change would be substantially increased. This is particularly feasible if we add to this group those who are uncertain as to their views regarding change. But even granting these most favorable, as well as unlikely, conditions, a proposal for reorganization is almost certain to meet with defeat in the large suburban areas. This is evident from the data presented in Table 7-5. In the large area suburbs, even when the factor of higher taxes is attached as a condition of maintaining the present district, nearly half (48 percent) of the residents state this as their preference over a single district with lower taxes. But this is not the case in the medium-sized and small area suburbs. Less than two-fifths of the former and only slightly more than one-fourth of the latter continue to favor maintaining their present separate districts when high taxes are included as a necessary condition. When the added cost factor is introduced, support for a single district increases from 29 percent to 47 percent in the medium-sized area suburbs, and in the small area suburbs the increase is from 36 percent to 57 percent. On the other hand, support for the present district declines in the medium-sized area suburbs from 61 percent to 39 percent. And in the small area suburbs, the decline is from 50 percent to only 29 percent.

But how would various segments of the population respond to this proposal? It is to this question that we now turn our attention. The present discussion will focus on the role of socioeconomic status. Our purpose here is to determine what role each of the socioeconomic variables plays in accounting for how residents view reorganization of school districts when the relative cost factor is stressed.

According to the data presented in Table 7-6, socioeconomic status differences play a highly important role in how residents view reorganization when the cost factor of alternative proposals is emphasized. In all areas, both city and suburban, in each size class, the college trained seem to offer the most resistance to change. For example, in the large metropolitan areas only 20 percent of the city residents at the grade school level would prefer the present district

TABLE 7-6

PERCENT FAVORING PRESENT DISTRICT WITH HIGHER TAXES AND SINGLE
DISTRICT WITH LOWER TAXES BY SELECTED EDUCATIONAL,
OCCUPATIONAL, AND INCOME GROUPS BY PLACE OF
RESIDENCE AND SIZE OF METROPOLITAN AREA

Selected Character- istics and Place of Residence	Percent Favoring					
	Present District (Higher Tax)			Single District (Lower Tax)		
	Large	Medium	Small	Large	Medium	Small
	%	%	%	%	%	%
Education						
Grade School						
City	19.5	17.8	19.9	59.7	60.3	61.7
Suburbs	31.4	30.7	21.1	52.9	48.0	59.9
College						
City	31.1	22.9	24.2	59.5	66.3	62.1
Suburbs	60.0	47.1	33.3	33.8	40.5	55.1
Occupation						
Below Skilled						
City	20.9	18.8	21.4	62.1	62.5	64.8
Suburbs	37.9	36.2	28.1	48.4	45.7	62.2
Professional-Managerial						
City	25.3	22.2	26.6	62.7	61.1	64.9
Suburbs	59.6	43.1	31.4	33.9	44.6	56.2
Income						
Under $75						
City	18.6	24.8	13.4	60.8	52.5	72.2
Suburbs	38.3	26.9	34.3	46.8	50.0	52.2
$150 plus						
City	32.3	26.2	32.7	61.3	69.0	57.1
Suburbs	60.6	53.5	32.9	31.9	33.7	59.2

with higher taxes, but the proportion increases to 31 percent in
the college category. In the large area suburbs, the variation of
such responses is from 31 percent to 60 percent. The same pattern
of difference is also found in the other areas, but the proportion
stating a preference for the present district declines appreciably by
size of metropolitan area. It is particularly noteworthy that while
60 percent of the college trained large area suburban residents
prefer the present district, this declines to only 33 percent among

those living in the small area suburbs. At the grade school level, the decline by size of area is from 31 percent to 21 percent. In both medium-sized and large area suburbs, we find a disproportionately high percentage of the residents at the college level stating a preference for maintaining the "status quo," even though this would involve higher taxes. But at the grade school level, less than one-third state such a preference.

The influence of limited education appears to be more important than place of residence in how residents view change. At any rate, at the grade school level, the central city-suburban differences tend to largely disappear. For the most part, a majority of the residents with limited education, regardless of where they live, tend to favor setting up a single district if it would mean lower taxes. At this level of education, size of metropolitan area seems to have little, if any, influence on their views. This is not, however, the case with the college trained. While education has no effect on the proportion of city residents who favor a single district, nor does size of area, we find that both variables are important among suburban residents. Among the latter, the college trained are not only less likely to favor a single district, but the size of metropolitan area has a pronounced effect on the proportion who do so. The most marked differences by education are found in the large area suburbs, where the proportion favoring a single district with lower taxes declines from 53 percent at the grade school level to only 34 percent among the college trained. The same pattern of difference is found in the other suburban areas also, but the size of the difference decreases substantially by size of area. The difference by education decreases from 19 percentage points in the large suburbs to only 5 percentage points in the small area suburbs. It is readily evident that educational differences become increasingly less important, as size of area declines, in accounting for views regarding change.

These views vary substantially among the college trained. In the large area suburbs, 60 percent state a preference for the present district with higher taxes, but this declines consistently by size of area, and reaches a low of only 33 percent in the small area suburbs. Thus it is only among the college trained in the large area suburbs that we find a majority stating a preference for the present district with higher taxes. On the other hand, it is only in the small area suburbs that a majority in the college group would prefer a single district with lower taxes, whereas at the grade school level this tends to be the stated preference in each size class. At the college level, only 34 percent in the large area suburbs would favor a single district, but this proportion increases to 55 percent in the small area suburbs, where a majority of the residents favor a single district with lower taxes; this preference persists at all educational levels. But in the larger areas, it is only at the grade school level that a majority make this choice.

The pattern of responses by place of residence, by size of metropolitan area, and by variations in level of education tends to be found again within both occupational and income groups. At each occupational and income level, suburban residents are more likely than central city residents to favor the present district with higher taxes, and the proportion who do so is larger in the high status than in the low status categories. The largest status difference between central city and suburbs tends to be found in the large metropolitan areas. The size of the differences declines continuously by size of area, and tends to largely disappear in the small metropolitan areas. Thus resistance to change, at least when that is tied into tax savings, tends to vary directly by size of area and is disproportionately concentrated among suburban residents and those in the higher status groups. Most opposition to change is found among the high status residents in the large area suburbs. Least opposition is, of course, found in the central cities, with little variation by size of area. Among suburban residents, least opposition is found in the small area suburbs, with little variation among status groups.

Use of the Schools and Preference for District Organization

Still another dimension to be considered is how actual use of the schools at the present time serves as an influencing factor in the preferences of residents for either the present district with higher taxes or a single district with lower taxes. These data are shown in Table 7-7. It is apparent that use of the schools does exert considerable influence on how city residents respond to this proposal, but even when this variable is taken into account, responses do not vary by size of central city. And in each "use" category, a sizable majority of the city residents state a preference for a single district

TABLE 7-7

PERCENT FAVORING PRESENT DISTRICT WITH HIGHER TAXES AND
SINGLE DISTRICT WITH LOWER TAXES BY TYPE OF SCHOOL
CHILDREN ATTEND BY PLACE OF RESIDENCE AND
SIZE OF METROPOLITAN AREA

Place of Residence and Type of School Children Attend	Percent Favoring					
	Present District (Higher Tax)			Single District (Lower Tax)		
	Large	Medium	Small	Large	Medium	Small
	%	%	%	%	%	%
Central City						
Public	28.0	24.0	29.4	66.7	65.3	59.4
Non-public	23.4	28.2	15.4	59.4	56.4	80.8
None	21.8	22.7	20.0	61.8	58.6	62.5
Suburban Area						
Public	57.0	49.7	34.3	34.9	39.6	51.5
Non-public	44.8	33.3	27.0	44.8	47.9	64.9
None	43.9	31.9	23.0	43.2	52.4	62.2

with lower taxes. Only a small minority, never exceeding 30 percent in any area, would favor maintaining the status quo, if this meant paying higher taxes. However, quite a different pattern is found in the suburbs.

When we control for use of the schools in the suburbs, we continue to find substantially different views by size of metropolitan area. Although the same pattern of difference as already noted by place of residence and size of area persists within each "use of school" category, the influence of use of schools in each size class is nevertheless marked. Most resistance to change, measured in terms of the proportion stating a preference for the present district, is found among the large area suburban residents who have children in public schools. This is the only category where a distinct majority state a preference for the present district. Least resistance is found among those who do not have any children in school and live in the small area suburbs. While residents who have children in non-public schools are somewhat more likely than those who are not currently using the schools to state a preference for the present district with higher taxes, they do so much less frequently than those

who do have children in the public schools. The same pattern tends
to persist in each size of area. But regardless of the use of the schools,
the proportion of residents who prefer the present district with
higher taxes declines by size of suburban area. For example, among
those with children in public schools, the proportion favoring the
present district with higher taxes declines from 57 percent in the
large to only 34 percent in the small area suburbs. But among
those with no children in school, the proportion declines from 44
percent to 23 percent in the same areas. The range between extremes is noteworthy; while 57 percent of those in the large area
suburbs with children in public schools want to maintain the
present district, even with higher taxes, only 23 percent of the
small area suburban residents who do not have any children in
school wish to do so.

If we consider those who would prefer a single district with lower
taxes, we find that support comes disproportionately from the small
area suburban residents, and particularly those who do not have
children attending the public schools. Least support for this alternative is reported by large area suburban residents who have children
in the public schools. In the medium-sized area suburbs, we also
find a disproportionately low percentage who would favor a single
district among those with children in public schools. Here too we
find that the proportion favoring a single district increases consistently, but inversely, with size of area within each "use of school"
category. It is also noted, in all suburban zones, that least support
for reorganization is found among the residents who have children
currently attending the public schools. It is only in the large and
medium-sized area suburbs, among residents with children in the
public schools, that we find a larger proportion favoring the present
district rather than a single district with lower taxes. In all other
subgroups, either the same proportion, or a higher proportion, would
favor a single district with lower taxes, but it is only in the small
area suburbs that a clear-cut majority respond thusly. But even
here the proportion is lowest among residents who have children in
public schools.

Again the reader is warned to be cautious in interpreting the
meaning of these findings, since many of the preferences may have
been stated with attention being focused on only one dimension of
the choices offered—that is, the residents may have responded pre-

dominantly in terms of the lower taxes that would result if they selected the single district approach. They may have tended to overlook, ignore, or at least not think about the full implications of the reorganizational proposal which would establish a single district for the area. Consequently, even though the above observations clearly illustrate the importance of the cost factor, the meaning of the findings is somewhat questionable in respect to the reorganization issue. We feel that much more confidence can be placed in the responses to the direct and unidimensional question of how residents would vote on setting up a single district as reported in Table 7-1. Nonetheless, it is important to note that when reorganization is proposed, along with decreased costs, a much larger proportion of the population appears to be ready to accept change.[5]

At this point we return to a further look at the responses to the more general question of how the residents would vote on a proposal to establish a single district for the city and suburban areas. In the present chapter, attention is focused only on how responses vary according to use of the schools. In the succeeding chapters, the question of reorganization will be analyzed more fully.

For the most part, even when we control for use of the schools, central city residents disproportionately tend to report that they would vote for a single district. And there is no consistent pattern of difference by "use of school" categories, except that the "don't know" responses tend to be consistently high among those who do not have children in school. Certainly one would get the impression from our data that central city residents generally, regardless of size of city, would support a reorganization proposal. Only about one-third of the residents have stated that they would vote against such a proposed change. This tends to be nearly the same in each "use of school" category and in each size class. But when we focus our attention on the suburban areas we find consistent and sizable differences by both "use of school" categories and size of metropolitan area. That is, the already observed differences by size of area con-

[5] However, this does not mean that it would be easy to find support for a proposed reorganization of school districts by claiming that tax savings would result. This would not necessarily follow; and regardless of whether taxes would be lower, the opposition forces would claim otherwise. As evidence of this, one need only to look at the usual techniques used by opponents to change. Regardless of what the proposal is, the universal attack tends to be stated in terms of the threat of increased costs. See, for example, Frank Smallwood, *Greater London: The Politics of Metropolitan Reform*, (N. Y.: Bobbs-Merrill, 1965).

tinue to be found within each "use of school" category. And the same pattern of difference by "use of school" categories is found in each size class. Consistently, the proportion who would vote for change is largest among those who have children in the non-public schools and lowest among those whose children are attending public school. The latter are the ones most likely to vote against such a proposed change.

It is noteworthy that a distinct majority of the residents in each "use of school" category, in both large and medium-sized suburban areas, would vote against reorganization of school districts. In the small area suburbs, we find a majority opposed only among those who have children attending public schools. Support for change in the small suburbs tends to come largely from those whose children attend non-public schools and, to a lesser extent, those who do not have any children in school. However, among the latter there is a very high proportion of "don't know" responses. In short, central city residents tend to view reorganization favorably, but strong resistance is found particularly in the large and medium-sized area suburbs. This tends to be most marked among the residents who have children in the public schools, but in all "use of school" categories a distinct majority appear to be opposed to change. It is only in the small area suburbs and among those who do not have children attending public schools that we find less than a majority opposed to change. The question now remains, what are the factors that account for resistance to change? It is to this question that we direct our attention in the next chapter, where we focus on resistance in relationship to the characteristics of the residents.

Before doing so, however, we will briefly describe some of the perceived consequences of change. No doubt much of the resistance to reorganization of school districts may be due to the fear of what may happen if change should come about. Thus, the question of concern here pertains to the anticipated consequences in respect to taxes and the quality of schools. This will be followed by a discussion of the advantages and disadvantages of a single district for the whole area.

Impact of Reorganization on Quality of Schools and Taxes

Looking first at what residents think would happen to the quality of schools, we find that the responses vary not only by place of residence, but by size of area as well. These data are shown in Table 7-8. City residents are more likely to feel that the schools would improve. But the proportion who do so declines by size of area. Just the opposite is found among suburban residents; the proportion

TABLE 7-8

EFFECT OF SINGLE DISTRICT ON QUALITY OF SCHOOLS AND TAXES
BY PLACE OF RESIDENCE AND SIZE OF METROPOLITAN AREA

Effect of Single District on:	Large		Medium		Small	
	City	Suburb	City	Suburb	City	Suburb
Total Number	477	495	457	493	488	492
	%	%	%	%	%	%
Quality of Schools						
Become better	31.2	11.9	28.4	14.4	22.5	21.5
Remain about same	31.9	29.9	35.0	35.9	42.4	43.1
Not quite as good	17.4	48.5	19.3	39.6	18.9	22.8
Don't know	16.8	9.7	15.3	9.3	13.5	12.4
No answer	2.7	—	1.5	0.8	2.7	0.2
Total	100.0	100.0	100.0	100.0	100.0	100.0
Taxes						
Increase	39.2	50.5	36.8	35.9	41.4	43.9
No change	22.2	21.8	29.3	34.9	29.5	24.0
Decrease	20.1	17.8	18.2	17.8	12.7	18.5
Don't know	16.4	9.9	13.6	11.4	13.9	11.6
No answer	2.1	—	2.2	—	2.5	2.0
Total	100.0	100.0	100.0	100.0	100.0	100.0

who feel that the schools would improve in quality increases as the size of area declines. As a result of this pattern, central city-suburban differences are largest in the large metropolitan areas. Of particular interest is the fact that in the small areas, nearly an equal proportion in both the central city and suburbs report that the schools would improve. But this view is shared by only slightly more than 20 percent, as compared with 31 percent in the large central cities and 12 percent in the large area suburbs.

In most areas, the predominant response is that there would be no change in quality following reorganization. And this view is most frequently expressed by residents in the small metropolitan areas, regardless of their place of residence. In the other areas, this view is shared by approximately one-third of the residents. This varies little by place of residence in either the large or medium-sized area suburbs.

But the most significant observation here is the large proportion of residents, particularly in the large and medium-sized area suburbs, who feel that there would be a decline in quality if a single district were established. In these areas, central city and suburban differences are marked. Suburban residents are more than twice as likely to feel that quality would decline, except in the small metropolitan areas, where the difference is only 20 percent. In short, suburban residents disproportionately feel that one of the consequences of setting up a single school district for the whole area is that the schools would not be quite as good as they are at present. It may very well be that this is an important factor in their resistance to change. At any rate, these data suggest that they perceive distinct disadvantages resulting from change.

Contrary to expectation, there do not appear to be any marked or consistent central city and suburban differences in the views on what would happen to taxes following reorganization. It is only in the large metropolitan areas that suburban residents are more likely to expect a tax increase. But it is noteworthy that while we do not find central city-suburban difference, a substantial proportion in all areas report that one of the consequences of change would be an increased tax burden. This view is shared by more than one-third of the residents in all areas. Another sizable proportion of the residents in all areas feel that taxes would remain largely the same even if a single system were established. And perhaps most important is the low proportion of residents who would expect a tax decrease. Only a slightly smaller proportion do not know what would happen to taxes as a result of change.

To the extent that "quality of schools" and "reduced taxes" are important factors in how residents would respond to change, these data suggest that not much support for change would be found, at least among suburban residents. It is particularly noteworthy that only a small minority of the latter share the view that the quality of schools would improve or that reorganization would lead to decreased taxes. On the other hand, a disproportionately high number of residents in both central city and suburban areas feel that taxes would increase. A large proportion of the suburban residents also feel that the quality of schools would decline. One would expect both of these factors to be important in resistance to change. Their importance will be examined in the next chapter.

Advantages and Disadvantages of a Single District

Pursuing the relative merits of reorganization further, residents were asked to state their opinions as to the advantages as well as the disadvantages of a single district for the whole area. These responses are shown in Table 7-9. It is noteworthy that a disproportionately high number of suburban residents feel that there would be no advantages. While central city residents are much less likely to report that there would be no advantages in having a single district, they are more likely to report that they "don't know" the specific advantages that would be gained. It is significant that more than two-fifths of the residents in most areas do not mention any specific advantage in response to this question. And the advantages that are reported cover a wide range and differ only slightly by place of residence and size of area.

One of the most common advantages mentioned is that there would be equality among the districts—that is, the standards would be uniform. This view is reported most frequently by the suburban residents in the large and medium-sized areas. While only 10 percent or less of the residents report that schools or education generally would be better, this type of response tends to increase among suburban residents as size of area declines. A much larger proportion feel that there would be cost advantages, in that the schools would be less expensive and taxes would be lower. However, these responses do not vary consistently by either place of residence or size of area. Central city residents are somewhat more likely to feel that there would be an improvement in both teachers and facilities under a single system. But again, each of these views is shared by less than 10 percent of the residents in any of the areas. Still others feel that there would be more efficient administration and less overhead. Here too the view is shared by only a small proportion of the residents in any of the areas. And an even smaller proportion feel that there would be more money for the schools because of the broader tax base. Thus, while at least a majority of the residents in all areas report at least some specific advantage in having a single district, there is little consensus. On the contrary, there is a wide variety of

TABLE 7-9

ADVANTAGES AND DISADVANTAGES OF A SINGLE DISTRICT BY PLACE
OF RESIDENCE AND SIZE OF METROPOLITAN AREA

Advantages and Disadvantages	Large		Medium		Small	
	City	Suburb	City	Suburb	City	Suburb
Total Number	477	495	457	493	488	492
	Advantages of a Single District					
	%	%	%	%	%	%
Less costly—tax savings	16.7	15.5	17.5	18.1	13.1	13.0
Better teachers and facilities	15.1	10.7	14.8	12.2	13.4	13.2
Equality among districts	16.6	22.2	20.3	21.3	16.6	11.2
More efficient administration	5.7	5.9	11.8	10.3	8.8	6.5
Broader tax base	5.7	4.8	2.8	3.7	5.3	3.5
Better schools—education	8.0	5.3	9.6	7.1	9.6	10.0
Don't know	26.8	15.4	20.1	15.2	31.3	27.6
None	11.3	24.2	13.1	24.5	11.5	19.1
No answer—Other	7.1	8.9	9.4	4.9	7.8	5.9
Total*	100.0	100.0	100.0	100.0	100.0	100.0
	Disadvantages of a Single District					
	%	%	%	%	%	%
Greater costs—higher taxes	11.4	12.4	9.7	9.8	12.7	10.8
Problem of transportation—distance	4.9	3.0	2.6	3.0	8.2	6.7
Too big, unwieldly, inefficient	19.6	29.8	22.9	24.0	17.0	19.1
Loss of individual attention	3.8	13.8	7.7	14.6	2.9	6.7
Lower quality—teachers not as good	3.2	15.2	3.5	10.1	3.3	4.5
Problems vary by districts	4.2	6.3	6.6	7.3	3.9	3.0
Loss of control—certain districts would dominate	1.6	5.4	6.4	11.4	5.4	10.2
Don't know	31.2	15.2	24.8	14.4	32.4	28.2
None—No disadvantages	16.7	8.7	11.4	11.6	11.9	10.6
No answer—Other	9.9	9.2	15.4	12.5	13.3	10.3
Total*	100.0	100.0	100.0	100.0	100.0	100.0

* Adds to more than 100 percent because multiple responses are reported.

advantages reported, but no single one is shared by many of the residents, and the central city-suburban difference appears to be negligible. The only meaningful difference is that suburban residents are more likely not to see any advantage in having a single district.

Suburban residents were much more responsive when asked to give their views on the disadvantages of a single district. Also, the gap between city and suburban responses tends to increase directly by size of area. That is, central city and suburban views differ more in the large than in the small metropolitan areas. For example, in the large areas we find that 53 percent of the city-dwellers do not express any specific disadvantage, as compared with only 27 percent of the suburban residents. In the small metropolitan areas, the proportions are 51 percent and 43 percent, respectively. Thus, while there is little variation in this type response among city residents, there is a marked difference by size of area among those living in suburban areas. Among the latter, as the size of the area declines, there is less of a tendency to see disadvantages in a single district.

Regardless of size of area, however, suburban residents are more likely than central city residents to report specific disadvantages in respect to a single district. The most frequently reported disadvantage in all areas pertains to the size of a single district that encompassed the whole area. A disproportionate number feel that a single district would be too big, inefficient, and unwieldly, resulting in large classes and overcrowding. While this disadvantage is expressed more frequently by suburban than by central city residents, it is nonetheless the most frequent disadvantage reported by residents in all areas. However, the central city-suburban gap is least in the small metropolitan areas. It is noteworthy that the size factor is mentioned by at least one person in five in nearly all of the areas. A related disadvantage—that is, loss of individual attention—is also frequently reported by suburban residents, particularly in the large and medium sized areas. As one would expect, city residents are much less concerned about this issue.

Residents in the larger suburbs tend to be disproportionately concerned about a single district lowering the quality of teachers, while those in the smaller areas are more likely to be concerned about loss of local control and the danger that the large districts would dominate the combined districts. Both of these disadvantages are rarely mentioned by the city residents, regardless of size of area. Still another disadvantage, which is mentioned by a sizable proportion of the residents, is the danger of greater costs and higher taxes. This is a disadvantage that is reported by approximately 10 percent of the residents. And this response does not appear to vary by either place of residence or size of metropolitan area. Problems of transportation and the distance factor are only infrequently mentioned, but this seems to be of most concern to the residents in the small metropolitan areas. This is likely due, in large part, to the more limited public transportation systems in these areas. Consequently, if the schools were consolidated under a single system, there would be the problem of transporting the pupils to these central locations. In the larger, more densely settled areas, this is apparently less frequently viewed as a potential problem.

In an overall appraisal of the responses concerning the disadvantages of a single district, it would seem that most of the specific issues expressed by the suburban residents, in particular, are in one way or another related to the "bigness" of the single district. Even when this dimension is not reported as such, the disadvantages that are mentioned are largely a function of size and loss of local control. It is also evident from these data that suburban residents are more likely than those in the city to feel that there are specific disadvantages in having a single district for the whole area. But it is to be noted that city and suburban differences tend to decline directly as size of metropolitan area decreases. While substantial differences are found in the large metropolitan areas, city and suburban differences largely disappear in the small metropolitan areas. No doubt this is one of the reasons why we find less resistance to change in the small than in the large suburban areas.

Summary

In the above discussion, we have noted that there is much less resistance to change in cities than in suburban areas. Size of metropolitan area has little effect on how city residents view reorganization of school districts, but among suburban residents resistance to change varies inversely by size of area. When a differential cost factor is introduced, there is a substantial increase in all areas in the proportion favoring change; however, there seems to be a hard-core group in the suburbs that would resist change under any circumstances. They are opposed in principle, and they are willing to pay for the privilege of remaining separate from the city.

Most resistance to change is found in the suburbs among the higher status groups and those who have children attending public schools in the area. There seems to be little consensus as to the advantages of a single district while, at least among the suburban residents, there seems to be the fear that a single district would be too large and there would be loss of local control. It is noteworthy that as the size of the metropolitan area declines, the views expressed by central city and suburban residents, concerning all of the above issues, become more similar. Both place of residence and size of metropolitan area play an important role in how residents view reorganization of school districts.

8

Factors Related to Resistance to Change

ALTHOUGH THERE TEND TO be rather large and significant differences between central city and suburban residents in how they would react to a proposal to establish a single district for the whole area, there is still a sizable proportion in all areas whose responses differ from the majority view. Thus the purpose of the present chapter is to attempt to determine some of the salient factors that account for resistance to change. Essentially we are concerned with the question of whether or not those who are opposed to change differ in any important respects from those who would favor reorganization of school districts. In the present discussion, attention will be focused first on views regarding change held by different socioeconomic status classes. This in turn will be followed by an analysis of resistance to change in relationship to how residents evaluate the schools in their own areas, as well as in other parts of the metropolitan area. Lastly, we will be concerned with the relationship between resistance to change and the general views held by residents regarding taxation and the support of schools.

Type of Respondent

When we control for type of respondent, as we have done in Table 8-1, we continue to find very marked central city-suburban differences in the proportions who would vote for change. How-

TABLE 8-1

PROPORTION OF RESIDENTS THAT WOULD VOTE FOR A SINGLE DISTRICT
BY TYPE OF RESPONDENT BY PLACE OF RESIDENCE
AND SIZE OF METROPOLITAN AREA

Type of Respondent and Family Units	Large		Medium		Small	
	City	Suburb	City	Suburb	City	Suburb
	%	%	%	%	%	%
Total	46.5	22.0	44.4	29.0	44.9	35.8
Husband-Wife Households						
Male	55.1	25.8	50.6	35.9	51.9	37.1
Female	43.5	20.5	40.0	22.0	43.1	34.3
Other Type Households						
Male	35.7	22.7	52.6	37.0	41.2	46.7*
Female	40.7	16.0	37.9	22.5	36.4	32.4

* Less than twenty cases.

ever, within each area, there tends to be a rather consistent pattern
of difference by type of respondent. In all size classes and in both
central city and suburban areas, support for change is found primarily among males living in dwelling units composed of both hus-
band and wife. Consistently, males in such families are more likely
to favor change than females. Although the size of the difference is
substantial only in the medium-sized area suburbs, the persistence
of the pattern of difference in all areas is noteworthy. Even males in
incomplete family units, are more likely than females to favor
change. But in all subgroups, central city residents are much more
likely than suburban residents to favor reorganization.

There seems to be more similarity between males and females
living in complete family type units, even though these are not from
the same families, than is found among those with other types of
living arrangements. Among the latter, sex differences are much
more marked. Although not shown in the table, much of this difference is due to the disproportionately high percentage of "don't
know" responses among females. Rather consistently they are less
likely to take a firm position either for or against the proposed
change. But regardless of the family composition or sex of the respondent, persistent city and suburban differences are found. We
also continue to find among suburban residents, within each type

of respondent category, a general increase in the proportion favoring change as size of area declines. Least support for change is found in the large area suburbs, particularly among females. Most support for the reorganizational proposal among suburban residents comes from males in the small areas, but even here there is less support for change than is found in any of the central cities. Unlike suburban zones, size of central city appears to be unimportant. It is further noted that there is much more variation in the views held by place of residence than by type of respondent.

Income

Income differences within the populations appears to be one of the factors that helps to account for variations in views regarding school district reorganization. However, the influence of this variable is quite different among central city and suburban residents. In the former, most support for change is found among residents in the top income category. This is true of each size class, but the proportion favoring change is particularly high in the small cities, where seven out of ten top income residents report that they would vote to support the establishment of a single district for the whole city-suburban area. Most opposition is consistently reported by the middle income group, though in none of the cities is opposition reported by a majority. The lower proportion opposed to change in the lowest income category is due largely to the disproportionately large number who "don't know" how they would vote on such an issue. At any rate, at all income levels, substantial support for change is evident.

Quite a different pattern of attitudes, among income groups, is observed among suburban residents. Whereas most support for change comes from the top income group in the central cities, it is at this level that we find most opposition in the suburbs. However, within this income category there are substantial differences by size of area. The range is from a low of 54 percent in the small to a high of 78 percent in the large area suburbs. Thus at the income level where resistance to change is greatest, the proportion opposed is nearly 50 percent higher in the large than in the small area suburbs. On the other hand, the proportion favoring change is nearly twice as great at this income level in the small than in the large area suburbs. Also it is noteworthy that the number of undecided or who don't know how they would vote is substantially higher in the small area suburbs. Of particular significance here is the fact that in the large area suburbs, nearly eight out of ten residents in the top income group have already decided that they would be opposed to change, but the proportion declines to less than three-fifths in the lowest income category, while the proportion of "don't know" responses increases from 3 percent to 17 percent. A very similar pattern is found in the other suburban areas also, but the size of the difference is less marked.

In short, lower income groups are less likely to report that they are opposed to change, but this is due, in part at least, to the higher proportion who "don't know" how they would vote. But even at the lower income levels, where we tend to find the least opposition to change, approximately half of the residents have decided that they would vote against reorganization. In each of the suburban areas, the largest proportions who would vote for reorganization are in the middle income categories, although the size of the difference is not large and the proportion never exceeds 40 percent. It is also noteworthy that in the central cities, this is the income group most opposed to change. Here again we find that within each subcategory, support for reorganization tends to increase inversely by size of area, whereas resistance to change varies directly by size.

Education

The role of education as a factor in resistance to change is also substantial, as is indicated by the data shown in Table 8-2. Generally speaking, the proportion opposed to change tends to increase directly by level of education. However, the findings are not quite that simple or that direct in either segment of the metropolitan community. Focusing first on the suburban areas, we do consistently find that opposition to setting up a single district increases directly with education. This pattern recurs in each size class. The range is marked. For example, in the large area suburbs, the proportion opposed to reorganization increases from only 42 percent of those in the lowest education category to a high of 80 percent among the college trained. In the small area suburbs, where there is much less opposition, the range is from 33 percent to 51 percent. It should be noted, however, that at the low educational levels there is a very

TABLE 8-2

HOW VOTE ON SINGLE SCHOOL DISTRICT BY EDUCATION OF RESPONDENT BY PLACE OF RESIDENCE AND SIZE OF METROPOLITAN AREA

Education & Size of Metropolitan Area	Central City					Suburban Area				
	Number	Favor	Oppose	Other*	Total	Number	Favor	Oppose	Other*	Total
		%	%	%	%		%	%	%	%
Large										
Under 7	58	29.3	27.6	43.1	100.0	26	26.9	42.3	30.8	100.0
7–8	101	41.6	34.7	23.8	100.0	76	28.9	59.2	11.8	100.0
9–11	120	58.3	30.0	11.7	100.0	93	30.1	59.1	10.8	100.0
12	124	48.4	43.5	8.1	100.0	169	19.5	74.0	6.5	100.0
13 plus	74	44.6	43.2	12.2	100.0	131	14.5	80.1	5.4	100.0
Medium										
Under 7	53	39.6	17.0	43.4	100.0	16	25.0	75.0	—	100.0
7–8	93	45.2	32.2	22.6	100.0	59	33.9	54.2	11.9	100.0
9–11	108	49.1	34.3	16.7	100.0	98	32.7	53.1	14.3	100.0
12	116	37.9	44.0	18.1	100.0	166	33.1	60.2	6.6	100.0
13 plus	87	49.4	36.8	13.7	100.0	154	20.8	66.9	12.3	100.0
Small										
Under 7	40	30.0	17.5	52.5	100.0	36	25.0	33.3	41.7	100.0
7–8	101	38.6	40.6	20.8	100.0	111	39.6	44.1	16.2	100.0
9–11	113	52.2	31.9	16.0	100.0	134	36.6	50.0	13.4	100.0
12	167	46.1	42.5	11.4	100.0	133	30.8	57.9	11.3	100.0
13 plus	67	47.8	41.8	10.4	100.0	78	42.3	51.3	6.4	100.0

* Includes undecided, don't know, and no answer.

high proportion of residents in the "don't know" category. At the lowest educational level, we find that nearly one-third in the large and more than two-fifths in the small area suburbs do not know how they would vote on such a proposal. This accounts, in part at least, for the much lower proportion opposed to change. Even if we disregard this educational level, we still find that the proportion opposed increases directly with education. The range of difference is, however, less pronounced.

In the suburban zones of both the large and medium-sized areas, the college trained are distinct from all others in the low proportion who would support change. Not only does the proportion who would vote for change tend to be higher at the lower levels of education, but there is little variation below the completed high school level. The small area suburban residents show a different pattern. While the proportion opposed to change does increase directly with education up to the high school level, the proportion declines at the college level. This group has the highest proportion who report that they would vote for reorganization of school districts on an area-wide basis, which is just the opposite in the other suburban areas. At the other levels of education, the proportion favoring change does not follow any consistent pattern. However, it is noteworthy that the proportion of "uncommitted" responses decreases consistently as level of education increases. The range is from 42 percent at the lowest educational level to only 6 percent at the college level. At each level of education, the proportion of residents who do not know how they would vote tends to be higher in the small area suburbs than in the larger suburban areas. Thus in the small area suburbs, not only do we consistently find more support for reorganization, but there is also a larger proportion who are "uncommitted" as to how they would vote. The major difference here is the unusually high proportion at the college level who would support setting up a single school district, since this is the type of person most likely to resist change in the larger suburban areas. This again emphasizes the significant role that size of area plays in the resistance to change.

In the central cities, regardless of size of area, resistance to change tends to increase directly by education, as it does in the suburbs. But oddly enough, so does support for change. In each size class, least support for change is found in the lowest educational category and most support at the college level. This is, of course, contrary to the pattern observed in both the large and medium-sized area suburbs. This apparent inconsistency is due to the high proportion of city residents who do not know how they would vote. And this proportion is highest at the lower levels of education. As a result, we find fewer residents in favor of change, and also fewer opposed to change, as compared with those at the higher levels of education. Among the latter, residents are more likely to take a firm stand on the issue—that is, they know how they would vote. At each educational level, we continue to find more support for change in the cities than in the suburbs. While this pattern of difference is found in each size class, the size of the city-suburban difference tends to be least in the small metropolitan areas. Resistance to setting up a single district for the whole area is disproportionately concentrated in the suburban areas, and in each size class most resistance is found among the better educated residents.

Age

We had expected to find a close relationship between age and resistance to change, with most opposition, particularly in the suburbs, concentrated among the older residents and among those with children in school. Our data only partially support this expectation. In the large metropolitan area suburbs, the highest proportion opposed to change is found among those 25 to 44 years of age. The next highest proportion is found among those 55 years of age and over. Thus, least opposition is found among those under 25 years and those between 45 and 55 years of age. The first group has not yet started to use the schools; whereas among the latter their children, in most cases, would have completed their secondary school education.

In the medium-sized area suburbs the pattern is somewhat different; but still, basically, we find the same factors operating. Here, however, most opposition is expressed by the older residents, followed by those 25 to 45 years of age. And again, least opposition is found among those under 25 years and those in the age group 45 to 54 years. Thus in both the large and medium-sized area suburbs, age is one of the factors that accounts for variations in views regarding reorganization. In the small suburbs, there doesn't appear to be any consistent variation in the proportion who favor change, up to age

55 years, but after this point the proportion who would vote for reorganization drops substantially. Even in the central cities, there is a tendency for the proportion favoring change to follow the same pattern by age as found in the large and medium-sized suburbs, though the size of the differences among age groups is less marked. Nonetheless, most support for change tends to come from those in the 45 to 54 year category, and least support is found among those over 55 years of age. It is noted, however, that there is a disproportionately large number who do not know how they would vote among those in the older ages, which may account, in part, for the lower proportion favoring change.

For the most part, regardless of place of residence within the metropolitan community and regardless of size of area, residents over 55 years of age are less likely than others to favor change. In the suburban areas, in particular, older persons are consistently against a proposal for change. This resistance is also shared disproportionately by suburban residents in the 25 to 45 year category. We continue to find, within each age category, more resistance in the suburbs than in central cities, and more resistance to change in the large than in the small area suburbs. Thus while age is certainly a factor in helping to account for variations in views regarding reorganization, it is less a factor than place of residence.

Race

We turn now to how the different racial groups feel regarding reorganization of school districts. For this part of the discussion we are limited only to city residents, since Negroes are rarely found in any of the suburban areas. Even in the cities, the Negro accounts for only about 10 percent of the total households. However, given the limitations of size of sample, it is nonetheless significant that Negroes in the city are much more willing to accept change than whites. These data are shown in Table 8-3. In each size class, Negroes have a higher proportion who would vote for reorganization than is found among whites. And the gap is more pronounced in the small than in the large cities. On the other hand, Negroes are less likely than whites to oppose reorganization. Here too, we find that the Negro-white difference is more marked in the small than in the large cities. For example, while only 23 percent of the Negroes would vote

TABLE 8-3

HOW VOTE ON SINGLE SCHOOL DISTRICT BY RACE, CENTRAL CITY ONLY,
BY SIZE OF METROPOLITAN AREA

Race and Size of Metropolitan Area	How Vote on Single District				
	Number	Favor	Oppose	Other	Total
		%	%	%	%
Large					
Negro	44	52.3	22.7	25.0	100.0
White	424	46.0	38.0	16.0	100.0
Medium					
Negro	49	61.2	24.5	14.3	100.0
White	403	42.4	35.7	21.8	100.0
Small					
Negro	37	62.2	13.5	24.3	100.0
White	434	43.3	40.1	16.5	100.0

against reorganization, some 38 percent of the whites would do so. Thus, whites exceed Negroes by approximately 65 percent. In the small cities, only 14 percent of the Negroes would oppose change, as compared with 40 percent of the whites, which is nearly a three-fold difference. Some of the differences noted here are due to the higher proportion of Negroes who do not know how they would vote. In both large and small cities, Negroes are about 50 percent more likely than whites not to know how they would vote. But even given the larger undecided vote, Negroes still have a higher proportion who would favor change. The Negro view, however, is not likely to have much effect on how the residents of the area would vote on a proposal for change, since they constitute such a small proportion of the total population. It would be interesting to know whether Negroes would continue to favor change if they lived in the suburbs. Unfortunately, the limited number of Negroes in the suburbs does not permit even an exploratory analysis of this question.

Place of Work

Contrary to expectation, where suburban residents work does not have any influence on the views held regarding change in the organization of school districts. It was thought that if persons lived in the suburban part of the metropolitan community but worked in the central city, they would be more sympathetic to an area-wide approach to the school problem. That is not supported by the data, however. There is no consistent pattern of difference by place of work in any of the suburban zones. Apparently daily contact through the work situation does not alter the generally isolationist views regarding the organization of school districts. Persons in each place of work category are equally opposed to change, and in all suburban areas this view is shared by a majority; however, as previously noted, the proportion opposed does decrease as size of area declines.

Quite a different pattern is found among central city residents. In each size class, we find that those who work in the suburbs are more likely to be in favor of setting up a single district for the whole area than are those who work in the central city. At least for central city residents, frequent contact with the suburbs tends to make them more receptive to an overall area-wide approach. But the proportion of residents in the central city who work in the suburbs is relatively small and decreases substantially by size of area. On the other hand, half or more of the suburban residents work in the central city; the largest proportion doing so are in the small metropolitan areas, where seven out of ten suburban workers hold jobs within the central city. But this, as we have seen, is not an important factor in how residents react to a proposed reorganization. Regardless of place of work, suburban residents tend to be opposed to change.

Residential Experience

What influence does previous residential experience have on the views held by residents of the area? Here too, we would expect that those who had previously lived in the opposite part of the metropolitan community would be more favorable to an area-wide approach than those who had lived only in one segment of the community. However, the data only partially support this. In the central cities, most support for change does come from those who had previously lived in the suburbs, but moved into the central city more than five years ago. This holds for each size class. A somewhat different pattern is found for those who have more recently moved in from the suburbs. In the large metropolitan areas, the recent movers are more likely to support change than those who have only lived in the central cities, but in both the medium-sized and small areas, least support for change is likely to come from this group.

Still another pattern is found in the suburbs. In the large metropolitan areas, previous residence has little influence on how suburban residents view change, but in the medium and small area suburbs it is those who have moved from the city during the past five years who are most likely to support change. Least support would come from those who have lived only in the suburbs. In the latter areas, the proportion of residents who have lived in central cities and who support change is at least 25 percent higher than the proportion found among those who have lived only in the suburbs. But in all categories, support for change comes only from a minority, though the proportion increases as size of area declines. There doesn't seem to be any consistent pattern of difference in how residents view change, by length of time lived in the metropolitan community, among either central city or suburban residents in any size class. Those who have recently moved to the present metropolitan area, whether they live in the central city or in the suburbs, tend to express the same views regarding school district organization as the long-time residents of the area. If they live in the central city, they tend to favor change; but if they live in the suburbs, they tend to oppose change about as frequently as other suburban residents. This observation holds regardless of size of area. On the other hand, length of residence at the present address tends to show an appreciable influence in all areas. These data are shown in Table 8-4.

In the suburbs, at least, resistance to change increases directly with length of time lived at the present address, except in the large area suburbs, where the proportion opposed remains relatively constant. But even in the large area suburbs, the proportion favoring change is least among those who have lived the longest at their present address. This, however, is due to the larger proportion who are uncertain as to how they would vote, since the proportion opposed is the same as is found in the other categories.

If we focus on the proportion who report that they would vote in favor of reorganization, most support, in all areas, comes from those who have lived at their present address for less than three years; and least support is found among those who have lived at the same address for fifteen years or more. Also we find that the size of the difference, particularly in the suburbs, tends to increase

TABLE 8-4

HOW VOTE ON SINGLE SCHOOL DISTRICT BY LENGTH OF TIME AT PRESENT ADDRESS
BY PLACE OF RESIDENCE AND SIZE OF METROPOLITAN AREA

Time at Present Address & Size of Metropolitan Area	Central City					Suburban Area				
	Number	Favor	Oppose	Other	Total	Number	Favor	Oppose	Other	Total
		%	%	%	%		%	%	%	%
Large										
Less than 3 years	187	48.1	38.5	13.4	100.0	171	22.8	68.9	8.2	100.0
3–15 years	181	47.5	35.3	17.2	100.0	237	22.8	69.6	7.6	100.0
15 years plus	104	42.3	34.6	23.1	100.0	82	17.1	68.3	14.6	100.0
Medium										
Less than 3 years	176	46.6	34.6	18.7	100.0	170	30.0	56.5	13.5	100.0
3–15 years	180	48.3	33.9	17.8	100.0	242	31.0	59.5	9.5	100.0
15 years plus	96	33.3	36.4	30.2	100.0	78	21.8	71.8	6.4	100.0
Small										
Less than 3 years	168	47.6	35.7	16.7	100.0	177	42.9	42.4	14.6	100.0
3–15 years	222	45.5	37.8	16.7	100.0	236	36.0	51.2	12.7	100.0
15 years plus	96	39.6	39.6	20.8	100.0	78	19.2	61.5	19.2	100.0

inversely with size of area. Thus in the large suburbs, the proportion favoring change is 33 percent higher among those who have been long-time residents at a given address. In the small suburbs, the same difference exceeds 120 percent. Here we find that 43 percent of the recent movers favor change, as compared with only 19 percent of those who have lived at their present address for fifteen years or more. Conversely, except in the large area suburbs, the proportion opposed to change increases directly by length of time lived at the present address. In the medium-sized area suburbs, opposition increases from 57 percent to 72 percent, and in the small area suburbs the proportion opposed to change increases from 42 percent to 62 percent. Thus, opposition to change increases by more than 25 percent in medium-sized area suburbs, and by nearly 50 percent in the small area suburbs, when one compares the long-time residents with recent movers.

In the central cities also, in each size class, the proportion in favor of change declines with length of residence at present address, but the size of the difference tends to be less than that already observed among suburban residents. However, the significant point here is that there is no corresponding increase in the proportion who are opposed to change. Rather, as length of residence at the present address increases, more and more city residents are found in the "don't know" category. Thus while the suburban residents tend to become more opposed to change the longer they live at the same address, city residents do not. The latter show a marked tendency to shift from favoring change to the "don't know" category. In short, the long-time residents in the central city are more likely not to take a position on the proposal, whereas in the suburbs they tend to support the status quo.

Satisfaction with the Schools

One would expect views on change of the organizational structure of school districts to be influenced by the extent to which residents are satisfied with the schools in their area. That is, we would expect those most satisfied with the existing schools to be the least favorable to change. However, when we compare how people would vote on setting up a single district by their level of satisfaction with the schools in their district, no consistent pattern of difference is found in the central cities. By and large, central city residents generally favor reorganization, regardless of how satisfied they are with their schools. On the other hand, this dimension is of considerable importance in the suburbs. In each size class, least support for and most opposition to change is reported by those who are very satisfied with their schools. This level of satisfaction is reported by a substantial majority of the suburban residents. It is noteworthy that support for change is one-fifth higher in the large area suburbs among those who are less satisfied with their schools, while in both the medium-sized and small area suburbs, the proportion favoring change increases by more than one-third among those who are in the quite satisfied or dissatisfied categories.

Marked differences by size of metropolitan area are again found within each satisfaction category. Thus, for example, while less than 20 percent of those in the large area suburbs who are very satisfied favor setting up a single district, this proportion increases to 24 percent in the medium-sized and to 34 percent in the small area suburbs. In the quite satisfied category, the proportion favoring change is higher in each area and also increases consistently as size of area declines. In this satisfaction category, the proportion favoring change ranges from 24 percent in the large area to 44 percent in the small area suburbs. A similar pattern of difference is found among those who report that they are dissatisfied. Curiously, however, the most marked differences are found between the "very satisfied" and the "quite satisfied" categories. Support for change increases among those in the latter category. Even so, those in the suburbs who support change are always a minority.

When residents were asked if they were satisfied with the type of training provided at the high school level in their district, only a very small minority responded negatively. Thus their views on change would have very little impact on the overall proportions favoring change, but it is still significant that the proportion favoring change is consistently higher in each suburban zone among those who are not satisfied with the type of training provided by the high school. The most marked difference is found in the large suburban areas, where the proportion favoring change increases from only 21 percent among those who are satisfied to 49 percent among those who report that they are not satisfied. The same pattern is also found in the other suburban areas, but the size of the difference is less. At any rate, it seems quite clear that support for change among suburban residents is most likely to come from those who are least satisfied with their schools. Since this segment of the population constitutes a very small minority, their effect on the overall response pattern is negligible.

Evaluation of Schools

In Table 8-5, we see how residents in each area would respond to the proposal to establish a single district for the whole area according to how they evaluate their own schools, as compared with those in the opposite part of the metropolitan area. It is apparent that this factor has considerable influence on how suburban residents feel about a change in school district organization. Among the suburban residents, least support for change in each size class is found among those who rate their own schools as better, while most support comes from those who rate the city schools above their own. Those who feel the schools are the same in both areas fall midway between the two extremes in the proportion who would favor change. Actually, it is only among those who feel that schools in the city are better that we find less than a majority opposed to change. There is even less opposition within this group than is reported by city residents generally. And most significant of all, the proportion opposed to change is lower in the large area suburbs than in the other size classes. This is the least amount of opposition that we have found thus far in any subcategory. But here, too, it is noted that the proportion of suburban residents who rate city schools as better than their own is so small that this segment of the population would have little, if any, effect on the overall opposition to change. Yet it is significant that we should find a distinct majority (60 percent) favoring change in an area where opposition to change is so widespread.

In the medium-size area suburbs, and to a much greater extent in the small area suburbs, the proportion of residents who evaluate the city schools as better than their own increases. And here, too, we find the greatest amount of support for change, but even in this category it is only in the small area suburbs that a majority would vote for a single district. It is noteworthy that in neither area has a majority taken a position in opposition to the proposal.

TABLE 8-5

HOW VOTE ON SINGLE DISTRICT BY EVALUATION OF SCHOOLS BY PLACE OF RESIDENCE AND SIZE OF METROPOLITAN AREA

Evaluation of Schools & Size of Metropolitan Area	Central City					Suburban Area				
	Number	Favor %	Oppose %	Other %	Total %	Number	Favor %	Oppose %	Other %	Total %
Large										
Better in city	146	54.1	36.3	9.6	100.0	35	60.0	28.6	11.4	100.0
About the same	141	47.5	36.9	15.6	100.0	189	23.2	68.3	8.5	100.0
Better in suburbs	101	46.5	41.6	11.9	100.0	217	12.0	82.9	5.1	100.0
Don't know	87	33.3	29.9	36.7	100.0	53	32.0	41.5	26.4	100.0
Medium										
Better in city	145	46.2	42.1	11.7	100.0	57	40.4	45.6	14.0	100.0
About the same	142	43.7	35.9	20.4	100.0	193	34.7	54.9	10.4	100.0
Better in suburbs	78	50.0	34.6	15.4	100.0	177	16.9	77.4	5.6	100.0
Don't know	90	38.9	22.2	38.8	100.0	65	33.8	46.2	20.0	100.0
Small										
Better in city	231	51.9	33.3	14.8	100.0	135	53.3	37.0	9.6	100.0
About the same	157	42.7	40.1	17.2	100.0	232	32.8	52.2	15.1	100.0
Better in suburbs	42	31.0	54.8	14.3	100.0	89	21.3	66.3	12.4	100.0
Don't know	58	32.8	34.5	32.7	100.0	36	25.0	41.7	33.4	100.0

There is a close similarity between the proportion of suburban and city residents who would favor setting up a single district, among those who rate city schools as better. This is the only subcategory where central city-suburban differences tend to disappear. That is, regardless of place of residence, when city schools are considered better the proportion favoring change is approximately the same. That is not the case among those who feel that the schools are about the same in both areas. In the central city, these people also tend to favor reorganization in about the same proportion as found earlier, but support for change in the suburbs declines sharply. The decline is most marked in the large area suburbs, where the proportion drops from 60 percent to only 23 percent. The change is also substantial in the small area suburbs, where the proportion who would vote for a single district for the area declines from 53 percent to 33 percent. Thus, support for a single district is not readily forthcoming from residents who rate suburban schools as being about the same in quality as city schools.

Willingness to vote for change seems to be found only among the limited few who feel that the city schools are better. Apparently, if the quality of the schools does not differ, a majority of the suburban residents would prefer to maintain their separate districts apart from the city. And the tendency to remain separate is particularly marked among those who feel that the suburban schools are better than those in the central city. Among the latter, in the large area suburbs, we find that only 12 percent would vote for a single district, while 83 percent would vote against such a proposal. This contrasts sharply with the 60 percent favorable vote and 29 percent opposed among those who feel that city schools are better. The important point here, as far as the probable overall vote is concerned, is that there are six times as many who rate the suburban schools as better than the number who feel that the central city schools are better. And since it is the former who are most likely to oppose change, this, in large part, establishes the pattern of the overall vote. Even in the small area suburbs, where opposition to change is least, a substantial majority of those who feel that suburban schools are better would vote against a single district. We also find a disproportionately high negative vote among those who feel that the schools are about the same in both areas.

How residents evaluate the schools in different parts of the metropolitan area does not appear to have any consistent influence on how central city residents would vote on a proposal for change, but it is a highly significant factor among suburban residents. And the importance of this factor is evident in each size class. In all of the suburban areas, a sizable majority of the residents rate their own schools above or at least equal to those in the central city. And it is among such residents that the opposition to change in school district organization is most evident. This clearly is one of the important factors that accounts for resistance to change. The concern over quality of school is suggested by the high proportion of residents who would vote for change, among those who rate the city schools above the schools in their own area. At any rate, resistance to change is substantially reduced if suburban residents feel that the city schools are better than those in their own area. Perhaps they see in reorganization an opportunity to upgrade their schools, whereas those who predominantly oppose a single district see no comparable increase in the quality of schools that would obtain in the enlarged district. Consequently, they favor maintaining the status quo. Change under even the best of conditions is likely to be resisted, but resistance increases when no apparent advantages are expected to accompany the change. And this seems to be the general consensus among suburban residents, since most already feel that their schools are as good as or even better than those in the city. The impact of this perception is apparent in the data presented in Table 8-6.

Concern over the quality of the schools is a factor of major importance in how residents in all areas would vote on a proposal for change in organizational structure. In each metropolitan area, regardless of size, and in central cities as well as suburban areas, most support for change comes from that segment of the population who feel that a single district would produce better schools than the present organizational structure. Central city and suburban differences virtually disappear among those who feel that schools would become better under a single system. Equally important is the general lack of variation by size of metropolitan area. In all areas, 70 percent or more would vote in favor of change. And the proportion of suburban residents sharing this view who would vote against such a proposal ranges from only 21 percent in the small to 24 percent in the large area suburbs. This is clearly the least opposition that has been found in any subcategory. In the city the proportion opposed is even less. It must be noted here that while we find strong support for reorganization, particularly among suburban residents,

TABLE 8-6

HOW VOTE ON SINGLE DISTRICT BY WHAT WOULD HAPPEN TO QUALITY OF SCHOOLS UNDER A SINGLE SYSTEM BY PLACE OF RESIDENCE AND SIZE OF METROPOLITAN AREA

Change in Quality in Schools & Size of Metropolitan Area	Central City					Suburban Area				
	Number	Favor	Oppose	Other	Total	Number	Favor	Oppose	Other	Total
		%	%	%	%		%	%	%	%
Large										
Become better	149	73.8	18.8	7.4	100.0	59	71.2	23.7	5.1	100.0
Remain about same	152	53.9	32.3	13.8	100.0	148	35.1	54.7	10.2	100.0
Not quite as good	83	14.5	80.7	4.8	100.0	240	2.5	95.4	2.1	100.0
Don't know	80	16.3	31.3	52.4	100.0	48	18.7	35.4	45.8	100.0
Medium										
Become better	132	81.1	11.4	7.6	100.0	71	70.4	23.9	5.6	100.0
Remain about same	160	41.9	35.0	23.2	100.0	177	41.8	49.2	9.0	100.0
Not quite as good	88	13.6	78.4	8.0	100.0	195	4.6	87.2	8.2	100.0
Don't know	70	22.9	22.9	54.3	100.0	46	19.6	47.8	32.6	100.0
Small										
Become better	110	70.9	21.8	7.3	100.0	106	71.7	20.8	7.6	100.0
Remain about same	207	45.4	39.1	15.4	100.0	212	34.0	48.6	17.5	100.0
Not quite as good	92	28.3	62.0	9.8	100.0	112	14.3	83.0	2.7	100.0
Don't know	66	24.2	25.8	50.0	100.0	61	19.7	44.3	36.0	100.0

in this category, only a small minority of the residents share the view that schools would be better under a single district. Nevertheless, it is of interest to note that under such conditions a distinct majority of the residents in all areas would vote in favor of change. This is the only condition in which we have found a majority in favor of change in all areas.[1]

Support for change declines markedly in all areas among those who feel that schools would remain largely the same under a single system. Even in this category, size of metropolitan area does not appear to be important, in that the proportion favoring change and the proportion opposed tends to be nearly the same in each size class. The proportion who would vote for change in the large suburbs decreases from 70 percent among those who feel that the schools would become better to only 35 percent among those who feel that the schools would remain about the same, and to less than 3 percent among those who feel that the quality of schools would decline under a single system for the whole area. Conversely, opposition to change ranges from 24 percent to 95 percent, according to what residents think would happen to the quality of schools if reorganization occurred. A very similar pattern is found in the other suburban areas also, as well as in the central cities.

The point to be emphasized here is the very large proportion of residents, particularly among those in the suburbs, who feel that reorganization of school districts would not improve the quality of their schools. Actually, more than half of those in the large suburbs hold the opinion that the quality of schools would decline. And as already noted, less than 3 percent of the residents in this category would vote for change, while more than 95 percent reported that they would vote against it.[2]

School Expenditures

Views regarding change also vary by how residents feel about the amount that is being spent on education in their area. The highest

---

[1] This does not make the problem of bringing about change any easier. It merely focuses on one factor that might be used to bring about a favorable vote. How one could convince a population that schools would be better under a single system remains a difficult question.

[2] A fuller discussion of what residents think would happen to the quality of schools under a single district for the whole area has been presented in Chapter 7.

proportion favoring change, in all areas, is found among those who feel that not enough is being spent on education in their area. Most opposition, particularly in the suburbs, is reported by those who feel that about the right amount is being spent in their areas. But even within this category, support for change increases substantially as size of area declines, and the proportion opposed increases directly by size of area. Thus while only slightly more than half of those in the small area suburbs who feel that the right amount is being spent on education would vote against reorganization of school districts, this increases to three-fourths in the large area suburbs. For the same category of response, no such comparable difference is found among central city residents by size of area. While there is no consistent pattern of difference in any of the response categories by size of central city, we do find, even among central city residents, that the proportion favoring change is highest among those who feel that not enough is being spent on education in their area. On the other hand, least support comes from that segment of the city population who feel that too much is being spent.

A very distinct and consistent pattern of difference in the proportion who favor change is found among suburban residents, according to how they feel about the amount that is being spent on education in their areas. And within each category, the proportion favoring change increases as size of metropolitan area declines. Conversely, the proportion who would vote against change increases consistently as size of area increases. For example, among residents who feel that too much is being spent, the proportion who would vote against a proposed reorganization increases from 53 percent in the small area suburbs to 69 percent in the large area suburbs. Among those who feel the right amount is being spent, the comparable proportions opposed to change are 52 percent and 75 percent, respectively. And even in the category where resistance to change is least—that is, among those who feel that not enough is being spent—the proportion opposed ranges from 47 percent in the small to 57 percent in the large area suburbs. Thus while a substantial number of the suburban residents are opposed to change, we nonetheless note that how they feel about the amount spent on education is an important factor influencing their reaction to a proposed reorganization. Least opposition tends to come from those who feel that not enough is being spent.

And it is noteworthy that in this segment of the population, less than a majority are opposed to change in both the medium-sized and small area suburbs. But in the other response categories, from slightly more than one-half to three-fourths of the residents would vote against change.

The most significant observation here is the very low proportion of residents favoring change among those who feel that about the right amount is being spent on education. But here too, the proportion varies by size of suburbs, ranging from only 19 percent in the large area to 34 percent in the small area. The lack of support for change in this group takes on added significance when it is noted that in all areas this group constitutes a substantial majority of the total population. Thus, how they react to change largely determines how the total population would respond. For example, in the large area suburbs, nearly 70 percent report that the right amount is being spent, and three-fourths of these are opposed to change. The opposition in this group alone would be sufficient in size to constitute a majority of the total population. Thus, even if all others in the community favored change, which of course they do not, there would still be a majority opposed. It is this "contented" majority in all of the suburban areas that accounts for a disproportionate amount of the resistance to change that is found in the suburbs.

Expected Change in Taxes

The crucial importance of the cost factor is even more strikingly evident from the data presented in Table 8-7. Without exception, in all zones, central city or suburban, least support for change is found among those who feel that reorganization would result in increased taxes. In all size classes, central city residents are more likely to favor change than those in the suburbs, but the amount of support for change is substantially less than is found among those who feel that taxes would either remain largely the same or decrease. Also, there seems to be little variation in the proportion favoring change by central city size, but here too we find increased support for change in the suburbs as size of area declines. However, even in the small area suburbs where we find the highest proportion in favor of reorganization, support for change is 30

TABLE 8-7

HOW VOTE ON SINGLE DISTRICT BY WHAT WOULD HAPPEN TO TAXES UNDER A SINGLE SYSTEM BY PLACE OF RESIDENCE AND SIZE OF METROPOLITAN AREA

Change in Taxes and Size of Metropolitan Area	Central City					Suburban Area				
	Number	Favor %	Oppose %	Other %	Total %	Number	Favor %	Oppose %	Other %	Total %
Large										
Increase	187	34.8	57.2	8.0	100.0	250	10.8	85.6	3.6	100.0
No change	106	58.4	27.4	14.1	100.0	108	25.9	63.0	11.1	100.0
Decrease	96	81.2	9.4	9.4	100.0	88	58.0	35.2	6.8	100.0
Don't know	78	17.9	32.1	50.0	100.0	49	6.1	57.1	36.7	100.0
No answer	10	30.0	30.0	40.0	100.0	—	—	—	—	—
Medium										
Increase	168	36.3	55.4	8.3	100.0	177	11.9	82.5	5.6	100.0
No change	134	46.3	30.6	23.1	100.0	172	37.8	51.7	10.5	100.0
Decrease	83	75.9	16.9	7.2	100.0	88	56.8	37.5	5.7	100.0
Don't know	62	22.6	11.3	66.1	100.0	56	12.5	55.4	32.1	100.0
No answer	10	30.0	40.0	30.0	100.0	—	—	—	—	—
Small										
Increase	202	39.6	49.5	10.9	100.0	216	25.0	63.0	12.0	100.0
No change	144	55.6	28.5	16.0	100.0	118	39.8	44.9	15.3	100.0
Decrease	62	66.1	29.0	4.8	100.0	91	64.8	27.5	7.7	100.0
Don't know	68	19.1	29.4	51.5	100.0	57	22.8	43.9	33.3	100.0
No answer	12	41.7	33.3	25.0	100.0	10	30.0	60.0	10.0	100.0

percent less among those who would expect a tax increase under
a single system than is found for the total population. Whereas 36
percent of the total favor change, this declines to 25 percent among
those who feel that taxes would increase. The relative decline is
even more marked in the large area suburbs, where the decrease
is from 22 percent to only 11 percent. In the central cities also,
we find substantially fewer people willing to accept change if they
expect a tax increase to follow. The importance of the cost factor
is evident in all areas.

Of particular significance is the very high proportion of residents in all areas who would favor change when they expect taxes
to decrease under a single system. For example, in the central cities
the proportion favoring change ranges from a low of 66 percent
in the small to a high of 81 percent in the large metropolitan areas.
Even in the suburbs, a majority favors change in each size class,
but the pattern of increase in relationship to size is just the opposite of the one noted for cities. In the suburbs, most support for
a single district, even among those who think that taxes would
decrease, continues to be found in the small areas. In the latter
areas, if residents expect taxes to decline following reorganization,
one-third or less oppose change; but if they expect taxes to increase, as many as 86 percent would vote against such a proposal.
And this widespread opposition occurs in the large area suburbs
also. And it is noted that more than half of the residents in the
large area suburbs hold the view that taxes would increase if a
single district were established for the whole area. Even in the
small area suburbs, where we consistently find the least overall
resistance to change, nearly two-thirds of those who would expect
higher taxes to result would vote against reorganization. This exceeds the average for the total population by more than 25 percent, and is nearly two and one-half times larger than the proportion who are opposed among those who would expect lower
taxes. Very similar differences are found in both the large and
medium-sized area suburbs as well as in the central cities in each
size class.

A further observation of interest is the reaction of the group
that doesn't know what to expect regarding taxes as a result of
change. Generally speaking, the proportion favoring change is
lower in this category than in any other. This leads us to conclude

that when people do not know what would happen to taxes under a reorganization plan, they are not likely to vote in favor of change. Of equal importance, however, is that many of these people have not, at this point, taken a firm position in opposition. It is highly significant that a very large proportion report that they "don't know" how they would vote on such a proposal. More than half respond in that manner in the central cities, and more than one-third do so in the suburbs. In short, regardless of place of residence within the metropolitan area, most resistance to change is found among those who hold the view that taxes would increase under a single system. On the other hand, most support for change is expressed by those who think that taxes would decrease. Among the latter, even a majority of the suburban residents would vote in favor of change. Clearly it is in this group that resistance to change tends to be at a minimum.

Level of Government Responsible for Support of Schools

In all areas, as already noted, there is considerable variation among residents as to what level of government should bear the primary responsibility for providing funds to cover the costs of operations of the schools. This issue was discussed in Chapter 6. At this point we are concerned with how views regarding the level of government that should provide the primary support for the schools influence how residents respond to the proposed reorganization of school districts. These data are presented in Table 8-8.

Support for the reorganization of districts varies markedly and consistently, according to who the residents feel should be primarily responsible for the costs of operation.[3] For the most part, residents in all areas disproportionately feel that support of the schools is largely the responsibility of the residents living within the school district. And this is the segment of the population, particularly in the suburbs, that is most likely to oppose change. In each of the suburban zones, there is more resistance to change in this group than in any other. Also we find a consistent and direct variation in the proportion of suburban residents opposed to change by size of metropolitan area. The range is from 60 per-

---

[3] A very similar distribution was found when the question pertained to school buildings. Thus the latter is excluded from the present discussion.

TABLE 8-8

HOW VOTE ON SINGLE DISTRICT BY WHO SHOULD BE PRIMARILY RESPONSIBLE FOR COST OF OPERATION
BY PLACE OF RESIDENCE AND SIZE OF METROPOLITAN AREA

Responsibility for Cost of Operation & Size of Metropolitan Area	Central City					Suburban Area				
	Number	Favor	Oppose	Other	Total	Number	Favor	Oppose	Other	Total
		%	%	%	%		%	%	%	%
Large										
Residents in district	141	41.8	46.8	11.3	100.0	213	15.0	81.7	3.3	100.0
County government	103	51.5	37.9	10.7	100.0	52	21.2	67.3	11.5	100.0
State government	131	52.7	30.5	16.8	100.0	149	27.5	65.1	7.3	100.0
Federal government	51	58.8	25.5	15.7	100.0	43	44.2	37.2	18.6	100.0
Don't know	39	20.5	25.6	53.8	100.0	26	11.5	38.5	50.0	100.0
No answer	12	25.0	41.7	33.3	100.0	12	25.0	75.0	—	100.0
Medium										
Residents in district	144	50.0	34.0	16.0	100.0	232	22.0	69.8	8.2	100.0
County government	67	41.8	37.3	20.9	100.0	63	39.7	57.1	3.2	100.0
State government	148	47.3	41.2	11.5	100.0	122	35.2	54.9	9.8	100.0
Federal government	42	45.2	28.6	26.2	100.0	25	48.0	32.0	20.0	100.0
Don't know	46	23.9	17.4	58.7	100.0	40	20.0	50.0	30.0	100.0
No answer	10	30.0	40.0	30.0	100.0	11	36.4	54.5	9.1	100.0
Small										
Residents in district	180	45.6	38.3	16.1	100.0	186	27.4	59.7	12.9	100.0
County government	66	43.9	45.5	10.6	100.0	100	37.0	53.0	10.0	100.0
State government	141	54.6	38.3	7.1	100.0	122	47.5	40.2	12.3	100.0
Federal government	43	41.9	39.5	18.6	100.0	43	41.9	44.2	13.9	100.0
Don't know	41	19.5	19.5	60.9	100.0	30	30.0	23.3	46.7	100.0
No answer	17	29.4	29.4	41.1	100.0	11	27.3	54.5	18.2	100.0

cent in the small to 82 percent in the large area suburbs. On the other hand, least resistance to change is found among those who feel that the federal government, and to a much lesser degree the state government, should assume the primary responsibility for the costs of operations of the schools. The latter are very much in favor of setting up a single district for the whole area.

There appears to be a very definite relationship between willingness to accept local responsibility and wanting local control; those who prefer to give up local responsibility and turn to either the state, and more specifically to the federal government, for funds to run their schools, are also much more willing to give up local control. This finds expression in their willingness to vote in favor of setting up a single district for the combined central city and suburban areas. Here too we find that if people are uncertain as to who should be primarily responsible for the schools, they have a marked tendency not to favor change. This is due mainly to the very high proportion who do not know how they would vote on such a proposal.

It is particularly noteworthy that least resistance to change is found among the small minority of residents who feel that the federal government should be primarily responsible for providing funds for the local schools. In none of the suburbs is there a majority in this category who would vote against a proposal to set up a single district. In short, the larger the unit of government to which residents are willing to turn for the support of their schools, the more likely it is that they will not resist the reorganization of school districts on an area-wide basis. But in the suburban areas in particular, most residents view the support of schools as a local responsibility and prefer to remain autonomous units.

Pursuing the issue of support of the schools further and in more general terms, we continue to find that those who are willing to receive any aid whatsoever from the federal government, regardless of place of residence or size of metropolitan area, are more likely to favor change than those who are opposed to such aid. In response to the general question: "Would you be in favor of the federal government providing funds to help cover the costs of operations for local schools?" a majority of residents in all areas reported that they would be in favor of such aid. This question is quite different from the preceding one, which focused only on "primary" responsibility. Here we are concerned with the very general issue of whether the federal government should be involved in any way in the support of the local schools. While most residents feel that schools are largely a local responsibility, it is evident from the data presented in Table 8-9 that a majority, in all areas, are quite willing to accept federal aid as a supplement to their own efforts. Here too, we find that most resistance to change is expressed by those who would object to the federal government providing aid to the local districts, while those favoring federal aid are the ones most likely to support reorganization. The frequency of opposition, as well as support for change, varies by size of suburban area, but remains at about the same level in each of the city areas regardless of size. In the suburban areas, among those who are against federal aid, the proportion opposed to reorganization ranges from 57 percent in the small to 80 percent in the large area suburbs. Approximately the same range and the same pattern of difference, by size of area, is also found among those favoring federal aid, but the proportion opposed to change is substantially lower.

Viewed somewhat differently, we find that in the large area suburbs, the proportion who would vote in favor of change is nearly 60 percent higher among those who favor federal aid, as compared with those who are against such aid. In the medium-sized area suburbs, the proportionate difference is even larger. Those favoring federal aid are more than twice as likely to favor reorganization of school districts. While the same pattern is found in the small area suburbs, where support for change generally is more frequent, the size of the difference is substantially less.

Although most suburban residents are opposed to reorganization of school districts, most opposition comes from that segment of the population that would be opposed to local districts receiving any form of aid from the federal government. However, it is noteworthy that even among residents who would accept federal assistance, a majority, except in the small area suburbs, are not willing to accept a proposal to set up a single district for the whole area. While this group is much more receptive to change than others, the predominant view is still against a single district. Thus, while views regarding federal aid are important, they are of less significance as obstacles to change than either place of residence or size of suburban area.

TABLE 8-9

HOW VOTE ON SINGLE SCHOOL DISTRICT BY ATTITUDE TOWARD FEDERAL AID FOR OPERATIONS
BY PLACE OF RESIDENCE AND SIZE OF METROPOLITAN AREA

Favor Federal Aid for Operations & Size of Metropolitan Area	Central City						Suburban Area					
	Number	Favor	Oppose	Other	Total		Number	Favor	Oppose	Other	Total	
		%	%	%	%			%	%	%	%	
Large												
Yes	328	50.9	34.7	14.3	100.0		293	26.3	64.1	9.5	100.0	
No	113	40.7	46.0	13.3	100.0		174	16.7	79.9	3.5	100.0	
Don't know	31	29.0	22.6	48.4	100.0		28	10.7	50.0	39.3	100.0	
Medium												
Yes	291	46.4	34.0	19.6	100.0		294	37.4	53.7	8.8	100.0	
No	125	46.4	44.8	8.8	100.0		170	17.6	74.7	7.7	100.0	
Don't know	36	27.8	8.3	63.9	100.0		27	7.4	51.9	40.7	100.0	
Small												
Yes	286	48.2	36.0	15.7	100.0		269	39.4	47.2	13.3	100.0	
No	160	45.0	43.8	11.3	100.0		183	34.4	57.4	8.2	100.0	
Don't know	39	23.1	23.1	53.8	100.0		38	18.4	34.3	47.3	100.0	

Citizen Influence on School Expenditures

The final topic to be considered in this chapter as a factor in resistance to change pertains to the attitudes residents have concerning what local citizens can do about how school funds are spent in their districts. As noted earlier, suburban residents tend to feel that the ordinary citizen can do quite a bit about how school funds are used. In all suburban zones, a majority of the residents hold this view, whereas in the cities the most frequent expression is that the ordinary citizen "can't do much" about how school money is spent. It may be the belief that the ordinary citizen does have some control over the schools that accounts for the greater amount of resistance to change in the suburbs. At any rate, we would expect resistance to change to be more frequent among those who feel that the ordinary citizen does have control over the use of school funds, since these people may feel that this "control" would be largely lost in an area-wide district.

The overall impression that one gains from an inspection of these data is that this factor does contribute to resistance to change. But the relationship between resistance to change and views regarding the role of ordinary citizens is directly opposite in the central city and suburban zones. Whereas in the central cities those who feel that the citizen "can't do much" about how school money is spent are the ones least likely to favor change, in the suburbs this is the group that is most likely to vote in support of a proposal to set up a single district for the whole area. These findings represent fundamentally different ways of viewing some of the consequences of size of district.

Among central city residents, those who feel that the citizen does not "control" object to a larger district. One can only assume that part of this opposition to a single district is based on the expectation that in an even larger district the ordinary citizen would be even less able to have a say about how funds are spent. Consequently, they oppose change. Another segment of the population, which is only slightly smaller in size, feels that even in a large district the citizen can do quite a bit about how school funds are used, and they likely feel that the same "control" would be possible in an even larger district. Size of district is apparently not a deterrent for this group; at least they are more willing to accept change. But quite the opposite is the case in the suburbs. In the latter it is those who think that the ordinary citizen has already lost control over the schools who are most likely to favor change, and the least likely to be opposed to reorganization. Even here the size of the difference is not large, but the point worthy of note is the consistency of the pattern.

In all size classes, those who feel that the ordinary citizen can do quite a bit about how school funds are spent are the ones most likely to oppose setting up a larger area-wide district. Apparently, among suburban residents, control by the ordinary citizen is important, and they resist change because they feel that under the present system the ordinary citizen has that control. But, regardless of their views on what the ordinary citizen can or cannot do, a substantial majority of the suburban residents are opposed to an area-wide district. However, as already observed many times, opposition to change decreases as size of area declines. Size of area clearly accounts for more variations in the proportion opposed to change than do different views concerning the role of ordinary citizens. But the really crucial point, as observed throughout the study, is the different view regarding reorganization that is expressed by the residents according to where they live within the metropolitan community. In all subcategories, suburban residents persist in their opposition to setting up an area-wide district. Central city residents do not generally share this view. In short, it would seem that a proposal for change would likely be approved by city residents. At any rate, the chances would appear to be quite favorable. But in the suburbs, it would meet with almost certain defeat.

9

Community Involvement and Resistance to Change

ONE WOULD EXPECT THAT views regarding reorganization would vary according to the level of involvement of the population in school-related activities and community affairs. Involvement, however, is not easily measured, for its forms are manifold. In the present discussion, the indices of involvement center around knowledge of and participation in school-related activities, membership in formal organizations, informal contacts with friends and neighbors, community "ideological" orientation, and territorial scope of participation in the everyday life of the metropolitan community. Thus we are concerned here with the basic question as to what extent resistance to change is a function of the level of involvement of the residents in various aspects of local community life.

Knowledge of Schools

As has been noted earlier, only a small minority of the residents in any of the areas have children who are currently attending high school. Granting the uncertainties inherent in small numbers, we nonetheless find for this group that limited involvement, to the extent of knowing the name of the principal, is associated with resistance to change among suburban residents but with acceptance of change in the central cities.

In the suburbs, of those who have children in high school. the proportion opposed to reorganization is highest among those who at least know the name of the principal. Stated conversely, except in the medium-sized areas, this is the group that is least likely to favor change. In the large area suburbs, while 17 percent of those who know the principal favor change, the proportion increases to 29 percent among those who do not know the name of the principal. In the small area suburbs, the proportions who would favor reorganization are 33 percent and 50 percent, respectively. This index of knowledge proves to be particularly important in the suburbs of small areas, where the proportion opposed to change ranges from 63 percent among those who know the name of the principal to only 38 percent among those who do not. These data are shown in Table 9-1.

The importance of size of area is again evident. The proportion favoring change in the suburbs increases inversely with size, while the proportion opposed tends to decline. Just the opposite pattern is observed among central city residents. Among the latter, most support for change seems to come from the segment of the population that knows the high school principal, but even within this group support for reorganization declines directly by size of central city. Thus most support for change is found in the large central cities. On the other hand, we find that opposition to change among those who know the name of the high school principal increases as size of central city declines; while only 30 percent of those who know the name of the principal oppose change in the large central cities, opposition increases to 48 percent in the small central cities. But among those who do not know the principal, opposition declines by size of area. And the size of the difference is considerable, ranging from 46 percent in the large to only 32 percent in the small area central cities.

Regardless of the level of knowledge expressed by those who have children in high school, central city residents are much more likely than suburban residents to favor change. The only exception occurs in the small metropolitan areas, where central city-suburban differences disappear among those who do not know the name of the high school principal. It may well be that many of the small area suburban residents must send their children outside of their districts to attend high school. Consequently they have less knowledge of the high school officials, and they tend to favor reorganiza-

TABLE 9-1

HOW VOTE ON SINGLE SCHOOL DISTRICT BY KNOWLEDGE OF HIGH SCHOOL
AND ELEMENTARY SCHOOL PRINCIPAL* BY PLACE OF RESIDENCE
AND SIZE OF METROPOLITAN AREA

School Level and Place of Residence	Large		Medium		Small	
	Know	Not Know	Know	Not Know	Know	Not Know
High School*						
Central City						
Total Number	47	22	48	20	59	19
	%	%	%	%	%	%
Favor	61.7	40.9	50.0	40.0	44.1	47.4
Oppose	29.8	45.5	33.3	40.0	47.5	31.6
Other**	8.5	13.6	16.7	20.0	8.5	21.1
Total	100.0	100.0	100.0	100.0	100.0	100.0
Suburban						
Total Number	72	17	63	21	48	34
	%	%	%	%	%	%
Favor	16.7	29.4	28.6	28.6	33.3	50.0
Oppose	73.6	70.6	60.3	52.4	62.5	38.2
Other	9.7	—	11.1	19.0	4.2	11.8
Total	100.0	100.0	100.0	100.0	100.0	100.0
Elementary School*						
Central City						
Total Number	92	29	101	26	141	39
	%	%	%	%	%	%
Favor	51.1	48.3	51.5	57.7	48.9	59.0
Oppose	38.0	37.9	35.6	19.2	39.0	23.1
Other	10.8	13.8	12.9	23.1	12.0	17.9
Total	100.0	100.0	100.0	100.0	100.0	100.0
Suburban						
Total Number	142	31	171	43	186	49
	%	%	%	%	%	%
Favor	19.7	35.5	24.6	32.6	36.0	28.6
Oppose	74.6	58.1	66.1	53.5	54.3	57.1
Other	5.6	6.5	9.4	14.0	9.7	14.3
Total	100.0	100.0	100.0	100.0	100.0	100.0

* Data limited only to those who have children attending school at each grade level.
** Undecided, don't know, and no answer.

tion, perhaps so that they would have a high school of their own. At any rate, it is in this category that we find the least suburban opposition to change. In the suburbs generally, resistance to change varies directly by level of involvement in the high schools.

When we look at the families who have children in elementary school, we again find that the more knowledgeable suburban residents are the ones most likely to be opposed to change and the least likely to favor reorganization. At the elementary school level also, the proportion favoring change, among those who know the name of the principal, increases inversely by size of area; that is, least support for change is found in the large area suburbs. It is in these areas that we find most opposition to reorganization, as is shown in the lower portion of Table 9-1. While only 20 percent would favor change, 75 percent report that they would be opposed to it. But among those who do not know the name of the elementary school principal, the proportion favoring change nearly doubles —that is, 36 percent favor, while the proportion opposed declines to 58 percent. Although opposition is substantially reduced, it is still expressed by a clear majority. Thus even among those who are not sufficiently involved so as to know the name of the principal of the elementary school their children attend, a majority are opposed to any change in the organization of local school districts. No doubt a common justification for their opposition would be that they want to remain close to their schools. In the cities, opposition to change, in any of the knowledge categories or size classes, never reaches as high as 40 percent. That is, only a minority would oppose change, whereas in the suburbs, in all knowledge categories and size classes, a clear majority of the residents who have children in either the elementary or high school report that they would vote against a single district. And in most central cities, as well as suburban areas, those most involved in the schools are the ones most likely to resist change.

Still another rough index of level of knowledge of the schools pertains to whether or not the residents know anyone who is currently a member of the local school board. As is readily evident from the data presented in Table 9-2, this is another variable, which no doubt is a part of a syndrome, that is of some importance in accounting for resistance to change. The differences in the proportions opposed to change by level of knowledge are sizable

TABLE 9-2

HOW VOTE ON SINGLE SCHOOL DISTRICT BY KNOW ANYONE ON SCHOOL BOARD
BY PLACE OF RESIDENCE AND SIZE OF METROPOLITAN AREA

Know School Board Member & Size of Metropolitan Area	Central City					Suburban Area				
	Number	Favor	Oppose	Other	Total	Number	Favor	Oppose	Other	Total
		%	%	%	%		%	%	%	%
Large										
Yes	63	60.3	31.7	7.9	100.0	117	20.5	71.8	7.7	100.0
No	412	44.7	36.9	18.4	100.0	376	22.6	68.3	9.0	100.0
Medium										
Yes	69	55.1	23.2	21.7	100.0	156	18.6	76.9	4.5	100.0
No	384	42.7	36.7	20.5	100.0	336	33.9	53.0	13.1	100.0
Small										
Yes	112	49.1	39.3	11.6	100.0	201	31.8	59.2	9.0	100.0
No	375	43.7	36.8	19.5	100.0	288	38.9	42.7	18.4	100.0

and appear in all size classes. But equally important is the observation that this variable affects central city and suburban residents differently. Whereas in the central city, those who know some member of the board are the ones most likely to favor change, in the suburbs it is this group that is least likely to favor reorganization. Among suburban residents, most opposition comes from those who know some member of the board. This is no doubt partly a social class phenomenon, since those in the higher social status positions would more likely know members of the board and, as noted earlier, this group disproportionately opposes change. But there is likely more than social class involved. Knowing school board members is perhaps symptomatic of being a part of an on-going system. Suburban residents may enjoy and cherish being in a system where they know persons who hold public office, and they apparently do not wish to sacrifice this position by joining with the city in a single school district. Consequently, they are opposed to change. On the other hand, suburban residents who do not know any board member are much more willing to set up a larger district. Certainly a larger district would not deprive them of any direct access to the school board, since they do not now have such access.

Central city residents are much less likely to know a member of the board, but among those who do we find that a high proportion would favor reorganization of school districts on an area-wide basis. It may well be that these people feel that they could maintain contact with members of the board regardless of the size of the district. Or it may be that they do not value such contacts and would not resist change in order to maintain such a relationship with the school board. Regardless of the motivations involved, central city residents who have knowledge of the school board are willing to handle school problems on an area-wide basis, whereas suburban residents with such contacts want to maintain the status quo. Whether residents know any member of the board or not, least resistance to change is found in the central cities and the small area suburbs. Only a minority of the central city residents express opposition to change, but in the suburbs a clear majority oppose reorganization. The only exception is found in the small area suburbs among those who do not know any member of the board. But even within this category, more than two out of five are opposed to change and one other "does not know" how he would vote on such an issue. Here too, we find that resistance to change among suburban residents tends to decline by size of area. The "don't know" responses, at least among those who do not know any members of the board, increases consistently as size of area declines, which means that there is a larger uncommitted population in the small than in the large metropolitan areas.

Still another way to view knowledge of the schools is to combine the responses to several questions into a single score, as we have done in Chapter 3. At this point we wish to know how views regarding change are related to these overall knowledge scores. For analytical purposes we have divided the scores into four levels, as shown in Table 9-3. The concentration of scores at the low end of the range is noteworthy.

Focusing first on the central cities, we find, in each size class, that as the knowledge of schools scores increases the proportion in favor of reorganization also increases. While the same pattern is found in each class, the range is most pronounced in the large cities. But as is evident in the other central cities also, this is largely due to the marked relationship between level of knowledge of the school and the proportion who do not know how they would vote on such a proposal. Thus, for example, among those in the large cities who have a low knowledge score, some 22 percent do not know how they would vote, but this declines to only 3 percent among the small number who have high scores. In the same knowledge categories for the same areas, the proportion favoring change increases from 42 percent to 77 percent. Comparable differences are also found in both the medium-sized and small area cities. In other words, the greater the knowledge the more clearly formed is the opinion. It is noteworthy that while the proportion favoring change increases directly as level of knowledge of the schools increases, there is no comparable observed pattern in the proportion who are opposed to change. Quite the contrary, among central city residents approximately one-third express opposition to the proposed reorganization of districts, regardless of their level of knowledge of the schools. Consistently we find that those with high knowledge scores disproportionately favor change, whereas those with low scores do not know how they would vote. But even among the latter, approximately two out

TABLE 9-3

HOW VOTE ON SINGLE SCHOOL DISTRICT BY KNOWLEDGE OF SCHOOL SCALE SCORES
BY PLACE OF RESIDENCE AND SIZE OF METROPOLITAN AREA

Size of Metropolitan Area and Knowledge Scale Scores	Central City					Suburban Area				
	Number	Favor	Oppose	Other	Total	Number	Favor	Oppose	Other	Total
		%	%	%	%		%	%	%	%
Large										
4–5 High	31	77.4	19.4	3.2	100.0	54	13.0	87.0	—	100.0
2–3	44	59.1	31.8	9.1	100.0	61	23.0	70.5	6.6	100.0
1	144	43.7	42.4	13.9	100.0	90	24.4	67.8	7.8	100.0
0 Low	258	42.2	35.7	22.1	100.0	290	22.8	65.5	11.7	100.0
Medium										
4–5 High	73	52.1	35.6	12.4	100.0	88	21.6	71.6	6.8	100.0
2–3	55	45.5	36.4	18.2	100.0	62	30.6	64.5	4.8	100.0
1	79	48.1	39.2	12.7	100.0	91	30.8	61.5	7.7	100.0
0 Low	252	40.5	32.5	27.0	100.0	252	30.6	55.6	13.9	100.0
Small										
4–5 High	93	49.5	40.9	9.7	100.0	69	31.9	63.8	4.3	100.0
2–3	53	52.8	35.8	11.3	100.0	73	31.5	60.3	8.2	100.0
1	117	51.3	35.9	12.8	100.0	131	36.6	51.9	11.4	100.0
0 Low	225	37.8	37.3	24.9	100.0	219	37.9	40.6	21.5	100.0

of five would vote in favor of such a proposal. Thus, regardless of the level of knowledge of the schools, there is substantial support for change among city residents.

Level of knowledge of the schools plays quite a different role among suburban residents. Least support for change is found among those in the highest score category, but little variation is found among the other knowledge scores. This holds in each size class. But the significant point here is the close association between knowledge of schools and the proportion opposed to change. In each size class, the proportion who would vote against reorganization increases consistently and directly with level of knowledge of the schools. For example, in the large suburbs the proportion opposed to change ranges from a low of 66 percent among those with a low score to a high of 87 percent among those in the highest score category.

A closer inspection of the data in Table 9-3 again emphasizes the importance of size of metropolitan area in respect to the issue of reorganization of school districts. Within each level of knowledge category, the proportion opposed to change decreases as size of area declines. Among residents with low scores, the proportion who would vote against reorganization ranges from a high of 66 percent in the large to a low of 41 percent in the small area suburbs. In the high score category, the proportion opposed to change ranges from 87 percent to 64 percent, respectively. The same decline by size is also observed among the low medium and medium scores. Thus within each size class, resistance to change among suburban residents varies by their level of knowledge of the schools, but over and above this we find that resistance varies directly by size of area.

In short, in the city support for change increases directly with knowledge of the schools; but in the suburban areas, the more familiar residents are with the schools, the more determined they are to remain separate from the city. At any rate, the more knowledgeable persons clearly take the position that they would vote against a proposal to set up a single district for the whole area. Among city residents, size of area appears unimportant; but in the suburbs, as size of area increases, so does the amount of opposition to change. And this holds regardless of level of knowledge of the schools.

Participation in School-Related Activities

We turn now to an appraisal of the role of participation in school-related activities in accounting for resistance to change. We would expect to find most opposition, at least in the suburbs, among those who are active. This is based on the assumption that such persons would already have established themselves in an ongoing system, and would not want to jeopardize their position by changing the existing system. We have already seen that knowledge of the schools is associated with opposition among suburban residents. Looking first at the relationship between attendance at meetings and views regarding change, we find the expected pattern in the suburbs; but again, just the opposite pattern in the central cities. These data are shown in Table 9-4. Among central city residents, those who attend school board and PTA meetings are more likely to support change than the remaining portion of the population. The persistence of the pattern in each size class is worthy of note. In all areas, a majority of the city residents who attend such meetings report that they would vote in favor of a single district for the whole area. On the other hand, in none of the central cities do we find a majority in favor of change among those who have not attended such meetings. It should be noted that the latter includes all of the families who do not have children in school and who would thus not have any immediate contact with the schools. While the non-attenders are less likely to favor change, this does not mean that they have uniformly taken a position in opposition to such a proposal. Rather, such persons are found disproportionately among those who do not know how they would vote.[1]

Quite a different association is found in the suburbs. Not only is there a somewhat higher attendance rate in the suburbs, but those who are active are less likely than others to favor change. This pattern of difference is found in the suburbs of both large and medium-sized areas, but does not hold in the small area suburbs. In the latter, support for change tends to be slightly higher among those who attend school board meetings, while no differences are found in respect to attendance at PTA meetings.

---

[1] These data suggest that a substantial proportion of the non-active segment of the population would have to be effectively reached in order to carry a favorable vote on this issue, even in the cities.

TABLE 9-4

HOW VOTE ON SINGLE DISTRICT BY ATTEND PTA AND SCHOOL BOARD MEETINGS BY PLACE OF RESIDENCE AND SIZE OF METROPOLITAN AREA

Attend Meetings & Size of Metropolitan Area	Central City					Suburban Area				
	Number	Favor %	Oppose %	Other %	Total %	Number	Favor %	Oppose %	Other %	Total %
Attend PTA Meetings										
Large										
Attend	91	50.5	39.6	9.9	100.0	139	15.8	79.1	5.0	100.0
Never attend	385	45.7	35.6	18.7	100.0	354	24.6	65.0	10.5	100.0
Medium										
Attend	105	50.5	35.2	14.3	100.0	165	25.5	65.5	9.1	100.0
Never attend	338	43.5	34.6	21.9	100.0	327	30.6	58.4	11.0	100.0
Small										
Attend	135	51.9	33.3	14.8	100.0	169	36.7	54.4	8.9	100.0
Never attend	351	42.5	38.7	18.8	100.0	322	35.4	47.2	17.4	100.0
Attend School Board Meetings										
Large										
Attend	17	58.8	23.5	17.6	100.0	41	12.2	78.0	9.8	100.0
Never attend	458	46.3	36.7	17.0	100.0	451	22.8	68.3	8.8	100.0
Medium										
Attend	13	53.8	38.5	7.7	100.0	37	16.2	81.1	2.7	100.0
Never attend	430	44.9	34.6	20.5	100.0	456	30.0	59.0	10.9	100.0
Small										
Attend	25	52.0	32.0	16.0	100.0	49	40.8	51.0	8.2	100.0
Never attend	461	44.7	37.5	17.8	100.0	442	35.1	49.8	15.2	100.0

Most opposition to change in the suburbs comes from those who attend both school board and PTA meetings. This pattern of difference is found in each size class, but the size of the difference is least in the small area suburbs where only slightly more than half of the respondents are opposed to change. In the large area suburbs, the proportion opposed to change among those who attend PTA meetings is more than 20 percent higher than among those who do not attend. In the small area suburbs, the comparable difference is 15 percent. The opposition of those who attend school board meetings exceeds the proportion of others opposed to change by 14 percent in the large area suburbs, but by only 2 percent in the small area suburbs.

With the exception of the small area suburbs, the more active segment of the population is least likely to favor change and is most likely to be opposed to setting up a single school district for the central cities and suburban areas combined. There is, however, a sizable undecided vote, particularly among those who are not active, which tends to increase as size of area declines. That is, not only do we find more support for change in the small area suburbs, but we also find a larger proportion in the "undecided" category, at least among those who are not active in school-related activities. It may well be, as noted earlier, that much of the opposition to change is due to the threat of loss of contact with the schools, if the area were enlarged. Whether that risk is real or not is unimportant, since the consequence of this expectation is increased opposition to change. Persons who participate in these activities in the suburbs may well feel that their opportunities to do so would decrease if the whole area were encompassed within a single district. Consequently they resist change.

The crucial role of participation in school-related activities in fostering resistance to change is even more evident when viewed in terms of a composite score based on the responses to several questions.[2] Here, too, for purposes of presentation we have divided the participation scores into four levels. As is readily evident from the data presented in Table 9-5, a substantial majority of the residents in all areas are found on the low end of the participation scale. It is also evident that participation in school-related activities exerts considerable influence on how residents view the proposal

[2] See Chapter 3 for how scale was devised.

TABLE 9-5

HOW VOTE ON SINGLE SCHOOL DISTRICT BY PARTICIPATION IN SCHOOLS
BY PLACE OF RESIDENCE AND SIZE OF METROPOLITAN AREA

Participation in Schools Scores and Size of Metropolitan Area	Central City					Suburban Area				
	Number	Favor %	Oppose %	Other %	Total %	Number	Favor %	Oppose %	Other %	Total %
Large										
3–5 High	23	52.2	43.5	4.3	100.0	51	15.7	78.4	5.9	100.0
2	65	49.2	40.0	10.7	100.0	88	14.8	79.5	5.7	100.0
1	196	51.0	36.2	12.7	100.0	206	23.3	68.0	8.8	100.0
0 Low	193	40.4	34.2	25.4	100.0	150	26.6	60.6	12.7	100.0
Medium										
3–5 High	30	46.7	40.0	13.3	100.0	67	19.4	73.1	7.5	100.0
2	76	51.3	35.5	13.2	100.0	105	26.7	66.6	6.7	100.0
1	212	39.6	39.1	21.2	100.0	202	32.2	57.9	9.9	100.0
0 Low	140	47.8	26.4	25.7	100.0	119	31.1	52.9	15.9	100.0
Small										
3–5 High	43	60.5	25.6	14.0	100.0	81	37.0	55.5	7.4	100.0
2	83	44.5	45.8	9.6	100.0	74	36.5	54.0	9.5	100.0
1	191	44.5	38.2	17.2	100.0	152	35.5	51.3	13.1	100.0
0 Low	171	41.5	35.6	22.8	100.0	185	35.1	44.3	20.5	100.0

regarding reorganization of school districts in the area. Again it is evident that participation plays quite a different role in the suburbs than in the cities.

In the cities, most support for change tends to come from those who are most active, that is, those who have the highest participation scores. Also there is a similar tendency for the proportion opposed to change to be highest among those with the highest participation scores. This apparent inconsistency is due to the sharp and consistent differences observed between level of participation and the proportion who "do not know" how they would vote. For example, in the large cities only 4 percent of those who are most active are undecided as to how they would vote, but this increases to 25 percent among those with the lowest participation scores. Similar differences are found in the other cities also. At any rate, in the cities, most support for change tends to come from those who are most active in school-related functions.

But when we look at the same evidence for the suburbs, just the opposite relationship is noted, at least in the large and medium-sized areas. As the level of participation score goes up, the proportion who would vote in favor of change declines. In the small area suburbs, participation scores appear to have little or no effect on the proportion favoring change, but even in these areas the proportion opposed to change varies directly by level of participation. Here, as in both large and medium-sized area suburbs, the proportion opposed to change is highest among those with the highest participation scores. But the apparent influence of participation in school-related activities declines with size of area.

There is no question but that participation in school-related activities in the suburbs is one of the variables that help to account for resistance to change, but even when we control for this dimension the differences in the proportion opposed to reorganization by size of area remains striking. At each participation level, resistance to change declines by size of area. Most resistance is found in the large area suburbs and least is found in the small areas. Thus, while 78 percent of the most active residents in the large area suburbs are opposed to change, this declines to only 56 percent among those in the small area suburbs. And among those with the lowest participation scores, the proportion opposed to change ranges from 61 percent in the large to only 44 percent in the small area suburbs. Similar differences are also found at the other participation levels.

Even though overall participation, as reflected in these scores, is an important factor in accounting for resistance to change in the suburbs, it does not override the significance of size of metropolitan area.

Why involvement in school-related activities would have just the opposite effect in the suburbs than in the central cities is likely due to a combination of several factors. One such factor is that central city residents, who are active, may support change because they see no danger in size as such. They are already a part of a relatively large school system and have become involved in it. No doubt they feel that they could continue to be active in a larger district. On the other hand, suburban residents are active in a much smaller system. They may feel that in an area-wide district including the central city they would lose these contacts, and would be unable to participate as they have done in the past. They know what they can do in the present system, and they want to hold on to this aspect of involvement in community life. The doubts that this segment of the suburban population have concerning the quality of the central city schools is, of course, another factor. Consequently, they oppose change. At any rate, regardless of the motivation involved, most suburban residents are opposed to change, and resistance is most pronounced among those who are active in school-related functions.[3]

Involvement in Community Activities

We now turn our attention to the influences of other forms of involvement in the community. First, the discussion will focus on informal participation in the life of the local community. This is

[3] Part of the explanation for the observed relationships here may also be a function of socioeconomic status. At any rate, the higher status groups in the city are most likely to favor change, whereas in the suburbs most opposition is found at this level. In both areas these groups, because of their high aspirations for their children, are more involved in and more knowledgeable about school-related activities than those at the lower socioeconomic levels. Thus, while the high status city and suburban residents respond differently to the issue of change, both may do so for the same reason—that is, both groups may react as they do because of their concern with the quality of education available to their children. Suburban residents may want to remain separate because they perceive their schools as being "better," whereas city residents may favor reorganization so as to share in the quality of the suburban schools. Some support for this interpretation is found in Table 8-6. City residents are more likely to feel that schools would improve in quality following reorganization, whereas many suburban residents expect quality to decline.

measured in terms of frequency of contact with neighbors and of the place of residence of close friends within the metropolitan community. It is hypothesized that "segregated" informal relationships would encourage resistance to change, whereas those whose contacts are broader in scope would more likely favor reorganization. This hypothesis finds considerable support from the evidence regarding frequency of contact with neighbors, at least in the suburban areas. However, among city residents, contact with neighbors does not seem to have any systematic influence on how persons respond to the proposed reorganization. The only consistent difference found in each size class is the large proportion who are undecided among those who "never" have contacts with their neighbors. Otherwise the reaction to change, among central city residents, is erratic in terms of contact with neighbors. But in the suburbs we consistently find that frequent contact with neighbors is closely associated with resistance to change. In all suburban areas, most opposition to change is reported by those who have at least weekly contact with their neighbors. Apparently such contacts enhance the local orientation of the residents and result in opposition to change. Stated differently, they want to maintain local autonomy. On the other hand, least opposition to change is expressed by those who never have any neighborhood contacts. For example, in the large metropolitan area suburbs, we find that 74 percent of those who have weekly contacts with their neighbors are opposed to change, but this declines gradually with varying frequency of contacts, and reaches a low of only 57 percent among those who never interact with their neighbors. A similar variation is also found in the other suburban areas, but the pattern is much less marked. Here, too, the importance of size is readily apparent, for within each frequency-of-contact category the proportion of suburban residents opposed to change declines as size of metropolitan area declines.

It is particularly noteworthy that in the small area suburbs, except among those who have at least weekly contacts with their neighbors, less than a majority of the residents are opposed to change. In the other suburban areas, however, a clear majority oppose change, regardless of how often they get together with their neighbors. Among the latter, support for school district reorganization is never expressed by more than one-third of the residents.

Still another index of informal contacts within the community is the place of residence of friends. When we relate views concerning reorganization to where in the metropolitan area most friends live, we find sizable differences among suburban residents. However, among central city residents, this aspect of community life proves to be unimportant. Consequently, our attention is focused only on the suburbs. It is among those whose friends live in the central city that we find most support for change and least opposition. For example, in the large suburbs, we find that 28 percent of those whose friends live in the city favor change, while 59 percent are opposed; but among those whose friends live in the suburbs, support for change declines to only 20 percent, while the proportion opposed increases to 73 percent. A similar pattern of difference is found in the other suburban areas also. It is noteworthy that in the small area suburbs, nearly half of those whose friends live in the central city favor change, as compared with only one-third of those whose friends live in the suburbs. In the same categories, opposition to reorganization of districts on an area-wide basis increases from 39 percent to 54 percent. Thus it is abundantly clear that most opposition to change comes from suburban residents whose informal contacts with friends are limited predominantly to the local suburbs. When their informal contacts extend into the city, views on school district organization assume a corresponding scope. Such persons are much less locality-oriented and much less opposed to setting up an area-wide district.

Here too, the pattern of difference by size of area is worthy of emphasis. Whether friends live in the central city or suburbs, the proportion in favor of change increases as size of area declines, whereas opposition varies directly by size of area. Thus, while only 28 percent of those in the large area suburbs whose friends live in the city would favor change, this increases to 35 percent in the medium-sized and to 48 percent in the small area suburbs. Conversely, opposition to change declines from 59 percent to 39 percent, respectively. And even among those whose friends live in the suburbs, opposition to change ranges from a high of 73 percent in the large to a low of 54 percent in the small area suburbs. On the other hand, the proportion in favor of change increases from 20 percent to 32 percent in the same areas. Thus, while exposure of suburban residents to informal relationships beyond the immediate locality is an important influence, it does not override the importance of size of area. The latter persists as a significant variable in accounting for resistance to change.

Membership in formal organizations appears to be of less significance among suburban residents, in accounting for resistance to change in the organization of school districts, than are informal contacts. However, there is a slight tendency for persons who do or have held officer positions in formal organizations to resist change more than do non-officers or those who do not belong to such organizations. This effect is observable in each size class and in each residential zone, but the size of the difference is slight. Least support for change tends to come from those who currently hold or have held leadership positions in formal community organizations. It is in this group, in each size class, that we find the largest proportion who express opposition to change. The general members of organizations are less likely than officers to resist change, but more likely to do so than persons who do not participate in such organizations. No doubt the size of the difference would increase if we differentiated the organizations according to type, place of meeting, and area of residence of most of the members. The present classification is such that many counter influences are likely at work, with the result that their effects probably cancel one another. For example, while belonging to an organization does enhance resistance to change among suburban residents, this influence may be lost, in part, due to contacts outside of the immediate local suburbs, since members may come from the larger area and meetings may be held in the city.

Voting in local elections is still another measure of formal involvement in the life of the community. One would expect that those who frequently vote in local school elections would be more concerned and oriented toward their own areas than the non-voters, and would thus be more likely to resist change. According to the data presented in Table 9-6, this appears to be true among suburban residents, but not among those who live in central cities. Quite the contrary, the proportion who would favor change tends to be highest among city residents who vote in nearly every school election, and lowest among those who never vote. The only exception to this is found in the medium-sized cities, where the proportion favoring change is unusually high among the non-voters, a deviation from the pattern which is not readily understandable.

TABLE 9-6

HOW VOTE ON SINGLE SCHOOL DISTRICT BY HOW FREQUENTLY VOTE IN SCHOOL ELECTIONS
BY PLACE OF RESIDENCE AND SIZE OF METROPOLITAN AREA

Frequency of Voting in School Elections & Size of Metropolitan Area	Central City					Suburban Area				
	Number	Favor	Oppose	Other	Total	Number	Favor	Oppose	Other	Total
		%	%	%	%		%	%	%	%
Large										
Nearly everyone	270	50.0	37.8	12.2	100.0	313	19.2	72.8	8.0	100.0
Other	106	42.4	35.8	21.7	100.0	91	29.7	64.8	5.5	100.0
Never	71	35.2	38.0	26.7	100.0	62	21.0	61.3	17.7	100.0
Not able to vote	21	66.7	23.8	9.5	100.0	12	58.3	25.0	16.7	100.0
Medium										
Nearly everyone	284	43.3	38.0	18.7	100.0	332	26.8	64.2	9.0	100.0
Other	92	41.3	32.6	26.1	100.0	89	36.0	56.2	7.9	100.0
Never	62	53.2	22.6	24.2	100.0	56	32.1	44.6	23.2	100.0
Not able to vote	5	—	—	—	—	11	36.4	54.5	9.1	100.0
Small										
Nearly everyone	282	47.5	39.4	13.1	100.0	266	33.5	54.1	12.4	100.0
Other	110	43.6	41.8	14.5	100.0	121	36.4	45.5	18.2	100.0
Never	79	36.7	30.4	32.9	100.0	97	38.1	45.4	16.5	100.0
Not able to vote	11	36.4	27.3	36.4	100.0	6	75.0	25.0	—	100.0

In the central cities, the proportion opposed to change does not appear to be associated with frequency of voting. The proportion who would vote against a single district fluctuates between 30 percent and 40 percent regardless of how frequently residents vote in school elections. However, we do find that persons who vote frequently are much more likely to have taken a position regarding the issue, whereas the non-voters are disproportionately undecided as to how they would vote on such a proposal. This likely accounts, in part, for the lower proportion among the non-voters in the city who favor reorganization.

Suburban residents show quite a different pattern. As expected, those who vote in nearly every school election are the ones least likely to favor change. Conversely, it is in this category that we find the most opposition to reorganization. While the proportion of suburban residents opposed to change declines by size of metropolitan area, those who vote most frequently in school elections, in each size class, consistently show most opposition to change. And those who never vote are the least likely to oppose reorganization. But a point to be noted is that even among the non-voters in the suburbs, a substantial proportion are opposed to change. Here too, the non-voters include the largest proportions who are undecided as to how they would vote on such a proposal. It is quite evident that the suburban residents who vote regularly in school elections are the ones most likely to favor maintaining the status quo. This relationship takes on added importance when we note that a large proportion of the suburban residents vote in most school elections. Thus opposition is widespread. But, again, it appears to be less important than size of area, since an inspection of the data in Table 9-6 shows that there is more variation in the proportion of suburban residents opposed to change by size of metropolitan area than by frequency of voting within any of the suburbs.

Participation Range—Local and Metropolitan

Still another index of level of involvement in the community is the range of territory over which residents spread their daily life. One would expect that resistance to change would decline as the territorial scope of activity enlarges—that is, most opposition would be found among those who are largely restricted to their own local areas in most of their daily activities. Accordingly, in Table 9-7,

TABLE 9-7

HOW VOTE ON SINGLE SCHOOL DISTRICT BY PARTICIPATION RANGE BY PLACE OF RESIDENCE AND SIZE OF METROPOLITAN AREA

Participation Range & Size of Metropolitan Area	Central City					Suburban Area				
	Number	Favor %	Oppose %	Other %	Total %	Number	Favor %	Oppose %	Other %	Total %
Large										
1 Local	61	41.0	34.4	24.6	100.0	47	17.0	68.1	14.9	100.0
2	109	43.1	44.0	12.8	100.0	73	16.4	72.6	11.0	100.0
3	125	44.8	32.0	23.2	100.0	99	16.2	75.8	8.1	100.0
4	94	51.1	34.0	14.9	100.0	120	30.0	61.7	8.3	100.0
5 + Metropolitan	88	52.3	36.4	11.4	100.0	153	24.2	68.6	7.2	100.0
Medium										
1 Local	32	34.4	31.3	34.4	100.0	29	17.2	72.4	10.3	100.0
2	65	46.2	29.2	24.6	100.0	64	21.9	71.9	6.3	100.0
3	131	48.9	34.3	16.8	100.0	78	21.8	66.7	11.6	100.0
4	102	48.0	35.3	16.7	100.0	125	28.8	58.4	12.8	100.0
5 + Metropolitan	127	38.6	38.6	22.8	100.0	195	35.4	54.9	9.7	100.0
Small										
1 Local	38	44.7	31.6	23.7	100.0	12	16.7	66.7	16.6	100.0
2	97	45.4	38.1	16.5	100.0	36	36.1	50.0	13.9	100.0
3	148	44.6	38.5	16.9	100.0	80	28.8	50.0	21.3	100.0
4	105	45.7	36.2	18.1	100.0	100	29.0	58.0	13.0	100.0
5 + Metropolitan	99	43.4	39.4	17.1	100.0	204	42.1	41.2	16.7	100.0

we have presented data showing how views regarding reorganization vary by participation range.[4] It is readily apparent that this dimension of daily life is still another variable that exerts considerable influence on how suburban residents, in particular, respond to the proposal for change. But among city residents, it is only in the large metropolitan areas that the proportion favoring change increases directly with scope of participation. Also, the proportion of residents who are undecided is highest among those whose daily life is limited to the local area, and lowest among those whose range of activities is more metropolitan in scope. The "undecided" vote ranges from 25 percent to only 11 percent, respectively. There is a tendency for the latter pattern of difference to be found in the other city sizes also, but we do not find any consistent variation, by participation range, in the proportion who favor change nor in the proportion opposed, in either the medium-sized or small metropolitan area cities.

In the suburban areas, the influence of range of activities is much more evident and much more consistent. Regardless of size of area, the proportion favoring change is highest among those whose range of daily activities is most extensive. The differences by participation range are most marked in the medium-sized and small area suburban zones. For example, in the medium-sized area suburbs, the proportion favoring change ranges from a low of 17 percent among those whose activities are local to a high of 35 percent among those whose daily activities are more metropolitan in scope. In the small area suburbs, the comparable range is from 17 percent to 42 percent.

In both medium-sized and small area suburbs, opposition to

[4] This is a composite score based partly on distances travelled and partly on contacts outside the local neighborhood. Each item in the list represents one class of a dichotomy. The scale is built on a simple count of the number of affirmative answers given to the eight inquiries listed. Nine scale positions are possible, i.e., 0 through 8. But because of small numbers at the extremes, positions 0 and 1 are combined and reported as 1, while positions 6, 7, and 8 are grouped together as scale value 5. A scale value of 1 means that the individual leaves his neighborhood for none or only one of the eight activities; scale position 2 indicates that any two of the activities are beyond the local neighborhood, and so on. The activities included are: (1) Distance to work—3 miles or more; (2) Distance to church—3 miles or more; (3) Distance to school—1 mile or more; (4) Place where shopping is done—central business district or major shopping area, in contrast to neighborhood stores; (5) Trips to central business district for purposes other than work —2 or more times per month; (6) Acquaintance with neighbors—few or none; (7) Place where relatives live—in opposite zone, or none in area; (8) Place where friends live—in opposite zone, or none in area.

change declines consistently by range of participation. While nearly three-fourths of those in the medium-sized area suburbs whose daily life is largely limited to the local area oppose change, this declines to only slightly more than half of those whose activities are most extensive. In the small area suburbs, the proportion who would vote against setting up a single district declines from 67 percent to 41 percent for the same participation categories. Thus the relationship here is both consistent and sizable. However, in the large area suburbs, where opposition is widespread, it varies erratically by range of participation. Nevertheless, even here the "undecided" vote is largest among those whose activities are local, while favorable votes come disproportionately from those whose daily activities are more metropolitan in scope.

A point worthy of note is that among suburban residents, most support for change comes from those in the small suburban areas whose daily activities range throughout the whole community. Conversely, it is in this group that we find least opposition to school district reorganization. In general, except for the large area suburbs, opposition to reorganization of school districts comes disproportionately from those whose daily life is limited to the local area. Resistance appears to be, in part, a result of isolation from the rest of the community. At any rate, as isolation declines, support for change increases, though never is this view shared by more than a minority.

Efficiency and Economy of Operation

Support for the reorganization of school districts, regardless of place of residence or size of the metropolitan community, comes disproportionately from those who are concerned with efficiency and economy of operations. The evidence in support of this is presented in Table 9-8. A majority of residents in all areas who feel that the present system of multiple school districts in the area is wasteful favor change. However, even when this factor is considered, central city residents are still more likely to favor change than are suburban residents. It is of particular interest here to note the general lack of support that is expressed by the large number of central city residents in each size class who do not share the view that the present system is wasteful. While central city residents are nearly equally

TABLE 9-8

HOW VOTE ON SINGLE DISTRICT BY ATTITUDE TOWARD MULTIPLE DISTRICTS BY PLACE OF RESIDENCE AND SIZE OF METROPOLITAN AREA

Are Multiple Districts Wasteful & Size of Metropolitan Area	Central City					Suburban Area				
	Number	Favor	Oppose	Other	Total	Number	Favor	Oppose	Other	Total
		%	%	%	%		%	%	%	%
Large										
Yes	177	73.4	16.9	9.6	100.0	150	51.3	42.0	6.7	100.0
No	200	30.5	60.0	9.5	100.0	280	7.1	87.9	5.0	100.0
Don't know	90	33.3	22.2	44.4	100.0	63	17.5	49.2	33.3	100.0
Medium										
Yes	192	68.7	22.9	8.3	100.0	176	58.0	34.1	8.0	100.0
No	178	28.7	52.8	18.6	100.0	261	9.2	83.5	7.3	100.0
Don't know	79	24.1	25.3	50.6	100.0	54	29.6	37.0	33.4	100.0
Small										
Yes	214	70.6	22.9	6.5	100.0	197	60.9	32.0	7.1	100.0
No	201	25.9	59.2	14.9	100.0	241	17.4	68.9	13.7	100.0
Don't know	69	23.2	21.7	55.1	100.0	49	28.6	26.5	44.9	100.0

split on how they view the wastefulness of the present system, the views of these two groups concerning reorganization vary markedly. In all central cities, approximately seven out of ten of those who feel that the present system is wasteful favor change; however, among those who do not view the present system as wasteful, not more than three out of ten would favor change. On the other hand, a clear majority would be opposed to setting up a single district. There is little, if any, variation by size of city. In short, regardless of size, if central city residents view the present system as being wasteful, they clearly would support a proposal for change; but if they do not view the present system as being wasteful, and many do not, they are nearly equally opposed to change. Among the latter, a majority is opposed in each size class.

Although there is generally somewhat less support for change among suburban residents, the pattern of difference found in the city also obtains. The most striking observation here is that a distinct majority of the sizable proportion of suburban residents who view the present system as being wasteful would vote in favor of change. The proportion that would do so increases inversely by size of area, ranging from a low of 51 percent in the large to a high of 61 percent in the small area suburbs. On the other hand, support for change among those who do not feel that the present system is wasteful ranges from only 7 percent in the large suburbs to 17 percent in the small. But in this segment of the population, opposition ranges from a low of 69 percent in the small to a high of 88 percent in the large suburban areas. However, among residents who view the present system as wasteful, less than half this proportion would be opposed to reorganization—that is, only 42 percent in the large area suburbs, and this declines by ten percentage points in the small suburbs. This is the most pronounced association that we have found throughout our analysis.

Clearly, attitudes concerning the wastefulness of the present system play a crucial role in resistance to change. If residents feel that the present system is not wasteful, they oppose change. And it is noteworthy that a majority of suburban residents share this view. But it is equally noteworthy that a majority of the 30 percent to 40 percent who feel that multiple districts are wasteful would favor change. At least this points to an issue that might be exploited in any attempt to promote a reorganization proposal. We also note that among those who are undecided as to whether multiple districts are wasteful, less than a majority are opposed to change. In this segment of the population, we find a disproportionately large number who are also undecided as to how they would vote on setting up a single district for the whole area. Central city residents are similar in this respect. The proportion undecided regarding both issues is higher, however, in the central cities than in the suburban areas.

Again it is emphasized that support for change comes disproportionately from residents in the small area suburbs. Within each response category, the proportion favoring change increases as size of suburban area declines, while the proportion opposed tends to decline. And in all instances, not only are the differences consistent but they are sizable as well.

Ideological Orientation

We would expect that views concerning school district organization would be closely related to how residents view local government generally in metropolitan areas. For this reason, we have focused attention on the influence of what we have called an "ideological orientation" concerning local government.[5] Persons who tend to view local government problems as area-wide in scope would score high in respect to the ideological orientation scale (metropolitan ideology). On the other hand, low scores reflect a view that tends to favor the present system of multiple governmental units within the metropolitan community (local ideology).[6]

[5] A score of one was given for a positive response to each of the following questions: (1) Are multiple governments wasteful? (2) Have conditions in the suburbs reached the point where more services are needed? (3) Should suburban residents share in the responsibility of providing the services and conveniences in the city that they use? (4) If services were provided on an area-wide basis, would they be better? (5) If services were provided on an area-wide basis, would taxes decrease or not change? Scores range from 0 to 5. One would expect a high correlation between these responses and those regarding schools. The issue here is to demonstrate the extent to which schools and local government problems are viewed similarly and the extent to which they represent independent problems.

[6] In each size class, central city residents are "metropolitan" while suburban residents tend to be locally oriented. The difference, however, varies by size of area. In the large areas, average scores in the city (2.4) exceed the suburbs (1.6) by 50 percent, but the difference declines to less than 10 percent (2.3 vs. 2.1) in the small areas. City and suburban ideological orientation becomes more similar as size of area decreases.

Thus, in a broad sense, we are here concerned with the general relationship between views regarding the schools and views regarding local government in the metropolitan community.

According to the data presented in Table 9-9, the ideological orientation of the residents toward government is a much more significant factor in resistance to change in school district organization than is participation range within the metropolitan community. Actually, the relationship between ideological orientation and how residents would vote on a proposal regarding the reorganization of school districts is particularly striking in both central city and suburbs. But at each point along the ideological orientation scale, central city residents are more likely than suburban residents to favor change in school district organization.

The locally oriented central city resident is almost as resistant to school district reorganization as is his counterpart in the suburbs. Even though less than a majority of the locally oriented city residents would be opposed to reorganization of school districts, it is in this group that we tend to find most opposition to change. Also, it is in this group that we find the largest proportion who "do not know" how they would vote on setting up a single district for the central city and suburban areas. At any rate, it is highly significant that among the "locally" oriented, less than one in four of the city residents would favor the reorganization of school districts. On the other hand, approximately 80 percent or more of those who are "metropolitan" oriented would vote in favor of setting up a single district for the whole area. Ideological orientation represents one of the few instances in which the effects of a variable on the attitude toward change override the effect of size of area. The proportion favoring change is nearly the same in each size city within each ideological orientation category.

In the suburban areas also, support for change in school district organization comes disproportionately from those whose views tend to be more metropolitan in their orientation concerning local government. But such persons constitute a small minority of the suburban population. Least support comes from the large group of residents who view government in local terms. In the large suburbs, only 10 percent of the latter would vote in favor of a single school district, whereas 80 percent of the former would do so. On the other hand, the proportion opposed to change is 14 percent and 80

TABLE 9-9

HOW VOTE ON SINGLE SCHOOL DISTRICT BY IDEOLOGICAL ORIENTATION SCALE
BY PLACE OF RESIDENCE AND SIZE OF METROPOLITAN AREA

Ideological Scale & Size of Metropolitan Area	Central City					Suburban Area				
	Number	Favor	Oppose	Other	Total	Number	Favor	Oppose	Other	Total
		%	%	%	%		%	%	%	%
Large										
1 Local	120	21.7	43.3	35.0	100.0	275	10.2	79.3	10.5	100.0
2	139	40.3	45.3	14.4	100.0	122	24.6	68.0	7.4	100.0
3	127	53.5	36.2	10.2	100.0	63	36.5	55.6	7.9	100.0
4 Metropolitan	91	79.1	13.2	7.7	100.0	35	80.0	14.3	5.7	100.0
Medium										
1 Local	103	20.4	34.0	45.6	100.0	182	8.8	77.5	13.7	100.0
2	163	37.4	46.0	16.5	100.0	138	29.0	64.5	6.5	100.0
3	132	54.5	32.6	12.9	100.0	117	45.3	46.2	8.5	100.0
4 Metropolitan	59	83.1	10.2	6.8	100.0	56	60.7	26.8	12.5	100.0
Small										
1 Local	110	28.2	44.5	27.2	100.0	167	19.8	64.7	15.6	100.0
2	186	36.6	44.6	18.8	100.0	139	27.3	54.7	18.0	100.0
3	131	53.4	33.6	13.0	100.0	124	50.0	38.7	11.3	100.0
4 Metropolitan	61	82.0	11.5	6.6	100.0	62	69.4	21.0	9.6	100.0

percent, respectively. However, the point to be emphasized here is that most of the suburban residents tend to score low on the ideological orientation scale. That is, they tend more than do city residents to be locally oriented in respect to government in metropolitan areas. Their combined responses to a series of questions pertaining to government indicates that they favor the present segmented governmental structures. And these same people are predominantly opposed to change regarding the schools. Support for change, however, comes from that small segment of the population, particularly in the large suburbs, that tends to be "metropolitan area" oriented in respect to local government. Thus these data clearly show that the organization of school districts and the organization of local governments, although independent in one sense, are merely different aspects of the same thing. Residents in the metropolitan community tend to see both issues in the same light.

While city and suburban residents tend to view local government differently, it is noteworthy that when they do share the same views regarding government they tend to respond similarly to the proposal to set up a single school district for the whole area. Opposition to reorganization of school districts comes disproportionately and overwhelmingly from residents, regardless of place of residence or size of metropolitan area, whose ideology of government is locally oriented. And this ideology is particularly prevalent among suburban residents. Conversely, support for change comes disproportionately and from a distinct majority of those who tend to view governmental problems in the metropolitan context.

Views Concerning Governmental Reorganization

The close and consistent relationship between views concerning school district reorganization and views regarding local government is further evident from the data presented in Table 9-10, which show how residents would respond to the school issue according to how they would vote on a proposal to set up a single government for the central city and suburban areas. Again, we find the same pattern of difference in both the central cities and the suburbs, as well as in each size class. We continue, however, to find more support for change among central city residents than among those who live in the suburbs, regardless of how they would vote in respect to local

TABLE 9-10

HOW RESIDENTS WOULD VOTE ON SETTING UP A SINGLE DISTRICT BY HOW VOTE ON SINGLE GOVERNMENT BY PLACE OF RESIDENCE AND SIZE OF METROPOLITAN AREA

Vote on Single Gov't. and Size of Metropolitan Area	Vote on Single School District									
	Central City					Suburban Area				
	Number	Favor	Oppose	Other	Total	Number	Favor	Oppose	Other	Total
		%	%	%	%		%	%	%	%
Large										
Would vote for now	228	70.6	20.2	9.2	100.0	90	65.6	24.4	10.0	100.0
Would vote for later	45	40.0	51.1	8.9	100.0	62	24.2	72.6	3.2	100.0
Would never vote for	93	23.7	65.6	10.8	100.0	235	8.1	86.4	5.5	100.0
Don't know	90	21.1	40.0	38.9	100.0	99	15.2	68.7	16.2	100.0
No answer	21	9.5	33.3	57.1	100.0	9	11.1	33.3	55.6	100.0
Medium										
Would vote for now	228	68.9	20.6	10.5	100.0	150	61.3	32.0	6.7	100.0
Would vote for later	49	32.7	57.1	10.2	100.0	67	25.4	58.2	16.4	100.0
Would never vote for	72	16.7	68.1	15.3	100.0	150	14.0	81.3	4.7	100.0
Don't know	96	16.7	33.3	50.0	100.0	116	9.5	72.4	18.1	100.0
No answer	12	16.7	25.0	58.3	100.0	10	20.0	60.0	20.0	100.0
Small										
Would vote for now	262	61.8	27.1	11.0	100.0	186	60.2	28.0	11.8	100.0
Would vote for later	40	47.5	37.5	15.0	100.0	53	32.1	47.2	20.8	100.0
Would never vote for	88	21.6	62.5	15.9	100.0	176	17.6	71.6	10.8	100.0
Don't know	75	20.0	44.0	36.0	100.0	61	19.7	54.1	26.2	100.0
No answer	23	17.4	39.1	43.5	100.0	16	25.6	56.3	18.8	100.0

government reorganization. Conversely, there is more opposition to change in the suburbs; but within each suburban zone, marked and consistent differences are found in the proportion who would favor or oppose a single school district according to how they view the local government issue.

In both central cities and suburban zones, a majority of those who would presently vote for a single government for the area would vote in favor of setting up a single school district. Here we find approximately the same amount of support in the suburbs as in the central cities. Also, there is little variation by size of metropolitan area. However, support for a single district drops markedly, in both residential zones, among those who would not now vote for a single government but who claim that they would do so sometime in the future. Thus, for example, among suburban residents in each size class, support for school district change drops from three-fifths or more to less than one-third. On the other hand, opposition increases substantially and varies markedly by size of metropolitan area suburbs. The range is from 47 percent in the small to 73 percent in the large area suburbs, whereas opposition to a single school district never exceeded one-third, in any size class, among those who would now vote for a single government.

Among residents who would never vote for a single government —a view which is shared disproportionately by suburban residents —a clear and distinct majority, regardless of place of residence, report that they would be opposed to setting up a single school district combining the central city and suburban districts. Again we find much more opposition in the suburbs than in the central cities. A very substantial proportion of the suburban residents are clearly against change in both local government and school districts in their areas—that is, they oppose combining existing units into a single system. No doubt any effort to bring about change would have to be concerned about both local government and the schools, for these certainly appear to be but different dimensions of the same issue.

When we control for how residents would vote on setting up a single government, we find that the vote on the school issue does not vary by size of metropolitan area. With few exceptions, it is the view residents hold regarding setting up a single government for the metropolitan area that influences how they would react to the proposed school reorganization, rather than size of area as such. At any rate, when residents in different size suburban zones share a common view regarding how they would vote on a single government, size-of-area differences in how they would vote on the school issue disappear. In each response category and in each size class, we find approximately the same proportion of residents who would either favor or oppose the reorganization of school districts. The vote in favor of setting up a single government, however, is substantially larger in the small than in the large area suburbs. That is, resistance to change is more firmly established in the larger areas. Thus, this dimension would have less overall influence in the small than in the large suburban areas. For this reason, aggregate differences are found by size of area.

Further evidence concerning the close relationship between views on schools and local government is found when we relate the residents' first choice as to how local governments should approach present community problems to their views regarding the reorganization of school districts. These data are shown in Table 9-11. Among residents who feel that the best approach to solving service problems in metropolitan areas would be to either set up a single government for the whole area or annex the suburbs to the city, a substantial majority would vote in favor of setting up a single school district for the whole area. Again we find approximately the same amount of support for school district reorganization in the suburbs as in the central cities. Nor does the amount of support vary by size of metropolitan area. Thus, if central city and suburban residents share a common view regarding local government, they are likely to agree on schools also. However, central city residents are much more likely to favor area-wide government than suburban residents; consequently, we find much less support for an area-wide school system among suburban residents.

When residents of either area select any other organizational alternatives as the preferred approach to solving service problems of the metropolitan area—such as the city selling services to the surrounding communities, establishing special assessment districts, suburban areas combining, or maintaining the status quo—we find that a majority would be opposed to setting up a single school district for the whole area. This general pattern is found in both parts of the metropolitan area and in each size class. These alternative ap-

Preferred Solution and Size of Metropolitan Area	How Vote on Single District									
	Central City					Suburban Area				
	Number	Favor	Oppose	Other	Total	Number	Favor	Oppose	Other	Total
		%	%	%	%		%	%	%	%
Large										
Single government	136	73.5	14.7	11.7	100.0	64	60.9	29.7	9.4	100.0
Annex suburbs	58	67.2	17.2	15.5	100.0	11	72.7	27.3	—	100.0
City sell services	18	50.0	33.3	16.7	100.0	28	25.0	75.0	—	100.0
Special districts	28	53.6	35.7	10.7	100.0	18	33.3	66.7	—	100.0
Suburbs combine	43	37.2	55.8	7.0	100.0	77	14.3	80.5	5.2	100.0
No change	167	24.6	58.7	16.8	100.0	287	12.2	77.3	10.4	100.0
All other	27	7.4	14.8	77.8	100.0	10	30.0	20.0	50.0	100.0
Medium										
Single government	138	70.2	15.9	13.7	100.0	102	69.6	22.5	7.8	100.0
Annex suburbs	37	59.5	27.0	13.5	100.0	36	50.0	38.9	11.1	100.0
City sell services	17	23.5	64.7	11.8	100.0	18	16.7	72.2	11.1	100.0
Special districts	30	36.7	60.0	3.3	100.0	31	22.6	67.7	9.7	100.0
Suburbs combine	39	30.8	59.0	10.3	100.0	63	15.9	81.0	3.2	100.0
No change	166	31.3	44.6	24.1	100.0	234	13.7	75.2	11.1	100.0
All other	30	16.7	3.3	80.0	100.0	9	22.2	11.1	66.7	100.0
Small										
Single government	111	67.6	15.3	17.1	100.0	70	70.0	18.6	11.4	100.0
Annex suburbs	118	56.8	31.4	11.9	100.0	81	58.0	28.4	13.5	100.0
City sell services	22	27.3	59.1	13.6	100.0	40	27.5	60.0	17.5	100.0
Special districts	22	54.5	40.9	4.5	100.0	34	20.6	58.8	20.6	100.0
Suburbs combine	35	28.6	62.9	8.6	100.0	54	16.7	72.2	11.1	100.0
No change	154	29.2	49.3	21.4	100.0	188	22.9	65.4	11.7	100.0
All other	26	15.4	34.6	50.0	100.0	25	40.0	12.0	48.0	100.0

proaches referred to above are preferred disproportionately by suburban residents. And it is this segment of the population that accounts for most of the opposition to change regarding the schools, also.

Summary

It is evident throughout this chapter that the level of involvement in the life of the community, measured in terms of knowledge or participation, is a variable of considerable importance in how residents respond to a proposal to set up a single school district for the central city and suburban areas. However, involvement has just the opposite effect in the two residential zones. In the cities, the most knowledgeable and the most active residents tend to favor change, whereas in the suburbs these are the ones most likely to be opposed to change. Rather consistently, most support for change is found in the cities, while most opposition to reorganization is found in the suburbs. However, opposition among suburban residents declines by size of metropolitan area, so that least resistance is found in the small area suburbs. Level of involvement is an important variable in accounting for resistance to change in all size classes, but it does not override either place of residence or size of metropolitan area.

Perhaps the most significant observation in the above discussion is the large amount of support for change, regardless of place of residence or size of metropolitan area, that is expressed by the sizable number of residents who are concerned about "efficiency and economy of operations." Even among the suburban residents who see the present system of multiple districts as wasteful, a distinct majority would vote in favor of change. And the proportion who would do so increases as size of metropolitan area declines. We also found that a large majority of those who shared a metropolitan area "ideology" favored change in school district organization. It is highly significant that this ideology overrides even the importance of size of area, which has consistently been found to be an important variable in resistance to change. Opposition to reorganization comes overwhelmingly from residents, regardless of place of residence or size of metropolitan area, whose ideology of government is locally oriented.

If residents would vote for a single government for the city and suburban areas, a large majority would also favor reorganization of school districts, regardless of where they live. However, among those who would not support a single government, which is the view shared by most suburban residents, there is widespread opposition to school district reorganization. It is apparent from the consistency of the relationship between attitudes of residents concerning local government and views regarding the schools that neither of these issues can be effectively approached apart from the other. It would seem that, as noted in an earlier study, the school problem is only a small part of a much more complex problem—that is, the segmentation of government in metropolitan areas. If a single municipal government were established over the whole area, an effective solution to the school problem would likely be within reach.[7] It is a clear-cut issue of "integration" of the larger community in all respects versus segmented approaches to a wide range of individual functions. If residents accept the principle of "integration," they tend to accept "integration" of at least major functions. If they favor the "status quo," or any other segmented approach, in respect to any of the single functions, they are likely also to prefer the same type of approach for all functions. In a sense, the resolution of community problems in metropolitan areas appears to be an "either-or" proposition.

[7] B. G. Zimmer, "Searching Through Research," *Overview*, II (Jan., 1961).

10

Attitudes of Public Officials
Toward Schools and Changes

To THIS POINT, WE have been concerned only with how residents
in the metropolitan area view school issues and how they would
respond to a proposal to reorganize school districts on an area-
wide basis. Another dimension of the issue, which is likely to be
of crucial importance in resistance to change, is the views held by
local public officials. Thus the present chapter will attempt to compare the views of officials to those of the residents whom they serve.
The analysis will continue to focus on central city and suburban
areas, by size of metropolitan area. The primary objective is to determine the extent to which officials in different parts of the metropolitan area are likely to contribute to resistance to change. As in
our analysis of residents' responses, we will probe the views held by
officials on a variety of issues concerning the schools, in an attempt
to determine the amount of consensus among officials, as well as
between officials and the residents they represent.

One would expect that since local leaders have a vested interest
in the perpetuation of the existing systems, they would be more
opposed to change than the residents of their respective areas. We
also expect central city officials to favor reorganization, since this
would likely mean that their area of influence would be enlarged,
while suburban officials should oppose such a change for converse
reasons, in part at least. Further, we would expect opposition, particularly among suburban officials, to vary by size of area, since it

would be much more difficult for suburban officials to compete for leadership positions under a combined system in the large than in the small metropolitan areas. But regardless of size of metropolitan area, it is likely that many suburban officials would never have held office had they lived in a large municipality. That suburban public officials are clearly aware of this probability is suggested by their responses to the general question: "If you lived in the city, do you think you would have become a public official?" In the suburban zones of both the large and medium-sized areas, two-thirds of the school as well as municipal officials felt that they would not have become public officials if they had lived in the adjoining central city. Only one-fifth or less felt that they would have done so. A somewhat different response is found in the small area suburbs. Here the proportion of school officials who feel that they would not have held office is even higher; three out of four express the opinion that they would not have become public officials if they had lived in the central city, while one in five holds the view that he would have done so.

By way of contrast, more than one-third of the suburban government officials feel that even if they lived in the central city, they would have become officials, while less than half feel that they would not have done so. Roughly 10 to 20 percent of the government officials in each size class report that they are uncertain as to whether or not they would have become officials if they had lived in the city. It seems quite clear that between one-half and three-fourths of the persons currently holding official positions, in either the suburban school districts or other governmental units, feel that they would not hold such positions if they lived in the city. This is at least strong presumptive evidence that their public leadership positions depend, in large part, on the segmentation of governments and school districts in metropolitan areas. That they should have a vested interest in the status quo is more than a little probable.

Characteristics of Officials

Before considering the views held by officials, let us first look at the kinds of persons who become public officials in the different segments, as well as in different size metropolitan communities. In many respects, the age composition of public officials tends to reflect differences in the age composition of the population in their areas. That is, suburban officials tend to be younger than city officials, just as the suburban population generally tends to be younger than that of the central city. But quite apart from central city-suburban differences, we find that the proportion in the younger ages tends to decline by size of area; that association of age with size occurs among both central city and suburban officials. And still another difference is that school officials in all areas tend to be younger than government officials. The gap is particularly large in the suburban areas. Part of this difference is doubtless due to the fact that government officials hold not only policy-making positions, such as is the case among school board members, but many hold other administrative positions which are likely to be paid positions of a more permanent nature. Consequently, there is less turnover. Also one would expect school officials to be younger, since the type of people who would be most interested in serving on the board of education would probably be those who have children in school.[1] One would expect to find such persons serving on the school boards in the suburbs more frequently than in the central city, since the suburban areas would, in many instances, be in the early stages of attempting to develop a school program. And because of the emphasis placed on children in the suburbs, the younger adults would seek leadership positions.

A further factor here is that it is perhaps easier for a younger person to gain sufficient recognition in the suburban areas, so as to be able to win an election, because of the smaller population and greater opportunities for informal contacts. Whereas in the central city, because of the larger population and more impersonal relationships, one would need a more established community-wide reputation in order to win an election to such a position; so such persons are likely to be older. Thus there are a number of factors at work that tend to favor the election of younger persons to official positions in the suburban school districts than in the central city districts. These types of central city-suburban differences no doubt account in part for the large proportion of suburban officials who feel that

[1] Neal Gross, *Who Runs Our Schools?* (N. Y.: John Wiley, 1958). In a study of 508 school board members, 11 percent ran for the board because they "didn't like the way my children were being educated," and 20 percent disapproved of the way the schools were being run (p. 73). More than half of the school board members had children in the public schools (p. 79).

they would not have become public officials had they lived in the city.

When we focus on the educational level and income of public officials, we find that they differ markedly from the residents they represent.[2] This is as much the case in the suburbs as in the central cities. We also find that there are sizable differences between central city and suburban officials in respect to both variables. While public officials in all areas tend to be better educated and enjoy higher incomes than the residents, we also note that central city officials tend to rate above those in the suburbs, even though the opposite is the case in respect to the general population in each area. Consequently, the gap between officials and residents is less in the suburbs than in the central cities, but the size of the difference is only relative, since the absolute gap between officials and residents is substantial in all areas. It is noteworthy that the differences are least in the small area suburbs, but even there the same pattern is observed. These data are shown in Table 10-1.

In all areas, school officials tend to be better educated than government officials. Here too, the size of the difference is substantial in all areas except the small area suburbs, where the level of education of all public officials is markedly lower than in any of the other areas. While half or more of the school officials in all other areas are at least college graduates, we find that only 13 percent of the school officials in the small area suburbs have this amount of education. The significance of this is even more evident when we note that more than 80 percent of the school officials in the neighboring central cities are college graduates. These differences are probably due to the small size of the school districts in the small area suburbs. Many are only elementary school districts, and this type of system clearly attracts a different type of person than do the larger, more diversified districts. While the general level of education of the population is lower in the small area suburbs than in the other areas, it does not differ nearly as much as the amount of variation found among the officials in the different areas.

Incomes are only slightly lower among the small area suburban residents when compared to those in other areas, but the income of public officials is markedly lower in these areas. For example, while 15 percent or less of the school officials in both large and medium-

[2] This same difference is reported by Neal Gross, *ibid*.

TABLE 10-1

PROPORTION OF RESIDENTS AND OFFICIALS AT SELECTED LEVELS
OF EDUCATION AND INCOME BY RESIDENTIAL ZONES
AND SIZE OF METROPOLITAN AREA

Type of Respondent and Education and Income	Large		Medium		Small	
	City	Suburb	City	Suburb	City	Suburb
	%	%	%	%	%	%
EDUCATION						
Less Than High School Graduate						
School officials	13.4	10.0	—	11.3	—	34.5
Government officials	10.0	15.3	11.7	23.8	12.1	44.8
Survey population	58.6	39.4	54.6	35.1	52.1	57.2
College Graduate or More						
School officials	66.7	48.3	78.5	54.8	81.3	13.2
Government officials	55.8	30.6	57.2	30.2	59.1	16.4
Survey population	5.2	16.2	8.7	16.7	8.2	5.9
INCOME						
Less Than $125 per Week						
School officials	—	15.0	—	12.9	12.5	47.6
Government officials	9.9	23.8	6.5	25.3	4.5	47.7
Survey population	60.4	53.5	59.1	53.9	60.4	54.8
$150 or More per Week						
School officials	80.0	58.3	64.3	61.3	68.8	36.1
Government officials	80.0	61.0	79.2	58.7	80.3	29.9
Survey population	6.5	19.0	9.2	20.4	10.1	15.5

sized areas report weekly incomes of less than $125.00, this is the income that is reported by 48 percent of the school officials in the small area suburbs. On the other hand, while approximately two-thirds of the school officials in the larger area suburbs enjoy an income of $150.00 or more per week, only one-third of the school officials in the small area suburbs are in this income category. It should be emphasized that these are not incomes derived from the position, but rather represent the incomes from other sources of the residents who seek and fill these positions. These data indicate the segment of the population from which public leaders emerge.

It is noteworthy that while a clear majority of the residents in all areas report a weekly income of $125.00 or less, none of the central city school officials, and less than 10 percent of the central city municipal officials in either large or medium-sized metropolitan areas, are in this income category. But in the suburbs of the same metropolitan areas, approximately one-fourth of the government officials and 15 percent or less of the school officials have incomes of this size. In the small metropolitan areas, only a small minority of the central city public officials are in this income category. However, as already noted, this is the income level reported by nearly half of the public officials in the suburbs.

When we focus on the top income group, we find two-thirds or more of all central city public officials, but only 10 percent or less of the residents. In the suburban areas, one-fifth or less of the residents are in the top income group, as compared with approximately 60 percent or more of the public officials. The only exception is found in the small area suburbs, where the proportion of officials at this income level declines to only 36 percent.

The point to be emphasized here is that while we do find differences in the educational and income level of officials by size and type of area, the variations among officials are much less marked than the differences between officials and the residents they represent. Since public officials do differ in social and economic characteristics from the general population, we would expect that the views held by officials on various issues concerning the schools would differ from those held by residents of the area. For example, we would expect that the views expressed by public officials will be most similar to the views shared by the segment of the population in the upper socioeconomic status group, for by and large they appear to be recruited from that segment of the population.

Earlier it was suggested that suburban school officials would come disproportionately from families with children in school. This is based on the assumption that since suburban schools are in the early development stage, because of the recent growth in population, leadership positions would be sought by persons who have an immediate and practical interest in how the schools are run. Also, because of the small size, there would be less competition for such positions. Further, because of the composition of the population in the suburbs, as compared with the central city, one would expect that suburban governmental officials would also be more likely than central city officials to have children in school.

An inspection of the data presented in Table 10-2 clearly shows all of the expected differences. Of particular interest is the dispro-

TABLE 10-2

PROPORTION HAVING CHILDREN IN SCHOOL BY TYPE OF RESPONDENT
BY SCHOOL LEVEL BY RESIDENTIAL ZONES AND
SIZE OF METROPOLITAN AREA

Type of Respondent and School Level	Large		Medium		Small	
	City	Suburb	City	Suburb	City	Suburb
	%	%	%	%	%	%
Elementary School						
School officials	40.0	60.0	28.6	58.1	50.0	73.8
Government officials	38.6	35.6	33.8	28.6	36.4	32.8
Survey population	25.6	35.0	28.3	43.4	36.9	48.9
High School						
School officials	20.0	48.3	64.3	61.3	31.3	44.3
Government officials	22.9	37.2	22.1	31.7	25.8	32.8
Survey population	14.6	17.7	14.9	16.4	16.0	17.5

portionately large number of suburban school officials who have children in either elementary or high schools. While only one-third to one-half of the survey population have children in elementary school, the proportion of officials who do so ranges from approximately three-fifths to three-fourths. A similar situation is also found at the high school level. In each size class, school officials are not only more likely than the general population to have children attending school, but they are also more likely than government officials to have children in school. In each metropolitan area, suburban school officials are much more likely than comparable officials in the central city to have children currently attending school. The difference tends to be 50 percent or more in favor of the suburbs.

Even in the central cities, we find a higher proportion with children in school among school officials than in the general population and among other type public officials. However, the size of the difference at both the elementary and high school level tends to be less marked than in the suburbs. For the most part, use of the schools, at least at the elementary level, is approximately the same by government officials as by the general population. There is no consistent pattern of difference by either size or type of area. But at the high school level, suburban government officials are much more likely than the residents to have children in attendance. Actually, in each metropolitan area, in central cities and in the suburbs, a higher proportion of public officials have children in school than is found among the general population. No doubt much of this difference is due to the age composition of the populations involved. Government officials, when compared with the general population, tend to be disproportionately concentrated in those age groups which are most likely to have children of high school age. Thus the views public officials express concerning school issues will represent not only their vested interests as officials, but their comparatively greater involvement in the schools as parents.

Satisfaction with Schools

For the most part, there is a very high level of satisfaction with the schools. This is expressed by public officials, regardless of type or area, as well as by citizens. Actually, approximately 85 percent or more of the responses by all officials and citizens are in the somewhat or very satisfied categories. Only a very small minority report any dissatisfaction, and to the very limited extent that there are any differences, the general population expresses slightly more dissatisfaction than do school officials, while government officials are the ones who are most critical. But the point to be emphasized is that the range of responses varies only slightly; the proportion dissatisfied never exceeds 16 percent in any category. This degree of dissatisfaction obtains only among government officials in the medium-sized metropolitan areas, and it is of the same proportion in both segments of the communities.

It seems quite clear that there would be little interest in any effort to reorganize the school districts because of lack of satisfaction with the schools under the present structure. The response, however, to a general question such as: "Are you satisfied with your schools?" is likely to be quite nebulous in meaning. At any rate, when a more specific question is asked concerning the type of training offered by the high schools in their areas, responses show considerably more variation. But even here, a substantial majority appear to be satisfied.

Among school officials, approximately 85 percent or more are satisfied with the type of training offered by their high school. The proportion satisfied tends to be slightly lower among government officials and considerably lower among the residents. This pattern of difference is found in both central city and suburban areas. The low proportion of residents who are satisfied with the training offered in the high schools is due mainly to the much larger number of persons found in the "don't know" category. That is, nearly one-fifth or more of the residents do not have an opinion on the type of training offered. Thus their responses are not a matter of dissatisfaction, but a function of unfamiliarity with what is going on in the high school. On the other hand, few if any of the public officials did not have an opinion. And except for a sizable minority, the officials appeared to be satisfied with what is being offered. So here again it would seem unlikely that the level of dissatisfaction is such that one would expect it to generate any real interest in change. Quite the contrary, the level of satisfaction would likely be an important factor in maintaining the "status quo."

Evaluation of Schools

Let us turn now to a comparative evaluation of the schools in different segments of the metropolitan area—that is, how are the schools in one zone rated in relationship to the schools in the opposite part of the metropolitan community? These data are shown in Table 10-3. As expected, officials as well as residents rate their own schools as being better than those in the opposite area. However, officials are much more likely to do so than residents. This is observable in each size class. But perhaps it is even more significant that the evaluations vary substantially by size of metropolitan area, and the variation in the suburbs runs in a direction opposite from that in the central cities. As the size of metropolitan area declines, the proportion of central city officials as well as of residents who rate their own schools as better increases. For example, among city school officials the proportions range from 53 percent to 81 percent. A comparable range is also found among government officials. Residents are much less likely to concur in this judgment, but even here the proportion doing so is higher in the small than in the large metropolitan areas. The range is from 31 percent to 47 percent. But, as already noted, variations among the responses in the suburban areas follow the opposite pattern by size. However, in the suburbs also, in each size class, officials are more likely than residents to rate their own schools above those in the

TABLE 10-3

CITY AND SUBURBAN SCHOOLS COMPARED BY TYPE OF
RESPONDENT BY RESIDENTIAL ZONES AND
SIZE OF METROPOLITAN AREA

Type of Respondent and Evaluation of Schools	Large		Medium		Small	
	City	Suburb	City	Suburb	City	Suburb
	%	%	%	%	%	%
	Better in Own Area					
School officials	53.3	65.0	64.3	50.0	81.3	23.0
Government officials	54.3	59.3	26.0	30.2	75.8	29.8
Survey population	30.6	43.8	31.7	35.9	47.3	18.1
	Better in Opposite Area					
School officials	6.7	8.3	7.1	16.1	—	27.9
Government officials	8.6	8.5	9.1	17.5	1.5	13.4
Survey population	21.2	7.1	17.1	11.6	8.6	27.4
	About Same in Both Areas					
School officials	33.3	26.7	28.6	33.9	12.5	47.5
Government officials	32.9	32.2	48.1	49.2	19.7	52.2
Survey population	29.6	38.2	31.1	39.1	32.2	47.2

city. But this view is shared by a distinct majority of the officials only in the large area suburbs.

On this particular issue, we find substantial differences between officials and residents. And while there is a very high level of satisfaction with the schools in the area, as already noted, there is nonetheless an awareness on the part of many, at least in the smaller area suburbs, that central city schools are better than their own. As the size of the metropolitan community increases, central city officials are less likely to rate their schools above those in the suburbs; but it is noted that even in the large central city areas, a majority of the officials do so, though it is a less frequent response than in the smaller areas. On the other hand, as noted above, it is only in the large area suburbs that a majority of the local public officials, school or government, rate their schools above those in the city. No doubt these evaluations somewhat realistically reflect the variations in quality of schools in the suburbs, by size of area, as compared with neighboring central city schools. These differences we would expect on the basis of variations in the stages of development of the suburbs in different sizes of metropolitan areas. Again, these data give added support to our earlier observation and conclusion that as the suburban areas grow and mature to established communities, the amount of resistance to change increases. No doubt the more favorable evaluation of the schools in the suburban zones of large areas reflects their more advanced stage of development. Officials seem to be more aware of this difference than do the residents of these areas. At any rate, they are more likely to evaluate their own localities above the central city as far as schools are concerned. To the extent that they do so, we would expect increased resistance to change. We would expect officials to be more opposed to change than residents in all suburban zones, and we would expect resistance to change, even among officials, to decrease as size of metropolitan area declines. Before investigating this matter, let us inquire into the extent to which the present system of multiple districts is seen as being wasteful, and related economic attitudes.

Views Concerning Multiple School Districts

An inspection of the data presented in Table 10-4 indicates that central city officials are generally agreed that the present

TABLE 10-4

PROPORTION REPORTING THAT SEPARATE SCHOOL DISTRICTS ARE
AND ARE NOT WASTEFUL BY TYPE OF RESPONDENT
BY RESIDENTIAL ZONE AND SIZE OF
METROPOLITAN AREA

Type of Respondent and Attitude Toward Multiple Districts	Large		Medium		Small	
	City	Suburb	City	Suburb	City	Suburb
	%	%	%	%	%	%
Separate Districts Are Wasteful						
School officials	86.7	28.3	42.9	22.6	75.0	44.3
Government officials	70.0	23.7	70.1	36.5	84.8	26.9
Survey population	37.1	30.3	42.0	35.7	43.9	40.0
Separate Districts Are Not Wasteful						
School officials	13.3	71.7	42.9	77.4	18.8	54.1
Government officials	20.0	69.5	20.8	58.7	9.1	71.6
Survey population	41.9	56.6	38.9	52.9	41.2	49.0

system of multiple school districts is wasteful, whereas suburban officials are nearly equally in agreement that such is not the case. No difference appears among size classes in this respect, though the central city-suburban gap, particularly among school officials, declines as size of metropolitan area decreases. The reason for this is that while the proportion of central city officials who view the present system as wasteful tends to decline slightly by size of area, the proportions among suburban officials increase. For example, only 28 percent of the school officials in the large area suburbs report that separate districts are wasteful, but that rises to 44 percent in the small area suburbs. A very similar range is found among the residents, also.

In both large and small area cities, officials are nearly twice as likely as residents to view the present system as wasteful, whereas in the suburban areas the official-resident differences largely disappear. In the large central cities, 88 percent of the school officials report that multiple districts are wasteful, but only 37 percent of the residents respond thusly. The difference is due, in part, to the high proportion of residents who did not express an opinion. But in the suburbs, the responses of the school officials and residents are nearly identical. That is, about three out of ten hold the view that the present system is wasteful. While there are marked central city-suburban differences among officials in the proportion who view the present system as wasteful, only slight differences are found among the residents of the two zones in each size class. While only a small minority of the city officials report that multiple districts are not wasteful, a clear majority of the officials in the suburbs hold this view. There are, however, variations by size of area. In each of the suburban areas, public officials are much more likely than residents to defend and find justification for the present system; but in the cities, residents are more likely to view multiple districts favorably than are their officials. Again, this difference is due in large part to the disproportionately large number of residents who did not express a specific opinion regarding the issue.

A point to be stressed here, with reference to the potential for reform in metropolitan areas, is not only that central city officials tend to view the present system as wasteful but that a substantial number of the school officials and residents in the small area suburbs share that view. Only half of the residents and slightly more than half of the school officials in the small area suburbs took the position that multiple districts are not wasteful. However, in the larger areas, more than half of the residents and nearly three-fourths of the officials expressed this view. Thus it would seem that the setting for change is much more suitable in the smaller than in the larger metropolitan areas. At least in the smaller areas, there seems to be more general awareness on the part of the suburban officials, as well as the residents, of the shortcomings of having a number of separate districts in the area. But this view is shared much less frequently in the larger areas. On the contrary, just the opposite view is expressed. But in all suburban zones, officials are less likely to see, or at least to report, the wastefulness of the present system.

The Taxation Issue

We now turn to a discussion of how local officials view various dimensions of the tax issue in their areas, as compared with the residents. As is readily evident from an inspection of the data presented in Table 10-5, there is more criticism of the school tax burden in the suburbs than in the central cities. This is found in each size class. Regardless of type of area, residents are more likely than officials to view present school taxes as being too high. And school officials are less likely to share this view than government officials. Thus we find not only marked central city-suburban differences, but substantial differences between officials and residents in both central city and suburban areas. The largest proportion of residents reporting that school taxes are too high is found in the large area suburbs. This is also the case with government officials. But among school officials, there is only a small amount of variation by size of area, and to the extent that there is a difference, most criticism of taxes is found in the small area suburbs. Even there, the complaint is expressed by less than one-fourth of the school officials, but by nearly two-fifths of the residents.

While school officials are least likely to feel that taxes are too high, they are most likely to feel that not enough is being spent on education in their districts. Except in the small metropolitan areas, central city school officials are much more likely than suburban

TABLE 10-5

PROPORTION REPORTING SELECTED VIEWS CONCERNING SCHOOL TAXES
AND EXPENDITURES BY TYPE OF RESPONDENT BY RESIDENTIAL
ZONE AND SIZE OF METROPOLITAN AREA

Type of Respondent and Selected Views	Large		Medium		Small	
	City	Suburb	City	Suburb	City	Suburb
	%	%	%	%	%	%
Percentage Reporting That School Taxes Are Too High:						
School officials	6.7	18.3	7.1	19.4	6.3	23.0
Government officials	15.8	42.4	15.6	33.3	18.2	29.9
Survey population	29.6	45.1	21.9	32.3	30.5	38.2
Percentage Reporting That Not Enough Is Being Spent on Education:						
School officials	66.7	40.0	57.1	43.5	25.0	32.8
Government officials	8.6	5.1	14.3	11.1	10.6	1.5
Survey population	34.0	12.7	26.0	13.8	19.1	15.7
Percentage Reporting Preference for Cutting Taxes Over Better Schools:						
School officials	—	3.3	—	1.6	—	—
Government officials	5.7	5.1	1.3	6.3	6.1	9.0
Survey population	23.5	19.6	14.2	14.6	21.9	20.5
Percentage Not Willing to Pay More in Order to Improve the Schools:						
School officials	26.7	33.3	7.1	19.4	18.8	18.0
Government officials	32.9	42.4	26.0	42.8	34.8	35.8
Survey population	40.0	45.9	50.5	44.1	46.1	47.4

officials to report that not enough is being spent on education. In both large and medium-sized central cities, a majority of the school officials, from 57 percent to 67 percent, feel that not enough is being spent, but this drops to only 25 percent in the small area cities. From one-third to nearly half of the suburban school officials report that not enough is being spent in their zones. By way of contrast, residents are much less likely than school officials to share this view, but they are more likely to do so than government officials. The latter rarely feel that schools are under-supported. The proportion is consistently lower in the suburbs, but in none of the areas do we find even as many as 15 percent who feel that more funds should be spent for schools. This is quite different from a high of 67 percent among school officials and a high of 34 percent among the residents. But a point worthy of note is the very small proportion of suburban residents who feel that not enough is being spent on education. The proportion ranges only from 13 percent to 16 percent.

In short, it seems that when compared with the general population, school officials are much less likely to feel that taxes are too high and are much more likely to feel that not enough is being spent on education in their area. On the other hand, government officials tend to be more similar to the residents in the proportion who report that taxes are too high, but they are much less likely to feel that not enough is being spent on education. Clearly their interests and views reflect quite a different concern than those of school officials. At any rate, there appears to be considerable concern, particularly among suburban residents, over the size of the tax burden, and there is little interest in seeing more funds devoted to the support of their schools. The gap between school officials and residents is a substantial one. And this gap is found in each type and size of area category. Thus the gap between officials and residents seems to be quite independent of area of residence or size of metropolitan community.

Concern over taxes continues to be evident when we view the responses to the general question which provided a choice between better schools or cutting taxes. These data are shown in the lower portion of Table 10-5. Almost without exception, school officials, and to a lesser extent government officials, state a preference for better schools. That is, given the choice, they would prefer to see better schools than a reduced tax burden. But roughly one resident in five does not share this view, for this proportion states a preference for reduced taxes. Neither the pattern nor the size of response show any consistent difference by size of metropolitan area. The only meaningful difference here is that found between the residents in each area and their officials.

A closely related issue is presented in the bottom panel of the table, in which a similar distribution of responses appears. In all areas, residents are consistently less willing than officials, and particularly school officials, to pay more in order to improve their schools. And, contrary to earlier expectations, suburban residents are no more willing to do so than are central city residents. Nor do we find any appreciable differences among residents by size of area. Between four and five persons out of every ten, regardless of place of residence, would not be willing to pay more in order to improve their schools. However, among school officials, size of area is a factor, for it is in the large metropolitan areas that we find the least willingness to pay more in order to improve the schools. It is noted further that the proportion of school officials sharing this view is about 25 percent higher in the suburbs than in the central cities.

In an overall appraisal of the views regarding school taxes, it would seem that officials have quite a different conception of the issue than do the residents they represent. While the former tend to underplay the size of the tax burden and the amount spent on education, we find quite a different view among the residents. Among the latter, there are a disproportionate number who feel that taxes are too high and who are much less likely to feel that not enough is being spent on education. Residents would be much more willing than school officials to have reduced taxes rather than better schools, and they would be much less willing to pay more in order to improve the schools. On the other hand, practically none of the school officials would prefer reduced taxes over better schools, and all but a small minority would be willing to pay more in order to improve the schools. But, as already noted, these views are not shared by many of the government officials, nor by the residents within each area. In nearly every instance, the gap is substantial.

Level of Government That Should Support the Schools

Turning our attention to the general question of what level of government should be responsible for the support of the schools, we continue to find marked differences in the views expressed by residents and officials. And these differences tend to be consistent with the residents' general desire not to pay directly for the quality of education which they would like to have in their areas. For the most part, officials are much less likely than residents to favor federal aid for the cost of operations. With few exceptions, suburban officials are less likely to do so than central city officials. But the really significant difference is found between school officials and the residents in their zones. The gap is substantial in all areas, as is shown in Table 10-6. Among central cities, the proportion of school officials who would favor federal aid declines markedly by size of area, ranging from 40 percent in the large to only 6 percent in the small cities. But there is no variation among suburban school officials. In each suburban zone, approximately one-fourth of the officials report that they would favor federal aid, while more than half of the residents do so. And in the central cities, three-fifths or more of the residents

TABLE 10-6

PROPORTION REPORTING SELECTED VIEWS CONCERNING RESPONSIBILITY
FOR THE SUPPORT OF THE SCHOOLS BY TYPE OF RESPONDENT
BY RESIDENTIAL ZONE AND SIZE OF METROPOLITAN AREA

Type of Respondent and Selected Views	Large		Medium		Small	
	City	Suburb	City	Suburb	City	Suburb
	%	%	%	%	%	%
Percentage Favoring Federal Aid to Local Districts:						
School officials	40.0	23.3	35.7	25.8	6.3	24.6
Government officials	48.6	32.2	32.5	46.0	25.8	19.4
Survey population	68.8	59.2	63.9	59.6	58.6	54.7
Percentage Reporting Residents of District Should Have Primary Responsibility for Support of Schools:						
School officials	80.0	88.3	78.6	88.7	100.0	75.4
Government officials	74.3	89.8	77.9	77.8	87.9	85.1
Survey population	29.6	43.0	31.5	47.1	36.9	37.8
Percentage Reporting that Either State or Federal Government Should Have Primary Responsibility for Support of Schools:						
School officials	13.3	8.3	21.4	8.1	—	22.9
Government officials	11.5	1.7	5.2	12.7	1.5	10.5
Survey population	38.2	38.8	41.6	29.8	37.7	33.5

are in favor of the federal government providing funds to help cover
the costs of operations.

Thus, while federal aid is not generally viewed favorably by
school officials in any of the areas, it does find majority support from
the residents in all parts of metropolitan areas. However, in this instance residents are referring to federal funds only as a source of
help, and not as the primary source of support for the operation of
the schools. This is suggested by the responses to the next question,
which more specifically asked which level of government should be
"primarily" responsible for providing the funds for the daily operations of the schools.

Here it is even more evident that officials want to keep the support
of the schools primarily as a local responsibility of the residents
within the district. This view is, however, shared by only a minority
of the residents, but it is more frequently expressed by suburban
than central city people. We find that 75 percent or more of the
officials feel that the cost of operations is primarily a local responsi-

bility of the residents living within the district. These responses vary little by type of official. Nor do we find any consistent pattern of difference among officials, either by type of area or size of metropolitan community. Few local officials, in any of the areas, see this as a responsibility of either the state or federal government. Within each residential zone, there are marked differences between the views reported by officials and the views of the residents they represent. For example, only a minority of the residents in any of the areas report that the costs of operations should be primarily a local responsibility. This is what one would expect, in light of their more favorable view toward federal assistance. As is evident from the responses in the lower panel of Table 10–6, approximately one-third of the residents

TABLE 10-7

PROPORTION REPORTING THAT ORDINARY CITIZEN CANNOT DO MUCH
ABOUT HOW SCHOOL MONEY IS SPENT BY TYPE OF RESPONDENT
BY RESIDENTIAL ZONE AND SIZE OF METROPOLITAN AREA

Type of Respondent	Large		Medium		Small	
	City	Suburb	City	Suburb	City	Suburb
	%	%	%	%	%	%
School officials	6.7	5.0	7.1	8.1	—	21.0
Government officials	31.4	16.9	24.7	23.8	13.6	17.9
Survey population	50.3	39.4	53.2	47.3	52.5	41.7

hold the view that the costs of operations should be primarily the responsibility of either the state or federal government. By way of comparison, the latter source of support for the schools is rarely mentioned by officials in any of the areas.

Thus, officials and residents differ substantially in their views regarding the support of schools. Officials generally agree that financing the schools should rest primarily in the hands of the residents within the district. And only a small minority of the officials would be in favor of the federal government providing funds to help cover the costs of operations. Suburban officials are even less likely than those in the central cities to approve of such aid, except in the small metropolitan areas where the opposite is found. But quite a different response is reported by the residents. While a substantial majority in all areas are in favor of federal aid, only a minority report that the primary source of support of the schools should come from outside of their own local district. At the same time, only a minority of the residents share the view that the costs of operations should be primarily their own responsibility—that is, the responsibility only of the residents living within the district. Apparently they are willing to assume some of the responsibility, since they do not report this as the primary responsibility of another level of government, but it is readily evident that they approve of outside aid. In holding this view, they are at direct odds with their officials. Clearly there is a lack of consensus here.

Role of Citizen in How School Money is Spent

Since there is such a marked difference between officials and residents regarding who should support the schools, it will be interesting to learn just how much influence residents have in how school money is spent. The discussion is based on the general question: "Can the ordinary citizen do much about how school money is spent?" The responses are shown in Table 10-7. Again we find marked differences between officials and residents. Except in the small area suburbs, school officials rarely report that the ordinary citizen doesn't have much to say about how school funds are spent. These responses do not vary by type of area. However, this view is much more frequently expressed by government officials. The proportion of such responses increases directly by size of central city, but no comparable size variation is observed in suburban zones. Residents are even less sanguine about their influence on how school funds are spent. A majority of the residents in the central cities, and only a slightly lower proportion in the suburbs, report that they can't do much, and this proportion remains approximately the same regardless of size of area.

Thus, again it is quite clear that there is a substantial difference between the views reported by officials and by the residents they represent. School officials in particular are in almost unanimous agreement that the ordinary citizen can have considerable influence on how school funds are spent, but this view is not shared by many of the residents in any of the areas. We do find, however, that this view tends to be reported somewhat more frequently by suburban residents in each size class than by central city residents. But in all areas, central city and suburban, there is considerable disagreement between officials and residents.

Views Concerning Reorganization

We return now to the major point of the study, which is the extent to which public officials are opposed to change in the organization of school districts in the metropolitan community context. We have already observed rather widespread opposition among suburban residents, while central city residents tend to favor reorganization. At this point, the issue is how these views compare with the views that are expressed by the public officials in each area. An inspection of the data presented in Table10-8 would easily discourage anyone who was interested in bringing about a reorganization of school districts in metropolitan areas. For while central city of-

TABLE 10-8

PROPORTION IN FAVOR OR OPPOSED TO A SINGLE DISTRICT OR AREA-WIDE
HIGH SCHOOL BY TYPE OF RESPONDENT BY RESIDENTIAL ZONE
AND SIZE OF METROPOLITAN AREA

Type of Respondent and Selected Attitudes	Large		Medium		Small	
	City	Suburb	City	Suburb	City	Suburb
	%	%	%	%	%	%
Percentage Favoring Single District for Area:						
School officials	73.3	10.0	35.7	12.9	68.8	34.4
Government officials	51.4	8.5	59.7	28.6	54.5	10.4
Survey population	46.5	22.0	44.4	29.0	44.9	35.8
Percentage Opposed to a Single District for Area:						
School officials	26.7	88.3	50.0	79.0	25.0	63.9
Government officials	30.0	86.4	28.6	69.8	39.0	88.1
Survey population	36.3	68.9	34.8	60.6	37.5	49.8
Percentage Favoring Area-Wide High School:						
School officials	80.0	11.7	35.7	9.7	87.5	54.1
Government officials	74.3	8.5	62.3	26.9	66.7	19.4
Survey population	53.2	23.2	45.3	30.6	56.4	51.8
Percentage Opposed to Area-Wide High School:						
School officials	6.7	88.3	50.0	88.7	12.5	39.3
Government officials	17.1	91.5	27.3	73.0	30.3	77.6
Survey population	32.5	70.3	36.1	59.6	28.3	37.0

ficials tend to favor such a proposal, there is widespread opposition among suburban officials. And the opposition is particularly marked in the larger area suburbs. Three-fourths of the city school officials in the large metropolitan areas indicate that they would vote in favor of reorganization, but the proportion of school officials in the neighboring suburbs who would do so is a mere 10 percent. Even less support for change is found among the suburban government officials. While residents in the larger area suburbs are more than twice as likely as public officials to favor change, the number who would do so is only slightly more than one in five. On the other hand, 88 percent of the suburban school officials would oppose change, as would 70 percent of the residents. Clearly, any proposal for the reorganization of school districts in the larger metropolitan areas would almost certainly meet with defeat. And the opposition would be most emphatically expressed by the incumbent officials.

Yet opposition, not only among residents, but school officials as well, tends to decline as size of area decreases. Thus in the small area suburbs, we find that more than one-third of the school officials and the residents report that they would vote in favor of a reorganizational proposal. But among government officials, opposition continues at the same high level. Even in the suburban zones of small areas, where opposition is least, approximately two-thirds of the school officials and half of the residents claim that they would vote against such a proposal. Thus it is evident that opposition is still substantial, though it is much less general than in large metropolitan areas. As we move from the large to the small area suburbs, support for change increases more than threefold among school officials and nearly doubles among the residents. However, even though support for change is substantially higher in the smaller suburban areas, it is still expressed by only a minority. But the important point to note is that opposition has reduced to a level where a reorganizational proposal has a much greater chance for acceptance than in the larger areas.

Area-Wide High Schools

A very similar pattern of responses is also found in respect to administering high schools on an area-wide basis. Only a minority of either the central city officials or the residents would oppose such a proposal. In other words, such an issue would find ready support in the central cities. But this is not the case in the suburban zones, where only a very small proportion of the school officials would favor an area-wide high school. The only exception occurs in the small area suburbs, where a majority of the school officials and a majority of the residents report that they would favor handling high schools on an area-wide basis.

It is quite evident in the small area suburbs that both school officials and residents are much more likely to approve an area-wide high school than a single overall school district for the area. Apparently in the small area suburbs, the need for a consolidated high school is evident. Some districts do not have a high school of their own, and they seem to be quite willing to move in the direction of an area-wide high school; but they want to do so without any sacrifice of their independent school district status. While two-thirds of the school officials in the small area suburbs report that they are opposed to setting up a single school district, only 39 percent are opposed to setting up a consolidated high school to serve the same area that would be encompassed in the proposed single district. A very similar difference is also found among the residents. It is only in the cities and the small area suburbs that we find a majority of school officials expressing approval of an area-wide high school. In the other suburban areas, handling the high school on an area-wide basis is opposed just as much as setting up a single school district for the whole area.

But even in respect to setting up a consolidated high school, opposition is more frequently expressed by suburban officials than by the residents of those zones, whereas in the central cities, the opposite is found—that is, officials tend to favor change even more than the residents. Part of this difference is due to the larger proportion of residents who have not yet taken a position on this issue. That is, they are uncertain or do not know how they would vote on setting up a single district or in establishing a high school on an area-wide basis. Although the proportion of officials opposed to change is approximately the same in each central city, regardless of size, opposition in the suburbs tends to increase directly by size of area. And in each of the suburban areas, opposition is reported by a clear majority.

Assessment of Expected Opposition

Attention is now focused on the extent to which officials and residents are able to accurately assess the views regarding change that are held by the general population in their own zones and in the opposite parts of the metropolitan community. We have already noted that suburban officials are more frequently opposed to change than the residents whom they represent, while the opposite pattern is found in the central cities. The question here pertains to whether or not officials are aware of the gap that exists between their views regarding the reorganization of school districts and those expressed by the general population. These data are shown in Table 10-9.

TABLE 10-9

PROPORTION OPPOSED TO SINGLE DISTRICT AND PROPORTION WHO THINK
THAT OTHERS WOULD BE OPPOSED BY TYPE OF RESPONDENT BY
RESIDENTIAL ZONE AND SIZE OF METROPOLITAN AREA

Type of Respondent and Selected Attitudes	Large		Medium		Small	
	City	Suburb	City	Suburb	City	Suburb
	%	%	%	%	%	%
Percentage of Residents Opposed to Single District	36.3	68.9	34.8	60.6	37.5	49.4
Percentage Who Think People in Their Own Area Would be Opposed to a Single District:						
School officials	40.0	98.3	85.7	87.1	37.5	67.2
Government officials	38.6	88.1	51.9	71.4	50.0	85.1
Survey population	35.0	68.9	33.3	58.4	42.2	54.5
Percentage of Respondents in Opposite Area Who Think People in Area Would be Opposed to a Single District:						
School officials	50.0	80.0	71.0	92.9	49.2	62.5
Government officials	52.5	54.3	55.6	50.6	41.8	56.1
Survey population	42.7	43.0	42.8	35.2	41.5	39.3

It is particularly noteworthy that suburban officials have a gross misconception of how the residents in their areas feel about the issue of setting up a single school district for the whole area. Almost without exception, school officials, and to a slightly lesser extent government officials, hold the view that the residents in their areas would be opposed to such a proposal. However, as noted earlier, when the residents were asked how they would vote on such a proposal, only slightly more than two-thirds reported that they would vote against it. Thus, even in the large area suburbs, where maximum opposition is found, the proportion of residents opposed to change appears to be substantially lower than the officials seem to realize. It is not surprising then that officials would oppose change, when nearly all of them hold the view that the residents in their areas would be opposed to any such proposal. One must interpret these data with particular caution, however, since it is not possible to determine whether the officials actually think that the people in the area would be opposed to change or whether they attribute this view to the residents so as to justify their own opposition. At any rate, in each of the suburban areas, there is a marked difference between what officials think the residents would do and what the residents themselves say they would do.

On the other hand, the suburban residents seem to be quite capable of accurately assessing the views of their neighbors. At any rate, there is little, if any, difference between what the residents think others would do and what the residents report that they would do. For example, in the large area suburbs, nearly 70 percent of the residents state that the people in their zones would be opposed to setting up a single district for the whole area, which is the same proportion that reported that they would vote against such a proposal. In the small area suburbs, there is a slight tendency for the residents to overstate the amount of opposition, in that 55 percent report that the people in their area would be opposed to change, while only 49 percent said that they would vote against change. In the same zones, much larger proportions of both school and government officials expected the people to be opposed to change. The large gap between what officials think the residents would do and what the residents say they would do is not found in any of the central cities. That is, central city officials are much more accurate in their appraisal of how the residents in their areas would vote on such a proposal. The only exception is found among school officials in the medium-sized area cities, where the amount of expected opposition is grossly overstated.

An inspection of the data in the lower panel of Table 10-9 clearly shows that the officials in each area also tend to overstate the amount of opposition that would be found among the residents of the opposite area. While central city officials quite accurately appraise how their own residents would respond to change, there is a marked tendency for school officials to consistently overstate the amount of opposition that exists in the suburbs. In the large metropolitan areas, 80 percent of the central city school officials report that suburban people would be opposed to change, whereas only 69 percent of the residents report that they would vote against a proposed reorganization. In the small areas, these proportions are 63 percent and 49 percent, respectively. The difference is even more marked in the medium-sized areas. Likewise, a larger proportion of the suburban school officials would expect the central city residents to be opposed to change than is indicated by the responses of the residents. In the large metropolitan areas, while only slightly more than one-third of the residents of the city say they would vote against a single district, half of the school officials in the neighboring suburbs hold the view that the central city residents would be opposed to such a proposal. The same type of difference is observed in the other metropolitan areas, also.

It is noteworthy that except for the small metropolitan areas, a majority of the suburban officials feel that the people in the city would be opposed to change. In all instances, this markedly overstates the proportion of residents who respond thusly. And even in the small metropolitan areas, where less than a majority of the suburban officials express the view that city people would be against setting up a single district, the officials still substantially overstate the level of opposition that is reported by the residents. The same pattern of difference is also observed in respect to how city school officials appraise the level of opposition in the suburbs. In each size class, a much higher proportion of the city school officials expect the suburban people to be opposed to setting up a single district than is indicated by the responses of the residents regarding their views. On the other hand, among government officials, and to an even greater extent among residents in the city, there is a marked tendency for the proportion expecting opposition in the suburbs to be lower than the proportion of residents who report that they would vote against reorganization.

In short, suburban officials tend to overstate the level of opposition in their own areas as well as among residents in the central city. Suburban residents appear to be quite realistic in their judgment of the views of the other people in the area, but there is a slight tendency to overstate the level of opposition found among the central city residents. But in evaluating the views of the general population in their own zones, they are much more perceptive, or at least more nearly accurate, than any of the suburban public officials. Central city officials, however, both school and municipal, display a real capacity to correctly assess the views of the residents in their own areas, as do the residents also. Central city residents are much less accurate in reporting how suburban people would respond to a single district; their error, however, is a matter of degree rather than of kind.

These data suggest that one of the factors which may account for the high proportion of officials, particularly among those in the suburban areas, who oppose setting up a single district, is the notion that this view is shared by a majority of the residents not only in their own areas but in the contiguous central cities also. Similarly, suburban residents may oppose reorganization of school districts, in part at least, because they think that the other people in their area share this view. Perhaps one of the most interesting observations here is the marked similarity between how suburban residents assess the opposition that is likely among those living in the central city and how central city residents view the level of opposition that would obtain in the suburbs. In none of the areas do we find a majority of the residents holding the view that the people in the opposite part of the metropolitan community would be opposed to change. And these expectations do not vary either by size or type of area. However, while only a small minority of the city residents would expect others in the city to be opposed to change, we find that a majority of the suburban residents would expect others in the suburbs to be opposed to setting up a single district. Thus, to oppose change is to share what is thought to be the view of others in the area. But as these data show, opposition is not as widespread as suburban people or officials think it is. Yet it is quite likely that in responding to a proposal for change, suburban residents, as well as suburban officials, would react on the assumption that other people in their area would vote in opposition. No doubt this factor plays an important role in resistance to change, not only among officials, but the general population as well. At any rate, while city officials tend to favor the reorganization of school districts within the metropolitan community context, opposition is widespread among the suburban officials. And even though opposition is more frequent among officials than among suburban residents, nearly all of the suburban officials hold the view that the residents in their areas would be opposed to such a proposal. It is quite certain that they would act accordingly.

Views on Combining only Suburban Districts

There would be less resistance among suburban officials and residents to setting up a single school district which combined only the suburban areas than one that would include the central cities. But even a reorganization of school districts into a single suburban system is viewed with favor by only a small minority of the residents and officials in the suburban areas. Responses to this proposal, however, do not show the wide gap between officials and residents that was observed earlier in respect to setting up a single district for the whole area. Quite the contrary, as is evident from the data presented in Table 10-10: support for setting up a single district for the sub-

TABLE 10-10

PROPORTION REPORTING THEY WOULD VOTE FOR OR AGAINST A SINGLE DISTRICT FOR SUBURBAN AREAS ONLY AND HOW EXPECT OTHERS TO VOTE BY TYPE OF RESPONDENT BY RESIDENTIAL ZONE AND SIZE OF METROPOLITAN AREA

Type of Respondent and Vote on Single District	Vote In Favor			Vote Against		
	Large	Medium	Small	Large	Medium	Small
	%	%	%	%	%	%
How Vote on Setting Up Single School District for Suburban Areas Only:						
School officials	33.3	29.0	47.5	56.7	63.0	49.2
Government officials	30.5	31.7	46.3	59.3	58.7	43.3
Survey population	36.4	35.1	42.9	49.7	48.3	35.0
How Think Most People in District Would Vote on this Issue:						
School officials	16.7	17.7	41.0	70.0	69.3	49.2
Government officials	27.1	25.4	44.8	64.4	68.3	47.8
Survey population	20.4	18.9	28.3	44.0	39.8	28.9

urban areas only is reported as frequently by officials as by residents. Support for change within these limits also increases as size of area declines, but it falls short of finding majority support even in the small area suburbs. Actually, in the latter areas, the amount of support for change is about equal to the amount of opposition. But since not everyone has taken a position on the proposal, neither side of the issue succeeds in obtaining a majority of the total; whereas in the suburban zones of larger areas, at least one-half or more report that they would vote against such a proposal. In each size class, the proportion opposed to even this type of change tends to be higher among officials than among the residents in each suburban area.

Again in the responses to this proposal, there is a tendency to see less support for change and more opposition from others than is expressed by either the residents or the officials. For example, in the large suburban areas, one-third of the school officials report that they would vote in favor of a single school district for the suburban zones, but only half this proportion feel that most people in their district would favor such a proposal. On the other hand, while 58 percent report that they would vote against such a proposal, 70 percent think that most people in their district would do so. Only in the small area suburbs do we find general agreement between the proportion who say that they would vote against change and the proportion who feel that most people in the district would vote likewise. This is where we find least resistance to this type of change. Actually, the proportion who would vote in favor of setting up a single district for the suburban areas only is not far short of a majority.

At any rate, it seems quite clear that most suburban residents, and even a larger proportion of the officials, would be opposed to any proposal which would disrupt the status quo of their independent school districts. The resistance tends to decrease as size of area declines. Also, there would be less resistance to a proposal that was limited only to the suburban areas than one which included the central city. The evidence is quite convincing and consistent. Suburban officials and suburban residents are quite opposed to joining with the central city, and opposition is most marked in the larger metropolitan areas.

Cost as a Factor in Reorganization

There appears to be much more willingness on the part of public officials in the suburbs than among the residents in these zones to prefer the present school district with higher taxes over a single district with lower taxes. On the other hand, a substantial majority of the central city officials, as well as the residents, state a preference for a single district with lower taxes. Although in all areas the proportion making such a choice increases as size of central city declines, officials are even more likely than central city residents to select this alternative. Quite the opposite is found in the suburban areas where a clear majority of the officials in each of the suburban zones state a preference for the present district, even with higher taxes. The proportion making such a choice, however, declines as size of area decreases. Still, this view is not shared by a majority of the residents in any of the suburban zones. When the question is stated in these terms, opposition to a single district for the whole area declines appreciably. These data are shown in Table 10-11.

It will be recalled that approximately two-thirds of the residents in the large area suburbs reported that they would vote against a single district; however, when the issue is stated in more specific

TABLE 10-11

PROPORTION STATING PREFERENCE FOR PRESENT DISTRICT WITH HIGHER
TAXES OR SINGLE DISTRICT WITH LOWER TAXES BY TYPE OF
RESPONDENT BY RESIDENTIAL ZONE AND
SIZE OF METROPOLITAN AREA

Preference and Type of Respondent	Large		Medium		Small	
	City	Suburb	City	Suburb	City	Suburb
	%	%	%	%	%	%
Percentage Stating Preference for Present District With Higher Taxes:						
School officials	26.7	71.7	35.7	74.2	6.3	55.7
Government officials	15.7	79.6	15.6	53.9	19.7	68.7
Survey population	23.1	47.9	23.4	39.1	22.5	28.7
Percentage Stating Preference for Single District With Lower Taxes:						
School officials	73.3	21.7	64.3	19.3	93.8	37.7
Government officials	74.3	15.3	75.3	38.1	71.2	25.4
Survey population	62.1	41.0	60.4	46.9	63.5	57.3

terms and related to a differential tax burden, less than half would prefer the present district with higher taxes over a single district with lower taxes. Concern with costs is clearly evident. On the other hand, while only 22 percent would vote in favor of a single district, we find that double this proportion (41 percent) state a preference for a single district with lower taxes over the present district with higher taxes. Much the same kind of change in responses is found in the other suburban areas also. But it is only in the small area suburbs that a clear majority of the residents state a preference for a single district with lower taxes. This view is shared by less than two-fifths of the school officials and by only one-fourth of the municipal officials.

Although this question involves two different dimensions—school district reorganization and a differential tax burden—the responses differ so markedly from those noted earlier in reference to the more general question of how people would vote on setting up a single district, that it would seem safe to infer that the economic dimension is of crucial concern in such an issue. At least this is suggested by the marked changes in the responses reported by residents in all zones. The economic influence is also evident among officials in both central city and suburban areas. In the central cities, the tax dimension has the effect of increasing the size of the majority that supports change. But support for a single district, even given these conditions, falls short of a majority in both the large and medium-sized area suburbs. By the same token, less than a majority state support for the status quo. Among suburban officials, support for change increases when lower taxes are made a part of the proposal, but even under these conditions a sizable majority of the suburban officials state a preference for the present district with higher taxes rather than for a single district with lower taxes. Although the tax burden does have some influence upon the thinking of suburban officials, it is not of sufficient importance to win their support for setting up a single district for the whole area. The highly significant role that taxes play in how residents view the issue of reorganization of school districts in the metropolitan context is noteworthy. Certainly any reform movement would have to come to grips with this issue. It is clear, however, that the promise of lower taxes would not successfully overcome the resistance of the suburban officials, though it might contribute substantially to the outcome of a popular referendum.[3]

Impact of Reorganization on Quality of Schools and Taxes

If a single district were set up combining the existing central city and suburban districts, what would be the perceived consequences in respect to the quality of the schools and the tax burden? And more specifically, how do officials and residents differ in their views regarding these issues? According to the data presented in Table 10-12, there are marked central city and suburban differences as to what one might expect following reorganization. Moreover, the responses show the same pattern of difference that was observed earlier in respect to resistance to change. In general, the groups that were most likely to favor change, regardless of area or zone, are the ones most likely to see an improvement in the schools. The difference is not as clear-cut regarding the effect change would have on taxes.

Turning first to what would happen to the quality of the schools, it is noted that central city officials are much more likely than those in the suburbs, or even the residents of the central city, to feel that the quality of the schools would improve. It is particularly noteworthy that this view is shared by a majority of the school officials only in the large cities. As the size of the metropolitan area declines, there is a consistent decrease in the proportion of central city officials and central city residents who feel that the schools would improve in quality under a single system. But as already noted, officials in each size central city are much more likely than residents to expect the schools to become better. This type of variation does not obtain in the suburbs. In general, there are no differences between officials and residents in the proportion who feel that the

[3] In actual practice, this does not make reform any less difficult, because lower taxes would not necessarily result under a single district. And further, even though this might occur, the opposition would put up a campaign to confuse the issue and would make the counter-claim that taxes would increase. This is a standard format for any resistance group concerning any issue where public funds are involved. This invariably proves to be a very effective defense against change, because people are always suspicious concerning what will happen to taxes. Also, the general opinion is that reorganization would not result in reduced taxes. See discussion on this issue below.

TABLE 10-12

PROPORTION REPORTING EFFECT OF SINGLE DISTRICT ON QUALITY OF
SCHOOLS AND TAXES BY TYPE OF RESPONDENT BY RESIDENTIAL
ZONE AND SIZE OF METROPOLITAN AREA

Type of Respondent and Changes in Quality and Taxes	Large		Medium		Small	
	City	Suburb	City	Suburb	City	Suburb
	%	%	%	%	%	%
QUALITY OF SCHOOLS						
Percentage Reporting School Would Become Better:						
School officials	53.3	11.7	42.9	12.9	43.8	26.2
Government officials	41.4	10.2	32.5	14.3	34.8	16.4
Survey population	31.2	11.9	28.4	14.4	22.5	21.5
Percentage Reporting School Would Not be as Good:						
School officials	6.7	60.0	14.3	58.1	12.5	39.3
Government officials	7.1	64.4	9.1	44.4	10.6	32.8
Survey population	17.4	48.5	19.3	39.6	18.9	22.8
TAXATION						
Percentage Reporting That Taxes Would Increase:						
School officials	53.3	38.3	42.9	46.8	75.0	34.4
Government officials	41.4	45.8	45.5	34.9	47.0	55.2
Survey population	39.2	50.5	36.8	35.9	41.4	43.9
Percentage Reporting That Taxes Would Decrease:						
School officials	20.0	30.0	7.1	19.4	12.5	21.3
Government officials	24.3	13.9	13.0	15.9	12.1	13.4
Survey population	20.1	17.8	18.2	17.8	12.7	18.5

schools would improve. And in both the large and medium-sized area suburbs, this view is shared by less than 15 percent of either the officials or the general population. However, in the small area suburbs, slightly more than one-fourth of the school officials and more than one-fifth of the residents would expect an improvement in quality.

But much more substantial differences are found in respect to the negative aspect of reorganization. Again we find that the suburban officials are most critical, particularly in the large metropolitan areas. In these areas, suburban officials are nearly ten times as likely as city officials to report that the schools would not be as good after reorganization. This view is held equally by government and school officials. Among residents, the central city-suburban difference is slightly less than threefold. As the size of area declines, we find a lower proportion who feel that the schools would not be as good under a single system. Residents are much less likely to think so than the officials. In the small area suburbs, where we generally find most support for reorganization, only slightly more than one-third of the officials and less than one-fourth of the residents hold the view that the quality of schools would decrease, if organized in a single system. This is by far the least amount of criticism expressed in any of the suburban zones.

Thus it would seem that the judgment concerning what effect change would have on the quality of the schools is largely a function of whether or not officials or residents are opposed to or in favor of change. If they resist change, there is a marked tendency to report that reorganization would lower the quality of the schools. Whether this response is a defense of their position, or one of the reasons for their position regarding reorganization, is not at all evident. But the original source of this attitude is unimportant, for the mere fact that suburban officials in particular can claim this as a consequence provides them ready support as well as a justification for being opposed to reorganization. To oppose change for such a noble reason is to increase the influence of the officials among the residents of the zone.

The tax issue is much less clear. In all zones, in each size class, there is a very substantial proportion of the officials who feel that taxes would increase under a single system. This view is held about as frequently by officials in both zones, and there is little consistent difference between officials and residents in either the central city or the suburban areas. By and large, approximately two-fifths of the officials, as well as residents, report that they would expect taxes to increase if a single district were established for the whole area. On the other hand, only a small minority of the officials or the residents would expect a tax decrease. Again we find little or no difference between residents and officials. Even the usual central city and suburban differences are largely lacking. The only consistent difference observed is among school officials. In each size class, school officials in the suburbs are more likely to expect a tax decrease than are city officials, but in none of the areas does it exceed 30 percent. It is particularly noteworthy that less than one-fifth of the residents in any of the areas would expect a decrease in taxes.

In short, the most frequently expressed opinion is that a reorganization of school districts would result in a tax increase. Since this view is expressed as frequently by central city officials as by those in the suburbs, it is not possible to argue here, as we did above, that this is merely a defense for the status quo—for, as already noted, central city officials generally favor change, while a majority of the suburban officials are opposed to it. Of course, it should be noted that each is using a different point of reference. Since the view is quite widespread that change would cause a tax increase, it seems reasonable to conclude that the cost factor is an important one in resistance to change. This takes on added significance when we recall the large proportion, even in the suburbs, who would prefer a single district with lower taxes over the present district with higher taxes. And although suburban officials are less sensitive to the tax dimension than either central city officials or the residents in either area, resistance to change decreases even among suburban officials when lower taxes are incorporated into the reorganizational proposal. But still a majority supports the present system, even with higher taxes. Thus, it would seem from these data that public officials in the suburbs provide one of the major obstacles to change.

11

Summary and Conclusions

THE PAST HALF-CENTURY has witnessed the progressive development of the metropolitan community. This has resulted from a series
of different movement patterns. First, there was the concentration
of population in the central cities, which became the focal point
for later growth and development. This pattern of movement, in
turn, was followed by first a gradual, then more rapid, increase of
population in the outlying areas, particularly in the suburbs contiguous to the cities. And in more recent years, there has been either
a slow rate of growth in the central cities or, in many cases, an absolute decline in size, while the suburban areas have continued to
increase at very rapid rates. For the most part, all of these rather
radical changes in the territorial distribution of population have
been superimposed on an already existing political and educational
administrative framework. Even though the whole social structure,
technology, and size of the metropolitan community have experienced marked changes, the old administrative structures have largely
persisted in their earlier forms.

Many objective observers have frequently argued that the old
structures have become obsolete, wasteful, and inefficient, as well
as costly. Also, it is argued that they cannot effectively meet the
service needs of the population in the metropolitan setting. These
observers have consistently demonstrated the need for the reorganization of local government and school districts; yet change has not
come about. On the contrary, to the extent that there has been any
historical change in views concerning reorganization—or, for that

matter, any other adjustments in the traditional systems—it has been in the direction of increased opposition. The separate political as well as school district units which make up the present metropolitan community complex, have over time become highly crystallized autonomous structures. Efforts to bring about changes which would more clearly put the everyday life of the community and the administrative structures in equilibrium, have met with widespread opposition and failure.

This study, then, has asked the basic question: "What are the roots of this resistance to change?" The study has focused on resistances to change in the organization of school districts within the metropolitan community, with particular attention being concentrated on the influence of both place of residence and size of metropolitan area. And within each residential zone, we have examined how views regarding reorganization vary among different population subgroups, and by different life patterns within the community. The importance of this question is evident when one views some of the consequences of the present system of multiple school districts within the same community. The significance of the problem is perhaps best illustrated by the wide range of differences found among school districts within the same community, in their ability to support an educational system. Consequently, the quality of their separate programs varies substantially.

In addition to the basic question regarding change, the study has been concerned with several other aspects of the schools in the metropolitan setting—for example, the level of involvement of the metropolitan population in the schools; how residents evaluate the city and suburban schools; and what views residents hold concerning the broad question of the support of the schools. And lastly, how public officials compare in their views concerning school-related issues with the residents whom they represent. Although each of the above topics was thought to have descriptive merit in terms of the general school function within the metropolis, these variables were, in turn, examined in order to determine what role they played in resistance to change.

Regarding almost any dimension of the school issue, we have consistently found that not only do central city and suburban residents differ, but among suburban residents, in particular, substantial differences are found by size of metropolitan area. Although we do find sizable differences in how residents respond to a variety of school-related issues among various segments of the population, and according to different life patterns, it is nonetheless noteworthy that, with few exceptions, central city and suburban differences, and, to a lesser extent, size-of-area differences, largely persist even when we control for such influences.

Level of Knowledge

In looking back over the findings, one is impressed by how little the residents in all parts of the metropolitan area actually know about their schools. For example, even when we limited our observations only to families with children in elementary school, we found that about two out of five respondents did not know the name of the principal of the school their children attended. There appeared to be little variation either by place of residence or size of metropolitan area. When the total population was considered, we found that a majority of the residents in all areas did not know the name of the superintendent of schools in their district. And contrary to expectation, the level of knowledge concerning this position was even less among suburban residents than among those in the city. Lack of such knowledge was most widespread in the large area suburbs.

In all areas, there was an almost complete lack of knowledge as to who was chairman of the school board. In the cities, the proportion of residents who knew the name of the chairman ranged from a low of only 2 percent in the large areas to a high of 14 percent in the small metropolitan areas. But even more significant is the observation that the level of knowledge concerning the person occupying this position was even less in the suburban areas. However, when the question was extended to include the whole school board, suburban residents were more likely to know at least someone who was on the board. But here, too, the general lack of knowledge is striking. Even in the small area suburbs, where we found the largest proportion who knew a member, at least two out of three residents did not know anyone on the school board. And in the large cities, the proportion increased to 86 percent.

When an overall index of level of knowledge was constructed, based on the responses to a series of questions, there was a consistent tendency for the scores to be higher in the suburbs than in the cities. In both residential zones, the scores decreased by size of area. But the significant point here is that the overall knowledge scores varied more by size of area than by place of residence. And in each size class, in both residential zones, families with children in school had the highest scores. However, even when we control for use of the schools, size-of-area and place-of-residence differences persist. But the most striking and socially significant observation here is the very high proportion of households in all areas that have no knowledge of any of the questions included in the index.

It is noteworthy, however, that we found more variation in level of knowledge by educational attainment than by either size of area or place of residence. Of particular interest was the tendency for the knowledge scale scores, at the higher educational levels, to be higher in the cities than in the suburbs. At each educational level, scores tended to vary directly by population size in both segments of the metropolitan population. The same pattern of difference was also found by both income and occupation. As the status of the respondent increases, so does the level of knowledge of schools. While the overall level of knowledge tends to be somewhat higher in the suburbs than in the city, the differences are due more to the composition of the population than to place of residence or size of population. At any rate, when persons of comparable characteristics were compared, the overall suburban advantage was lost; in fact, city residents with high status characteristics seem to have a higher level of knowledge concerning the schools than those living in the suburbs.

Level of Participation and Ideological Orientation

Among families with children in school, suburban residents are more likely to attend school board meetings than are city residents. However, the proportion who do so never exceeds 16 percent. Thus, direct contact with this group is very limited. Residents are somewhat more likely to have discussed issues with board members informally. In all areas, residents are more likely to have discussed school problems with a board member than with the superintendent of schools. Apparently contacts with the superintendent are very limited, but they tend to increase as size of area declines. Although it is generally argued that officials are more accessible and one can have a greater voice in how things are done in the smaller districts, in actual practice this occurs very infrequently.

When an overall index of participation in school-related functions was constructed, central city-suburban differences became much more marked than when each of a series of school-related activities was considered separately. In each size class, suburban residents had the higher average scores. But again, level of participation varied more by whether or not families had children in school than by place of residence. While the overall participation scores differed between cities and suburbs, as well as by size of community, the differences were less marked than those found within each area according to the personal characteristics of the respondent. In all areas, participation scores increase by socioeconomic status, but within each status category—that is, education, income, or occupation—suburban residents had the highest scores. And regardless of status, participation scores tended to increase in both residential zones as the size of the metropolitan area declined. However, differences by size of area were less marked and less consistent than those observed by place of residence or status levels.

The extent to which residents are "metropolitan area" oriented in their views of community problems varies substantially by place of residence as well as by size of community. In each size class, city residents are much more "metropolitan" in their views, whereas suburban residents tend to be much more locally oriented. Among the latter, the proportion with local orientation decreases as size of area declines. The gap in orientation between city and suburban residents increases directly by size of metropolitan area. These data suggest that as metropolitan areas develop, and the suburban areas attain a larger population and become increasingly self-sufficient, they are likely to become more locally oriented and place more emphasis on local autonomy. Consequently, the resolution of common problems of metropolitan scope becomes increasingly complex and difficult, since the more locally oriented a population is, the greater the resistance to reorganization of school districts or local government.

Evaluation of Schools

Generally speaking, we have found that residents in metropolitan areas are satisfied with their schools. It is only in the small area suburbs, and in medium-sized cities, that the proportion dissatisfied even exceeded 10 percent of the total households. Yet when asked how the schools could be improved, only a minority of the residents reported that "no improvements" were needed. Suburban residents were not only more satisfied with their schools, but they were much more likely to feel that no improvements were needed. It is the residents in the large area suburbs who appeared to be the most satisfied, whereas least satisfaction was reported by those living in the large metropolitan area cities. The most frequently mentioned improvement that was needed pertained to physical facilities, i.e., schools and classrooms. But a substantial proportion of the residents also reported the need for more and better teachers as well as higher pay for teachers. City residents, particularly those in large areas, were most likely to emphasize these needs. It is readily evident that any proposal for change would be presented to a population that is generally satisfied with what they already have in their own area.

In evaluating city and suburban schools, residents tended to rate their own schools as being better, regardless of place of residence. The only exception occurred in the small area suburbs. Most suburban residents either rate their own schools as being better than those in the city or they state that the schools in the two areas do not vary in quality. But rarely, except in the small suburbs, do they rate city schools as being better than their own. While in the larger metropolitan areas, residents in both zones tend to feel that their own schools are superior to those in the opposite area, quite a different pattern of responses is found in the small metropolitan areas, where both city and suburban residents rate the city schools above those in the suburbs. It is only in the small metropolitan areas that the evaluation of the schools favors the city over the suburbs.

Views concerning the wastefulness of having multiple school districts within the metropolitan community vary not only by place of residence but also by size of metropolitan area. Central city residents tend disproportionately to view multiple districts as being wasteful. While the proportion expressing this view increases as size of city declines, it is not shared by a majority of the residents in any of the city areas. Similarly, while residents in the small suburban areas are more likely than those in the large area suburbs to share this view, the proportion does not exceed 40 percent. This view tended to be expressed most frequently by those in the higher socioeconomic status categories, regardless of place of residence.

Views Concerning Taxes and Support of Schools

While most residents in all areas feel that school taxes are about the right amount, a substantial minority feel that taxes are too high. Suburban residents are even more likely than city residents to express the latter view. This difference is found regardless of size of metropolitan area. But the important point here is that views on taxes vary much more by socioeconomic status—i.e., education, occupation, and income—within each residential zone than between central city and suburban residents. In all areas, the lower the status, the higher the proportion of residents who feel that taxes are too high. But at every status level, suburban residents are more likely than city residents to feel that taxes are too high, regardless of size of area.

It is also noteworthy that city residents are more likely than those in the suburbs to feel that not enough is being spent on education in their area. The proportion expressing this view declines as the size of city decreases. Many residents apparently want more from their schools than they are willing to pay for through taxes. For example, while 30 percent of the large city residents reported that their taxes were too high, only 7 percent felt that too much money was being spent on their schools. Conversely, while only 7 percent thought taxes were too low, nearly five times as many (34 percent) felt that not enough was being spent on education. Similar differences between what residents want to pay in taxes and the amount they want spent on education were found in all of the other areas, also. It is apparent that residents would like a well financed school system, but they would rather not pay for it through taxation. Much of this, however, is due to the views expressed by the older, longtime residents in the suburbs, who are most likely to feel that too much is being spent on education. This is also the group most likely to report that school taxes are too high. This is not surprising, since this is the segment of the suburban population that has experienced the full impact of the rapid expansion of school needs in the suburban areas, and they, more than any other segment of the population, have experienced tax increases to pay for the developing school systems in these areas—all of which represents substantial changes from the type of suburbs they experienced prior to these developments.

When residents were given the choice between better schools or reduced taxes, an overwhelming majority (70 percent or more) in all areas stated a preference for better schools. Although only a minority would favor a tax cut over better schools, the residents least likely to do so are those who currently have children attending public schools. While families whose children attend non-public schools are somewhat more likely to favor a tax cut, the persons most likely to do so are those who do not have any children in school. This pattern holds in every area, regardless of size, in the suburbs as well as in the cities. While a very large proportion of the residents in all areas stated a preference for better schools over a cut in taxes, we found that a much smaller proportion would be willing to pay more in order to improve their schools. Actually, residents are more likely to oppose than to favor such an increase. However, city residents seem to be more willing than those in the suburbs to pay more in order to improve the schools. The only exception was found in the small metropolitan areas, where the responses are the same in both zones. Here too, it is noteworthy that there is much more variation in willingness to pay more to improve the schools, by socioeconomic status levels than by place of residence.

A distinct majority of the residents in all areas reported that they would be in favor of the federal government contributing funds to local districts to help cover the costs of operations. We noted a tendency, however, for suburban residents to be somewhat more opposed to such support than central city residents. Also, views regarding federal aid were found to vary substantially among different segments of the population. In all areas, most opposition to federal aid comes from those with higher education. With each increase in education, the proportion opposed increases. Opposition to federal aid also tends to be slightly higher in the smaller metropolitan areas.

Actually, the range of difference in the proportion opposed to federal aid is substantially larger among educational levels within each area, than by place of residence within the metropolitan community. Also, as the level of occupational status increases, and as the size of income increases, we found consistently that opposition to federal aid increased, regardless of place of residence or size of metropolitan area. But in all instances, suburban residents were found to be more opposed to federal aid than central city residents.

Here too, we found much larger differences by variations in occupational status and income than by place of residence. But rarely in any subgroup was opposition expressed by more than one-third of the residents. In other words, we found substantial support for federal aid—that is, most of the metropolitan area residents, both city and suburban, would favor the active role of the federal government in the support of their local schools.

Although there is considerable support for federal aid to local schools, this clearly is not desired as the major source of support. Rather, the most frequent response in all areas is that the residents of the local school district should bear the primary responsibility for both buildings and the cost of operations at the local level. Even though this is the most common response, it is noted that in none of the areas do a majority of the residents agree as to what level of government should have primary responsibility for the support of the schools. We found, however, that suburban residents are more likely than those in the city to see the support of the schools as primarily the responsibility of the local residents. And if not a local responsibility, it should be assumed by the state.

Regardless of the variable used, we found a substantial increase in the proportion who view support of the schools as primarily a local responsibility, with each increase in socioeconomic status. Differences in views were much more marked by variations in socioeconomic status than by either place of residence or size of metropolitan area. Disproportionately, residents in the lower socioeconomic categories look to a level of government outside the local district, and beyond the area in which they are directly taxed, for the support of the schools.

Views on Reorganization of School Districts

Central city residents are much more likely than those in the suburbs to favor the reorganization of school districts on an area-wide basis. Regardless of size of area, or use of the schools, city residents favor change; but in the suburban areas, resistance to change increases markedly and directly by size of metropolitan area. Opposition is most pronounced among those who have children attending public schools. Even in the small metropolitan areas, where suburban resistance is least, approximately half of the residents have already decided that they would vote against a proposal to combine the city and suburban areas into a single district. In the other suburban areas, a distinct majority are opposed to change. Even if change is limited to the establishment of an area-wide high school, majority support is found only in the small area suburbs. While there is much more support for an area-wide high school, in the small area suburbs, than for a single area-wide school district, suburban residents in both the large and medium-sized areas, are as much opposed to an area-wide high school as to a single district.

When residents were offered, as part of the proposal for reorganization, a single district with lower taxes, the amount of support for change increased substantially in all areas. However, most resistance to change was found in the higher income groups, those with children in public schools, and in the large area suburbs. Consistently, suburban residents, more frequently than those in the city, stated a preference for the present district, even with higher taxes, rather than to join a single district with lower taxes. Although the cost factor proved to be important, it did not overcome the influence of either place of residence or size of area.

Income was found to be an important factor in how residents viewed change, but the association is different in the cities than in the suburban areas. In cities, most support for change is found in the high income group, whereas in the suburbs this is the group that expresses the most opposition. However, the proportion declines by size of area. Similarly, in suburban areas, opposition to change varies directly by education, whereas in the cities most support for change is found among those in the college group.

While central city residents tend to favor change, no matter how satisfied they are with their schools, in the suburbs we find least support for and most opposition to change reported by those who are very satisfied with their schools. And this is the level of satisfaction that is reported by a substantial majority of the suburban residents. Concern about quality of schools is suggested by the high proportion of suburban residents who would vote for change among those who rate city schools as better, and the high negative vote among those who feel that the suburban schools are superior to those in the city. When suburban residents feel that the city and suburban schools are of equal quality, a majority prefer to maintain the status quo; but, as noted, if they feel that their own schools are better, they

overwhelmingly oppose reorganization. In central cities, the proportion favoring change appears to be largely unrelated to how they
rate the schools.

It is of special interest to note that central city and suburban
differences, in the proportion favoring change, largely disappear
among those who feel that the quality of schools would improve
under a single system; this is the case regardless of size of area.
Under these conditions, less than one-fourth of suburban residents
would vote against change; and in the central cities, opposition is
even less. While in this category we find strong support for change
even among suburban residents, it is noted that only a small minority
of residents shared the view that the schools would be better under
a single system. Yet when they do share such a view, a distinct
majority in all areas would vote in favor of change. However, support for change declines markedly among those who feel that the
quality of the schools would remain largely the same under a single
system. And many of the suburban residents share this opinion.
Actually, more than half of those in the large area suburbs would
expect the quality of schools to decline; in this group, almost everyone (95 percent) reported they would vote against change.

When attention was focused on attitudes toward what was being
spent on education in their areas, we found that most opposition to
reorganization was expressed by those who felt that the "right
amount" was being spent in their areas. It is this "contented" majority, in all of the suburban areas, that accounts for a disproportionate amount of the resistance to change that is found in the
suburbs. In all residential zones, least support for change was found
among those who feel that reorganization would result in increased
taxes. On the other hand, a high proportion of the residents, in all
areas, favor change when they expect taxes to decrease under a
single system. It is in the latter category that resistance to change
is at a minimum. But if people do not know what to expect, as far
as taxes are concerned, there tends to be little support for change.

Among central city residents, those who attend PTA and school
board meetings are more likely to favor change than those who do
not attend. This holds for each size class. However, just the opposite
is found in the suburbs. Not only is there a higher attendance frequency among suburban residents, but those who are most active are
the ones least likely to favor change. Even when an overall school

participation scale was constructed, based on the responses to several questions regarding school-related activities, it was found that most support for change in the cities came from those with the highest scores. But here too, in the suburbs, as the participation scores increased, the proportion who would vote for change declined and opposition increased. However, at each level of participation, opposition to change declined substantially in the smaller metropolitan areas.

Resistance in the suburbs appears to be, in part, a result of isolation from the rest of the community. At any rate, as isolation in daily activities declines, support for change increases, though never is this view shared by more than a minority. For example, most opposition in the suburbs is found among those who have frequent contact with their neighbors, and whose friends live largely in the suburbs. Regardless of size of area, the proportion favoring change is highest among those whose territorial range of daily activities is most extensive. While this has no apparent effect on city residents, opposition among suburban residents declines consistently as the range of participation increases in scope. While suburban residents tend to have a much broader spatial range of participation in the community, they nonetheless are more likely than city residents to cling to a more local orientation concerning community problems, which is likely an important factor in accounting for their greater resistance to change. Most resistance to change is found in the large suburban areas, where the participation range in daily life is least, whereas most support for change is found in the small area suburbs, where the participation range is greatest and the residents are less locally oriented.

Support for change, regardless of place of residence or size of metropolitan area, appears to come disproportionately from residents who are concerned with efficiency and economy. At any rate, most support for reorganization is reported by those who express the view that multiple districts in the area are wasteful. However, if residents feel that the present system is not wasteful—and a majority of suburban residents share this view—resistance to change is widespread; although more so in the suburbs than in the cities.

The locally oriented central city resident on an "ideological orientation" scale is almost as resistant to school district reorganization as his counterpart in the suburbs. In all areas, opposition comes overwhelmingly from the locally oriented. This ideology is, however, most prevalent in the suburbs. On the other hand, residents who share a "metropolitan ideology," regardless of where they live, tend to favor change in school district organization. Actually, ideological orientation represents one of the few instances in which the effects of a variable on the attitude toward change overrides the effect of size of area.

Rather consistently, most opposition to change was reported by the suburban residents who felt that the ordinary citizen can do quite a bit about how school funds are spent. It is noteworthy that the latter opinion was expressed by a majority of the residents in all of the suburban zones. In the cities, however, this is the group that is most likely to favor change. Perhaps in the city, residents feel that the ordinary citizen would continue to have the same amount of control even in a larger district. At any rate, they favor change. But in the suburbs, where control by the ordinary citizen appears to be particularly important, at least traditionally, residents resist change because they feel that under the present system the citizens have that control, and they do not want to risk losing it. On the other hand, among the suburban residents who feel that such control has already been lost, there is less opposition to reorganization. While the weight of evidence throughout this study suggests that the suburban residents rarely if ever exercise more control over school issues than city residents, the significant point here is the more general belief that they could effectively exert control if they wanted to. Apparently they feel that this would not be possible in a larger district. It may not be so much what they actually do as what they think they can do that leads them to defend the present system.

Our data clearly show that the organization of school districts and the organization of local government in metropolitan areas, although independent in one sense, are merely different aspects of the same thing. While residents in city and suburban districts tend to view local government differently, it is noteworthy that when they do share the same views regarding government, they tend to respond similarly to the proposal to establish a single school district for the area. If either suburban or city residents would vote against a single government for the area—and a majority would do so—they tend to be opposed to reorganization of school districts. On the other hand, among those who would vote for a single government, a majority would vote in favor of change for the schools. Here too, size-of-area differences largely disappear.

Public Officials

Turning to the public officials, we found that, as compared with the residents they represented, school officials were even more satisfied with the schools in their area, and also more frequently rated their own schools as being better than those in the opposite zone. These evaluations vary substantially by size of metropolitan area, but the significant point is that the influence of size is just the opposite in the two residential zones. For example, while only slightly more than half of the school officials in the large cities rate their own schools as better, the proportion of such responses exceeds 80 percent in the small cities. In this case, there is an inverse relationship between size and the proportion who rate their own schools above those in the suburbs. But in the adjoining suburbs, the proportion of school officials who rate their own schools as better declines markedly and directly by size of area. Such responses range from two-thirds in the large to less than one-fourth in the small area suburbs. It is quite evident that only a minority of the residents in the small area suburbs hold the view that their schools are better than those in the city. While the same pattern was also found among the residents, the size of the differences was considerably less.

In the small area suburbs, the degree of consensus among school officials and residents concerning this issue is particularly notewothy. Slightly more than one-fourth of the school officials, and about the same proportion of residents, rate city schools above their own. And further, nearly half of both the officials and residents do not make any distinction as to the relative qualities of the city and suburban schools. By way of comparison, city school officials in this size class overwhelmingly rate their own schools above those in the suburbs, as do nearly half of the residents. No doubt the lower level of satisfaction with the schools in the small area suburbs, and the tendency for most residents, as well as officials, to evaluate the schools as being the same in both areas, or even better in the city, accounts in large part for the increased amount of support for change that one finds in the small area suburbs.

Our data show that a sizable majority of the central city officials are agreed that the present system of multiple school districts in the area is wasteful, whereas nearly as many suburban officials express the view that such is not the case. In both large and small area cities, officials are nearly twice as likely as residents to view the present system as wasteful, whereas, in the suburban zones, the official-resident differences largely disappear; but to the extent that differences are found, public officials are more likely than residents to defend and find justification for the present system.

A point to be stressed with reference to the potential for reform in metropolitan areas is that not only do central city officials tend to view the present system as wasteful, but a substantial number of the school officials and residents in the small area suburbs share that view. School officials, as well as residents in the small area suburbs, seem to be much more aware of the shortcomings of having a number of separate districts in the area. This is still another factor which likely accounts, in part, for the decline in resistance to change in the smaller areas.

Regardless of type of area, residents are more likely than public officials to hold the view that present school taxes are too high. School officials are not only much less likely to share that view, but they are most likely to report that not enough is being spent on education in their districts. And except in the small metropolitan areas, central city school officials more frequently express this view than do suburban school officials. By way of comparison, residents in all zones are much less likely to agree that not enough is being spent. A point to be stressed is that the gap between school officials and residents is a substantial one, and for the most part, the size of the gap seems to be quite independent of either area of residence or size of metropolitan community.

Consistent with these differences, we continued to find, in all areas, that residents are much less willing than officials, and particularly school officials, to pay more in order to improve their schools. This, of course, does not necessarily mean that the residents are any less interested than the officials in seeing their schools improved; instead, it may well reflect marked differences in how they think the schools should be supported. For example, residents would look to the federal government for assistance to improve their schools, whereas this source of help is not viewed with favor by the school officials, particularly those in the suburban areas. At any rate, we have found that officials are much less likely than residents to favor federal aid to local districts, and with few exceptions, suburban officials are even less likely to do so than those in the city.

Turning to the issue of reorganization, three distinct patterns of difference were found. First of all, as already noted, suburban residents are much more opposed to change than city residents. Secondly, when residents and officials are compared, just the opposite pattern of difference is found in the suburbs and in the central cities. For example, in the central cities, school officials are less likely than residents to oppose change, whereas in the suburbs much more opposition is expressed by the officials. Thirdly, opposition among officials as well as residents, although always higher in the suburbs, nonetheless declines by size of metropolitan area. But even in the suburban zones of small areas, where suburban opposition is least, approximately two-thirds of the school officials, and half of the residents, reported that they would vote against the establishment of a single district for the whole area.

An overall appraisal of the data indicates that while central city officials tend to favor change, there is widespread opposition to reorganization among suburban officials. And opposition is particularly marked in the large area suburbs. Rarely do the officials in these areas favor change. Although we consistently find size of metropolitan area differences, particularly in the suburbs, support for change within each area is most frequent among central city school officials and is least frequently reported by the officials in the suburbs.[1] In the large metropolitan areas, the proportion in favor of change ranges from only 10 percent of the suburban school officials to 73 percent of the city school officials. In the small metropolitan areas, where support for change is more frequent in the suburbs, the comparable proportions are 34 percent and 69 percent. The

[1] A point worthy of emphasis here is the marked similarity between the views held by school officials and the residents in their areas in the higher socioeconomic status groups. This similarity is particularly significant, since it is found in both city and suburban areas, even though the officials in the two areas represent entirely different and frequently directly opposite views. With rare exceptions, and regardless of the issue, officials more closely represent the views of the higher status residents than the general population. This is to be expected, since it is from this group that such officials are largely recruited. It would seem, then, that suburban officials, in particular, oppose change not only because of their vested interest as officials but also because this is the general climate of opinion that is most frequently shared by persons in the community in the same general social class position.

rank order of the proportions in favor of change follows the same pattern in each size class—that is, support for reorganization declines among each type of respondent in the following order: city school officials, city residents, suburban residents, and lastly, suburban school officials. Conversely, opposition varies in the opposite direction, ranging from a high of 88 percent among suburban officials in the large metropolitan areas to only 27 percent of the city officials. Even though opposition is less frequent in the small areas, the pattern is identical. Very similar patterns were also found in the responses to an area-wide high school, support for a single district with lower taxes, or the present district with higher taxes. These data are summarized in Table 11-1.

TABLE 11-1

PROPORTION OF SELECTED RESPONDENTS WHO FAVOR OR OPPOSE
REORGANIZATION BY SIZE OF METROPOLITAN AREA

Type of Reorganization and Size of Metropolitan Area	Central City		Suburban Area	
	School Officials	Residents	Residents	School Officials
	%	%	%	%
Favor a Single District				
Large	73	47	22	10
Small	69	45	36	34
Oppose Single District				
Large	27	36	69	88
Small	25	38	50	64
Favor High School on Area-Wide Basis				
Large	80	53	23	12
Small	88	56	52	54
Favor Single District—Lower Taxes				
Large	73	62	41	22
Small	94	64	57	38
Favor Present District—Higher Taxes				
Large	27	23	48	72
Small	6	23	29	56

As we move from the large to the small area suburbs, support for change increases more than threefold among school officials and nearly doubles among the residents. Although support for change is substantially higher in the smaller suburban areas, it is still expressed by only a minority. But the important point to note is that opposition declines to a level where a reorganizational proposal has a much greater chance for acceptance, even in the suburban areas. Of particular interest is the amount of support that is reported for a proposed area-wide high school, at least in the small area suburbs, and the degree of consensus that is found among residents and officials regarding this limited form of change. This is the only proposal for change that is not opposed more by suburban officials than by the residents.

Central city officials, as well as residents, would support an area-wide high school; but except in the small areas, only a very small proportion of the suburban school officials would favor such a proposal. It is highly significant that in the small area suburbs, a majority of the school officials, and a majority of the residents, favor handling the high school on an area-wide basis. However, it is readily evident that they want to do so without any sacrifice of their independent school district status.

Among suburban officials, support for change increases when lower taxes are made a part of the proposed reorganization, but even under these conditions, a sizable majority of the suburban officials state a preference for the status quo along with higher taxes, rather than to establish a single district with lower taxes. Although an additional tax burden would have some influence upon the thinking of suburban officials, it is not of sufficient importance to win their support for setting up a single district for the whole area. While the promise of lower taxes does win some additional support for change, even in the suburbs, it does not successfully overcome the widespread resistance of the suburban officials. However, lower taxes may contribute substantially to the outcome of a popular referendum, for this dimension has a marked influence on how the suburban residents would vote on such a proposal.

Conclusions

It is highly significant that a substantial majority of the suburban officials, both school and government, feel that they would not occupy such positions if they lived in the city. Thus their leadership position, as perceived by themselves, depends on the segmentation of school districts and governments in metropolitan areas. This likely accounts for much of the widespread opposition that is expressed concerning the establishment of a single school district for the whole area. Because of the consistency of the relationship between attitudes concerning government and views regarding the schools, it would seem that neither of the issues could be effectively resolved apart from the other. If residents, or officials, favor the status quo for local government they tend also to resist change for the schools.

Resistance to change is such in the larger metropolitan areas that any proposal for reorganization would be faced with overwhelming odds, but in the smaller metropolitan areas it would seem as though residents, and to a lesser extent officials, would be quite receptive to a proposal to reorganize the schools on an area-wide basis. It is in such areas that we have consistently found the least amount of resistance to change. However, the longer efforts to bring about change are put off, the more difficult the task becomes. Already the larger metropolitan areas have reached the stage of development where a reorganization proposal would not survive a referendum. It would be approved in the cities, but not in the suburban areas. Many future problems of segmented districts could be avoided if reform were initiated in the hundreds of smaller communities before they emerged as larger metropolitan-like areas, highly crystallized into a number of autonomous units. Clearly, efforts to be effective should be "preventive." For as long as change is to be decided either by public officials or by a referendum, the chances for success decline sharply as size of area increases. The relationship between size of area and resistance to change has been very evident throughout the study.

At least in the small metropolitan areas, some form of functional unity, if not administrative change, would be approved by a popular vote in all parts of the metropolitan area. Even though suburban residents want to maintain their independent districts, a distinct majority want and would support an area-wide high school. It is noted, however, that if the high school were established on an area-wide basis, the chances of complete reorganization of school districts in these areas may decline appreciably. Nonetheless, an area-wide high school is a form of change which would help resolve many of the current issues facing the schools in such areas, and one that would be readily accepted, even in the suburban zones, in the small metropolitan areas. This form of change would not, however, be accepted by the suburban residents, in particular, in the larger metropolitan areas.

As metropolitan areas increase in size, the suburban areas become increasingly crystallized in separate and independent political units, and there is a concomitant decrease in the chances of bringing about change in the organization of school districts or local government in such areas. The findings of this study, in terms of the relationship between stage of development, as measured by size, and resistance to change, clearly emphasize the need for reorganization efforts at the early stages of development. As already noted, this study points to the need for "preventive" efforts—that is, reorganization, to be accepted, must be initiated at the early stages of urban development. In order to avoid the further proliferation of multiple school districts in metropolitan areas in the future, attention should be focused on small metropolitan areas and quasi-metropolitan areas, that is, those urban communities which have not yet reached metropolitan status but are likely to emerge as such in the future.

To the extent that a single school district, or a single government, for the whole area is a desirable goal, attention should be focused on these smaller areas, since it is in these areas that the suburban populations and officials are more receptive to change. The residents in these areas have not yet built up the widespread opposition that is so prevalent in the larger metropolitan area suburbs. But this is only temporary; for, as the findings of this study show, there will be increased opposition to a single district as the size of the population increases. Actually, in the large metropolitan areas, change of the type discussed here is for all practical purposes not possible, as long as it can come about only through a referendum in the separate districts, or through the initiative or approval of local public officials. While proposals for change would be approved in the cities, it is almost certain that they would meet with defeat in the suburbs. If legislation were passed which would permit a referendum on a community-wide basis as a single unit, reorganizational proposals would be approved; but as long as separate majorities are needed in sub-areas of the larger community—that is, within each of the independent school districts—the full impact of the opposition in the suburbs would be effective in blocking any proposal for reorganization, at least in the larger metropolitan areas.

Opposition to reorganization in the large area suburbs is so extensive that, under the existing procedures for change, reorganization can be ruled out as one of the alternatives available to help resolve the problems of education associated with multiple school districts in metropolitan communities. However, this is not the case in the small metropolitan areas, where opposition to change is much less extensive; as size of area declines, so does opposition to change. This has important implications for the future, since many of the problems presently found in the small metropolitan areas could be corrected through change, and future problems of multiple districts could be prevented, if efforts to reorganize school districts were concentrated in the small urban communities which are likely to emerge as metropolitan areas in the future. To postpone the effort is to perpetuate the status quo, the maintenance of which is already firmly established in the larger areas. It also increases the amount of opposition that is likely to develop.

And finally, to end the discussion on a practical note, from the point of view of an action program designed to bring about change in the local metropolitan setting, the findings of this study emphatically demonstrate that the type of campaign that may be effective in winning support in the city would probably meet with failure in the suburban areas, because of the marked central city and suburban differences in how the residents view the schools and school-related issues. The fact that a number of variables were found to have just the opposite effect on attitudes toward change, in the two residential zones, suggests the need for approaches which are specifically designed for the separate areas.

The overall findings of this study quite dramatically show that the major effort should be focused on the suburban areas, for it is in these zones that the real obstacles to reorganization are concentrated. Although there are certain segments of the population, even in the suburbs, that would favor change, the predominant feeling is one of opposition. And it is to be noted that the frequency of opposition is most pronounced among the officials. But it should also be noted that while suburban and city officials tend to take opposite views concerning reorganization, it is quite likely that their motivations in doing so are not dissimilar. No doubt suburban officials oppose change because they want to maintain the status quo, so that they can retain their leadership positions. This, of course, represents a vested interest. For many, resistance to reorganization is a matter of survival as leaders. However, this may not be too different, at least in kind, from what the city official has in mind when he favors change. For it is quite likely that even under a single system, the city officials would be able to continue in the same or comparable positions. In the reorganized system, the influence of the position, which the incumbent would likely continue to occupy, would be enhanced, for it would extend to an even larger population as well as land area. In this case, change is not a threat to survival; on the contrary, it would offer, for most city officials, an opportunity to extend the power of their office. Clearly, the potential consequences of reorganization would be much different for suburban and city officials. This likely accounts for much of the widespread opposition that is found among the suburban officials.

Appendix

Sample Selection[1]

Initial Sample

While each of the six central cities had a city directory more or less exclusively devoted to it, the directory listings for any particular suburban municipality tended to be intermixed with those for other suburbs. This led to the employment of somewhat different sampling procedures in the two situations.

In sampling a central city directory, the first stage involved the systematic selection, with equal probability, of approximately fifty pages from the street address section. The following procedure was then employed with respect to *each* of the pages thus selected at the first stage:

1) A count was made of the entries which were apparently residential and apparently located within the 1960 boundaries of the central city.

2) A cluster size, C_p, proportionate to the residential count was computed. The average size of C_p was set at 5.5.

3) Starting with a randomly selected entry, C_p successive apparently residential entries were drawn into the sample.[2]

---

[1] Prepared by National Opinion Research Center, University of Chicago, August, 1962.

[2] Usually the successive entries referred to housing units which were geographically proximate; in fact, they would normally be located within the same structure, contiguous structures, or across the street from each other. But occasionally a series of commercial structures or undeveloped land intervened between suc-

Since by the foregoing procedure the number of entries drawn from a particular page was proportionate to the number of residential entries appearing on it, every entry in a city directory had the same probability of falling into the sample.

In directories where the street address listings for several suburbs were mixed together, the first stage involved the systematic selection, with equal probability, of a relatively large number of pages—usually about three or four times as many pages as the number of segments to be selected from the directory. A count was then made for each page of the number of apparently residential entries listed for each of the suburbs to be sampled. These counts were employed as measures of size in the second stage of selection. For each relevant suburb, the first-stage pages containing entries for that suburb constituted the sampling frame. Pages were systematically selected with probability proportionate to the aforementioned measures of size. A random start for each page thus selected was derived from the random number which had fallen into the interval of cumulated measures of size assigned to that page for the particular suburb. Starting with the page's n-th entry for that suburb, alternately five or six consecutive entries located in the suburb were selected for the sample.[3]

Usually the only locality identifications appearing in city directories are the post office names to be employed in addressing mail. The post office designation for a given area is sometimes different from the official name of the political subdivision in which the area is located. Particularly, unincorporated areas and small suburbs are often served by the post office of a nearby larger city or suburb. Since the universe for the present study was defined in terms of April, 1960, legal boundaries, particular care was exercised to insure that the directory sample coverage for a particular locality was neither broader nor narrower than it should have been. All geographic clusters selected for the sample were plotted on maps showing the appropriate boundaries, and those clusters found to be located outside the proper community were dropped from the sample. The

---

cessive entries, thereby reducing the geographic clustering. In other cases, the listing for a particular street came to an end within a cluster of entries, with the result that two or more geographic clusters, sometimes located miles apart, were drawn from a single page of a directory.

[3] As in the case of the central city sample, consecutive entries were sometimes geographically distant from each other.

problem of under-coverage was handled through the block supplement, as is discussed in a later section of this exposition.

The sampling plan for the survey specified that one interview was to be obtained in each housing unit.[4] Since the concept of household employed in the compilation of the city directory was not necessarily congruent with the survey concept of housing unit, two or more directory entries sometimes resulted in the assignment of only one survey interview and, conversely, one directory entry sometimes resulted in the assignment of two or more interviews. The situation where the directory contained two or more entries for a single housing unit was especially simple to handle. In the course of enumerating a household, the interviewer asked a specified series of questions concerning the living arrangements of all the people living at the particular "address." Whenever it turned out that a directory entry referred to an individual or family which merely shared the living quarters of some primary individual or family, the interview designated by this entry was simply dropped from the assignment.

When two or more housing units were found at an address for which the directory contained only one entry, the interviewer's assignment was expanded to include the additional unit(s). The procedure was different in cases where the directory contained more than one entry for an address, and inspection revealed even more housing units than there were entries. Interviews were, at this stage, conducted only at those housing units for which entries appeared in the directory, insofar as the identity of such housing units could be determined from the householders' names.[5] Housing units which were located at addresses with more than one directory entry, but which were themselves omitted from the directory, were drawn into the sample through the procedure described below.

[4] A housing unit was defined in accordance with the 1960 census procedure: "A room or group of rooms is a *Housing Unit* if it contains individuals who live and eat separately from the other persons in the structure, *and* if their rooms *either* (1) have direct access from the outside or through a common hall *or* (2) contain a kitchen or cooking equipment for the exclusive use of the occupants."

[5] A housing unit, rather than a particular family, was the unit of assignment. Interviewers were given householders' names solely to help them identify housing units. Owing to turnover, the names in the directory were, of course, frequently out of date. Nevertheless, it was usually possible to determine which housing unit had been occupied by the family listed in the directory. The interviewer then attempted to conduct an interview in that particular housing unit.

Block Supplement

In order to correct for the omission of new construction, as well as the other types of directory errors mentioned previously, the samples derived from city directories were supplemented by the canvass of a sample of blocks. Blocks were drawn from each of the municipalities for which a city directory had served as the sampling frame. A list of all entries in the city directory which pertained to a given block was assembled. An interviewer was then instructed to visit the block and to check the completeness of the list. Interviews were conducted in a sample of the housing units for which no entry appeared in the directory.[6] The sampling ratios employed in selecting blocks and in selecting omitted housing units within blocks were established in such a manner that, for any given block, the product of the block's probability of being in the supplementary sample and sampling ratio employed within the block was exactly equal to the probability which any entry actually appearing in the city directory had of falling into the original sample. In other words, housing units appearing in a city directory and those omitted from it were sampled at exactly the same rate.

Areal Sampling

The first stage of sampling in suburban areas not covered by a city directory involved the selection of a number of census enumeration districts. All the enumeration districts within the uncovered suburban area were listed in serial order within minor civil divisions. A sample of enumeration districts was systematically selected, with probability proportionate to their 1960 housing unit counts.

Each selected enumeration district was tentatively divided into segments on a map. An interviewer then visited the enumeration district and made a rough count of the number of housing units within each tentative segment. The desired segment size was approximately twenty-five housing units, so interviewers were instructed to modify the original segmentation accordingly.

---

[6] Housing units for which no entry appeared in the directory, but which were located at addresses for which there was exactly one directory entry, were excluded from this phase. Directory omissions of that type were compensated in the process of interviewing the original directory sample.

The segments thus created constituted the secondary stage sampling units. Two or three segments were selected within each enumeration district, with probability proportionate to the housing unit count. Each sample segment was then thoroughly canvassed by an interviewer. This process involved making a list containing every housing unit located within the segment boundaries. For each segment, the interviewer was sent sealed instructions indicating which line numbers on his listing were to be sample cases. When the listing was completed, the interviewer opened the instructions and then returned to the sample housing units to obtain the names of the residents so that an advance letter could be sent to potential respondents explaining the character of the survey. The listings were returned to the office and checked before the actual interviewing was initiated.

The sampling rate employed within a segment was the ratio of the household probability established for the suburban area of the particular city to the probability that the particular segment had of having fallen into the sample. The expected number of housing units falling into the sample from a particular segment was set at approximately 5.5. The actual number of cases assigned varied rather widely from the expected value, owing to changes in the enumeration district population from April, 1960, to the time of the survey, and owing to approximation errors in the field count of housing units in the segment.

Sample Execution

Prior to being visited by an interviewer, each sample household was sent a letter from the project director. The letter described the study as dealing with opinions about urban problems, and contained reassurances as to the legitimacy of the enterprise. Press releases were sent to all the local newspapers and to a number of other local institutions in a further effort to encourage participation. Stories describing the survey and its objectives actually did appear in a number of metropolitan and suburban newspapers.

The interviewers began approaching the sample housing units several days after the explanatory letters were mailed. At each housing unit, the interviewer first obtained a complete enumeration of all the people living there and their relationship to each other. This

DISTRIBUTION OF ASSIGNED HOUSEHOLDS BY INTERVIEW OUTCOME

Metropolitan area	Central City				Suburbs			
	Completed interview	Refusal, Breakoff	Other Loss*	Total (net assignment)**	Completed interview	Refusal, Breakoff	Other Loss*	Total (net assignment)**
	%	%	%	%	%	%	%	%
Buffalo.........	71.8	20.4	7.8	100.0 (323)	82.6	11.9	5.5	100.0 (293)
Dayton.........	75.8	11.6	12.6	100.0 (310)	83.9	13.4	2.7	100.0 (298)
Milwaukee.....	83.4	11.5	5.1	100.0 (295)	89.1	7.0	3.9	100.0 (284)
Rochester......	75.5	11.6	12.9	100.0 (294)	85.0	11.2	3.8	100.0 (286)
Rockford......	82.8	14.4	2.8	100.0 (291)	86.2	12.0	1.8	100.0 (275)
Saginaw.......	81.8	12.6	5.6	100.0 (302)	89.2	7.0	3.8	100.0 (286)

* This category includes households where the designated respondent was not at home after five or more calls, where language problems made an interview impossible, where the designated respondent was too ill or senile to be interviewed, where an interview was ostensibly completed but misplaced by the interviewer or lost in the mail, and where a variety of other mishaps occurred.
** The net number of assigned cases originally excludes originally assigned housing units which were found to be vacant, seasonal, occupied by transients, or not to be in reality separate housing units. It includes housing units which were not originally assigned but which were discovered in the process of interviewing.

information could be obtained from any responsible person who happened to be at home at the time of this initial visit. In the course of the enumeration, one person was designated as head of the household. In those households where the head was unmarried or where the head's spouse was not a member of the household, the head himself was considered as the only eligible respondent. In the more usual case, where the male head and his spouse were both household members, the interviewer assignment sheet pre-designated for each household whether the male or whether the female head was to be interviewed. The pre-designation involved assigning male and female head interviews alternately to the housing units as they appeared on the original assignment sheet. The specification as to the sex of the eligible respondent was simply ignored in households where the head did not have a spouse living there.

The pre-designated individuals were the only acceptable respondents for the survey. No substitutions were allowed. Once a given person in a given household was designated as being part of the sample, repeated attempts were made to interview him or her. Even with considerable interviewer persistence, though, it was not possible to obtain interviews with some individuals. The response rates in the various communities are shown in the accompanying table.